CW01658637

Kronik

OTTOMAN STUDIES

—

İLBER ORTAYLI

KRONİK BOOKS: 105
History: 3

CHIEF EDITOR
Adem Koçal

EDITOR
Cüneyt Dalgakıran

COVER DESIGN
Kutan Ural

First Edition, İstanbul Bilgi University Press, Ekim 2004, İstanbul

Seventh Edition, December 2021, Istanbul

ISBN
978-605-7635-08-2

KRONIK BOOKS
Şakayıklı Sk. N°8, Levent
Istanbul - 34330 - Turkey
Telephone: +90 212 243 13 23
Fax: +90 212 243 13 28
kronik@kronikkitap.com

Republic of Turkey
Ministry of Culture and Tourism
Certificate Number:
49639

www.kronikkitap.com
kronikkitap

PRINT AND COVER
Optimum Basım
Tevfikbey Mah. Dr. Ali Demir Cad. No. 51/1
34295 K. Çekmece / Istanbul
Telephone: +90 212 463 71 25
Press Certificate Number: 41707

OTTOMAN STUDIES

İLBER ORTAYLI

Kronik

İLBER ORTAYLI

Professor İlber Ortaylı was born in 1947. He attended primary and middle school in Istanbul and Ankara before completing his secondary education in 1965, at the Atatürk High School in Ankara. He graduated from Ankara University's Faculty of Political Sciences and the same university's Department of History, within the Faculty of Languages, History and Geography. Prof. Ortaylı studied Slavic and Oriental Studies at the University of Vienna. He wrote his MA thesis at the University of Chicago under the supervision of Prof. Halil İnalcık, completed his doctorate on the subject "Local Government in the post-Tanzimat Era" and gained his associate professorship with a study on "The German Influence in the Ottoman Empire". In 1983, he resigned from the post he then held and worked as a visiting scholar and lecturer at universities in Vienna, Cambridge, Jerusalem, Oxford, Tunis and Berlin. He also published articles in Turkish and foreign academic journals on Russian history and on Ottoman history between the 16th and 19th centuries. In 1989, Prof. Ortaylı was appointed head of the sub-department for Administrative History at Ankara University's Faculty of Political Sciences. Between 2005 and 2012, he was in charge of the Topkapı Palace Museum. From 2002 until 2014, he taught legal history in the Faculty of Law at Galatasaray University, a university at which he is still a guest lecturer. Prof. Ortaylı has a knowledge of German, English, French, Italian, Russian and Persian and is a member of the International Scientific Academies of Bosnia, Macedonia and Montenegro as well as of the European Society for Iranology.

English works by İlber Ortaylı published by Kronik

The Empire's Longest Century

Discovering the Ottomans

CONTENTS

PROVINCES

FAMILY

RUSSIA AND TURKEY

FORWARD TO THE FIFTH EDITION

Fifteen years passed since the first edition of this book; and after these fifteen years Kronik Publishing Company has asked me for a fifth edition. The interest of students and English-speaking readers only gives me great honor and I owe my gratitude to Fahri Aral. This last (fifth) edition is this time taken over by Kronik Publishing Company.

İlber Ortaylı
Istanbul, 2019

FOREWORD

Almost twenty years ago, my distinguished colleague Sinan Kuneralp of ISIS, İstanbul edited and published my articles on Ottoman studies that had previously appeared in English, French and German, under the title *Studies on Ottoman Transformation*. Recently, Bilgi University in İstanbul began to compile and publish scattered articles from different scholarly journals. And when they asked to publish my articles I was very honored and accepted the offer with pleasure. I would like to extend my thanks to my friend, the editor of these series, Fahri Aral and his assistant editor Can Cemgil.

İlber Ortaylı
Bilkent University Ankara, 2004

OTTOMAN MILLETS'

A gravure illustrating
the first assembly of Ottoman Parliament (Meclis-i Mebusan).

1

Ottoman Jewry and the Turkish Language

In the nineteenth century Jews throughout the world confronted a problem of language; education had become widespread, books and newspapers were read in almost every home, and, most importantly, everyone was a nationalist and language was the primary vehicle for expressing national identity. The real problem surfaced when Jews became integrated into the societies in which they lived, with the emergence of cultivated individuals who had mastered the national language and made contributions to the national literature. The question that arose was whether Jews should speak a language of their own.

In the Middle East, that is to say in the Ottoman lands, they spoke a variety of tongues. Perhaps none could be classified as specifically Jewish, like Hebrew and Yiddish; nevertheless, Judeo-Spanish, a dialect of Spanish which had taken on a Jewish cast, was spoken only by Jews and had become the predominant language of Ottoman Jewry. By the nineteenth century, however, it could no longer meet the needs of education and the printed word, or be the vehicle that would allow Ottoman Jewry to keep pace with the rapid changes taking place at that time.

It is well known that modern education came to the Jews of Turkey via the *Alliance Israélite Universelle* and that the language of instruction in their institutions was French (which, in fact, they taught extremely well). This meant that Judeo-Spanish began to lose its importance in the life of the society, while in everyday affairs the elite began to speak and write in French. Indeed, more of the newspapers directed at the Jews of Turkey that tended to remain in print were published in French rather than Judeo-Spanish. Yet, the truly important point was that scholarly and literary works (novels and books, such as those authored by Avraham Galante, for instance) were also written and published in French (About forty years ago the situation changed and Jews in Turkey now read and write only Turkish. The newspapers *Şalom* and *Tiryaki* are essentially Turkish, and Jewish authors have been achieving fame in the context of Turkish letters). By way of clarification, it should be emphasized that, until the mid-nineteenth century, Ottoman Jews did not really have a problem with language, but the rise of French in the second half of the century upset the linguistic balance. As that language started to predominate, Judeo-Spanish began to decline, and the question of Turkish was also thrown into the language debate, at least in terms of outlook and atitude.

The activities of the Jewish press also prove that, starting in the late nineteenth century, Turkish gained acceptance among Jewish intellectuals. For example, between 1888 and 1890 the *kethuda* (bailiff of representative) of Chief Rabbi Moiz Fresco published a newspaper in İzmir called Üstad, which was printed in Hebrew letters although its language was Turkish. During the second constitutional period, Nissim. Masliah put out a magazine called *İttihad* (union), and from 1915-1918 Moiz Kohen produced the journal *İktisadiyat* (Economy).[1] Moreover, it is worth noting that during the years of the republic, Moiz Kohen's journal, renamed *Tekinalp*, was not only an advocate of the use of Turkish, but also of "Turkification," the cultural integration of the Jewish community with the larger surrounding community.

---

1 For the names of the newspapers, see N. Benbanaste, *Örneklerle Türk Musevi Basınının Tarihçesi* (The history of Jewish-Turkish printing with examples), İstanbul, 1988, pp.57-62.

In terms of geography the Jews were the most widely distributed group in the empire, living not only in all the Arab provinces as well as in Mesopotamia, where, of course, they spoke Arabic, but also in upper Mesopotamia, where Aramaic and Kurdish were spoken. Indeed, after the founding of the state of Israel and the subsequent mass exodus of the Jewish population from that area, the Aramaic tongue was dealt a severe blow.

Judeo-Spanish was the chief language of the Jewish communities of Ottoman Europe, in nearly every city of western Anatolia, including İzmir and Bursa, in the cities of central Anatolia, and in Salonika, which could actually be described as a Jewish city; historical-demographic studies reveal that it had become predominantly Jewish as early as the sixteenth century. When the central government instituted educational reform in the nineteenth century, the use of Turkish was made compulsory in non-Muslim Ottoman schools and it was the Jews who adhered most strictly to this regulation. Students were taught not only the Turkish language, but also Turkish literature, history, and geography. Moreover, this policy continued to be pursed after the founding of the *Alliance Israélite Universelle* schools.

Although it had been peculiar to Ottoman Jewry, Judeo-Spanish had absorbed the Yiddish of the Eastern and Central European Ashkenazi Jews who had emigrated to the Ottoman lands, as well as the Italian spoken by the Jews who moved to these areas from Italy, but it fared less well against both the French language and French cultural influences. Given the insular nature of this community, which for two centuries had been undergoing a severe economic and cultural decline, French proved to be a life-giving window on the world. Yet, there were those who wanted Turkish to replace Judeo-Spanish (which was popularly called *Yahudice* among the Turks). We are not certain just what these individuals thought of French, but it is definitely the case that the leading Jewish intellectuals who espoused the Turkish language cause were thoroughly grounded in French themselves.

Although French was the language of instruction in the Jewish *Alliance* schools, the curriculum was much like that which developed in the wake of the *tevhid-i tedrisat* (standardization of education) law of 1925. Indeed, the course of instruction at the *Alliance* schools all but paralleled that of Galatasaray (the *Mektebi Sultani*) with equal emphasis given to Turkish and French. Concentrating of Turkish history and geography, as well as Turkish language and literature, this curriculum may well have served as a model for the course of studies followed in foreign schools operating in Turkey after 1925. There is no doubt that in Jewish schools the pupils gained a thorough mastery of written Turkish.

Few if any scholars have noted that, although there were not many highly placed Jews in the empire's administration, numerous Jewish civil servants were to be found in the ministries, and outside the capital, in provincial administrations, and particularly in the ranks of the *Maliye* (Ministry of Finance). The fact that they were able to master Turkish in these schools was an advantage for all of them. Some of these civil servants were employed in such local bodies as the *Nafia ve Ziraat Komisyonu* (Commission of Public Works and Agriculture) or the *Menafii Umumiye Sandığı* (Public Chest Fund), while others had been posted by the central government. As Carter Findley pointed out, non-Muslims in later-day Ottoman bureaucracy worked mainly in central offices, particularly the Foreign Ministry.[2]

Information related to this topic can be found in documents located in the Turkish archives, which have recently been catalogued and made available to scholars. A report of 16 Zilhicce 1321 (March 4, 1904) sent by the *Rumeli Vilayat-ı Şahanesi Müfettiş-i Umumiliği Memuriyet-i Celilesi* (General inspector of the Rumelian provinces), contains a list of non-Muslim civil servants employed by the *Adliye* (Ministry of Justice), *Mülkiyye* (civil home service), and *Maliye* in the provinces of Manastır,

2 C. Findley, *Ottoman Civil Officialdom*, Princeton, 1989, pp.143-168.

Salonika and Kosovo.[3] According to these lists, three Jewish civil servants were posted from the capital to Manastır, while in Kosovo there was one Jew working in the Dahiliye Dairesi (home office) and one in the Adliye. The postal service of the same province employed four Jews, and in the *nafia* (public works) there were twelve Jewish police officers. The significance of these figures should not be underestimated, for the Jewish population in those regions was low, while the number of civil servants in the Ottoman Empire was itself not excessive.[4]

At the turn of the century, the Jewish population in the empire is estimated to have been at least 400,000, with 120,000 living in and around Palestine and more than 200,000 in the heart of the empire, where Judeo-Spanish had succeeded in absorbing other languages, such as Italian and Yiddish. Indeed, Judeo-Spanish soon became the language used even in the Ashkenazi synagogues. In contrast, in the speech delivered at the inauguration of the *gymnasium* he had founded, Rav. Dr. Markus, a leading rabbi of the Ashkenazi community, pointed out how important it was to study Turkish.[5] It may be concluded that in the waning years of the empire, even if the lower strata of the Jewish population had no awareness of "Ottomanism" or "Turkish," it did indeed exist among the Jewish intellectuals, to the point where certain individuals espoused "Turkishness." In this context, the movement founded to replace Spanish with Turkish as the community language of Ottoman Jewry and the commission which was formed to implement this policy are very significant.

---

3 For the new classification, see *Başbakanlık Osmanlı Arşivi (hereafter: BOA) – Rumeli Müfettişliği Evrakı*, TFR-IUM-1326, 1321-12-21-26, nos. 2907/2, 3, 4, 7, 9, 10.

4 *BOA* TFK-I-UM-1321-12-26 of the same document, lists no. 2907/4, 2, 3, 7.

5 M. Grossman, *Dr. Markus-Osmanlıdan Cumhuriyete Geçişte Türk Yahudilerinden Görünümler* (Portraits of the Turkish Jews during the transition from Ottoman rule to republic), İstanbul, 1992, p.29, quoting the *Ha-Mevaser* of December 3, 1911.

On 23 Zilhicce 1317 (April 24, 1900), a petition bearing the signature and seal of His Excellency Mosheh HaLevi, *locum tenens* of the Dersaadet (İstanbul) Jews, was submitted to the *Adliye ve Mezahib Nezareti* (Ministry of Justice and Religious Sects). It requested that *lisan-ı Osmanî* (i.e. Turkish) be accepted and recognized as the *lisan-ı millî* (community language) of Ottoman Jewry. The points made in this petition may be summarized as follows:

> As a gesture of gratitude to the Ottoman Empire, which for centuries has protected and bestowed its blessings on us, the loyal Jewish community wishes to adopt the Ottoman language (Turkish) and to promote its use among the Jewish people, dispensing with the Spanish, which has served them to date, and instituting Turkish as the language of instruction in presently existing Jewish schools (see doc. 1). To this end a *"tamim-i lisan-ı Osmanî komisyonu"* (commission for the propagation of Turkish) has been established and a list of its members is attached herein.

Approval of this request was granted by the Minister of Education on May 9, 1900, the Foreign Minister on May 28, 1900, and the Minister of Justice on May 25, 1900, and submitted to the *Sadaret* (prime ministry). On September 5, 1900 (10 Cemaziyelevvel 1318), acting on the report submitted by the deputy chief rabbi *locum tenens*, the Ottoman cabinet recognized the existence of the commission and authorized its activities for the purpose of changing the language of the Jews from Spanish to Turkish and propagating the latter (see doc. 2). The palace issued an *irade imperial* (imperial decree) to this effect the same day.

This commission was composed of well-known members of the Ottoman Jewish community, who were to play an important political and cultural role in subsequent years (see doc. 3). The following is a list of the commission's members:

a. *Rusumat emanet-i celilesi tercüme kalemi müdürü muavini Harunaçizade Saadetlu Jak Bey* (The Honorable Mr. Jak, Deputy Director of the Translation Office in the Ministry of France)
b. *Bahriye nezaret-i celilesi Sertercümanı kaymakam Izzetlu Moiz Bey* (Chief Translator of the Naval Ministry, Lieutenant Captain Moiz Bey)
c. *Daire-i celile-i hariciye ve umur-ı şehbenderî kaleminden Hakî Izzetlu Yusuf Bey* (of the consul general's office in the Foreign Ministry)
d. *Maarif Nezaret-i celilesi encümen-i teftiş ve muayene azasından refetlu Ishak Efendi* (an inspector in the Ministry of Education)
e. *Daire-i celile-i hariciye ve umur-ı ticariye kaleminden Izzetlu Jak Menashe* (Foreign Ministry/Department of Commerce)
f. *Istişare odası müşavirlerinden Izzetlu Ishak Yenşa Efendi* (The Prime Ministry, adviser to the prime minister)
g. *Etibba-ı bahriyeden kolağası refetlu Viktor Efendi* (a physician, Captain Viktor Efendi of the Naval Ministry)
h. *Muallimin-i Musevîyyeden haham Haim Nahum Efendi* (R. Hayim Nahum – a teacher in the Jewish *gymnasium*)
i. *Şark demiryolları idaresi hukuk müşaviri refetlu Jak Samanon Efendi* (legal consultant of the Société Chemins de Fer d'Orient)
k. *Etibba-i mülkiyeden refetlu Jak Mandil Efendi* (civilian physician)

Only one person on this list, Hayim Nahum Efendi, was not a civil servant; eleven years after the formation of this commission he became the empire's Chief Rabbi. All the others were in the government bureaucracy, either military or civilian. Jak Mandil Efendi became the palace physician; his granddaughter Matilda is the wife of a renowned Turkish novelist, Yaşar Kemal Gökçeli.

Apart from being a member of the young Jewish intelligentsia we have alluded to, Jak Samanon, legal consultant to the railway company, was also friendly with such Turkish aristocrats as Prince Yusuf Izzeddin and Galib Pasha, and participated with them in a literary group.[6]

Although the historian Avraham Galante mentions the endeavors of the commission, he does not discuss its membership or any related bureaucratic procedures; information on these subjects can only to be found in the archives of the prime ministry. As Galante points out in his *Türkler ve Yahudiler* (The Turks and the Jews), it is certain that exegetic translations into Turkish of both the Talmud and Torah existed prior to the introduction of the Ottoman language into the schools.[7] Nonetheless, the undertakings of the commission are the first serious attempt we know of to conduct educational activities in spoken and literary Turkish, and this was a historically vital step toward the integration of Turkish Jews into the language of the country in which they lived. Despite the fact that very little information exists about the actual accomplishments of the commission, from that time forward Spanish was largely confined to the home and abandoned in the schools. Although it persisted for a while in worship and in journalism, it was gradually to decline in these areas as well. For the Jews in today's Turkey, Judeo-Spanish has become an archaic language.

---

6 L. Behmoroas, "Jak Samanon Efendi ve Türkçe Aşkı – Asrımız Doğarken", *Şalom*, 21 Haziran 1995, p.5. Lizi Behmoroas is Jak Samanon's granddaughter.

7 A. Galante, *Türkler ve Yahudiler*, İstanbul, 1998, pp.156, 162.

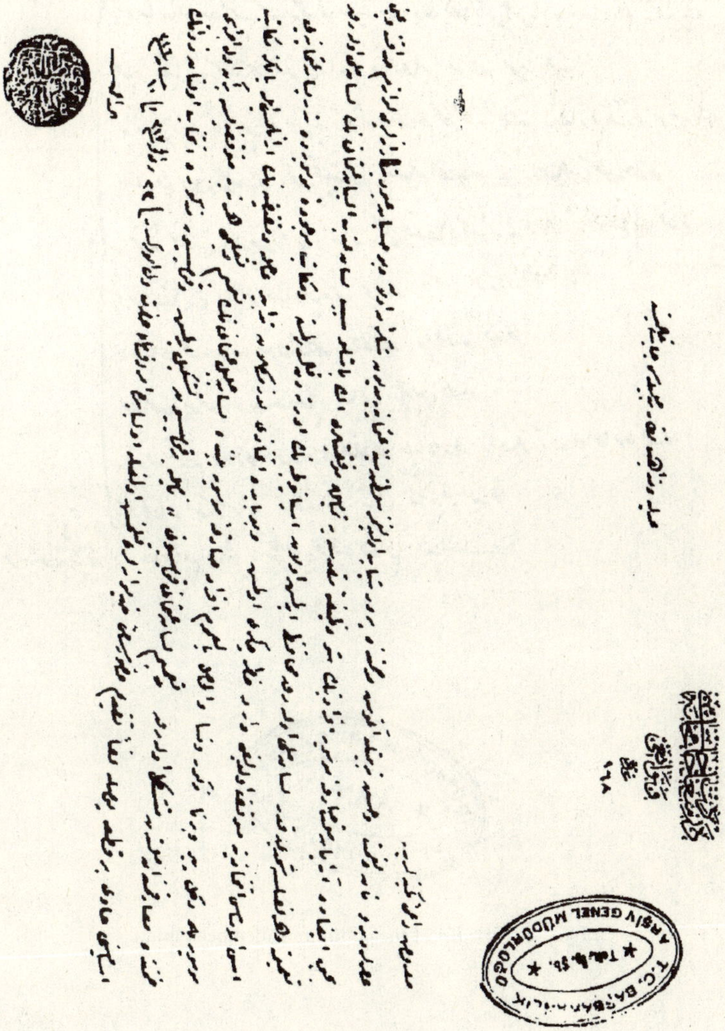

Doc. 1 – The petition of the chief rabbinate dated 23 Zilhicce 1317/24 Nisan 1900, *BOA*, *İrade Adliye ve Mezahîb*, Nr.6.

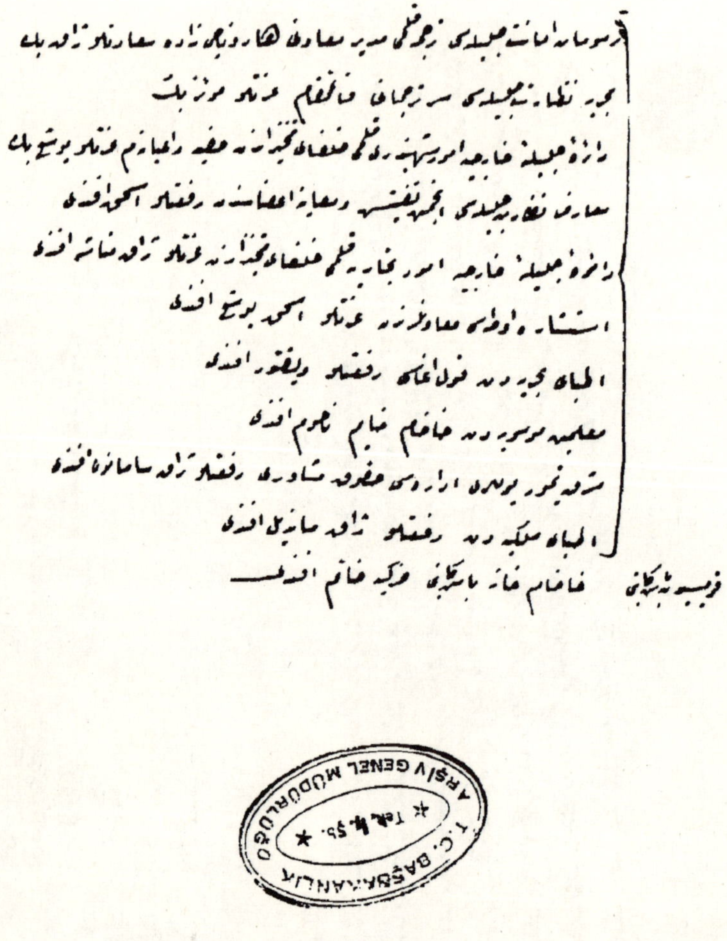

Doc. 2 – The list of the committee members, ibid.

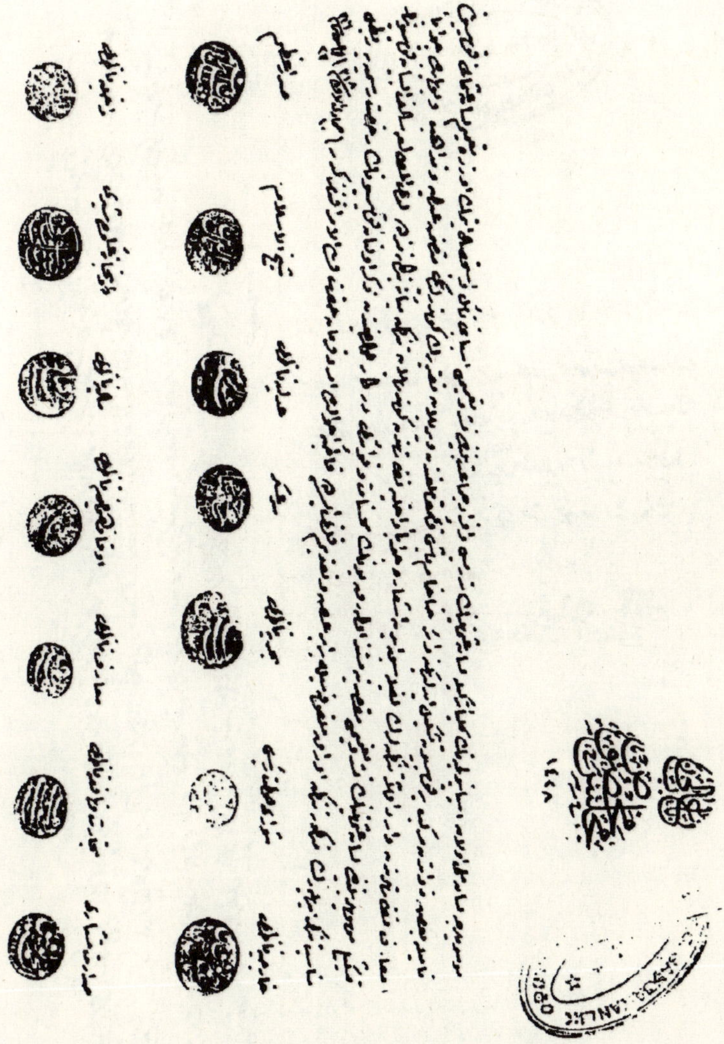

Doc. 3 – The decision of the Ottoman supreme council of ministers to authorize the organization of a "committee for the instruction and propagation of the Turkish language in the Jewish Community" dated 10 Cemaziyelevvel 1318/5 Eylül 1900, ibid.

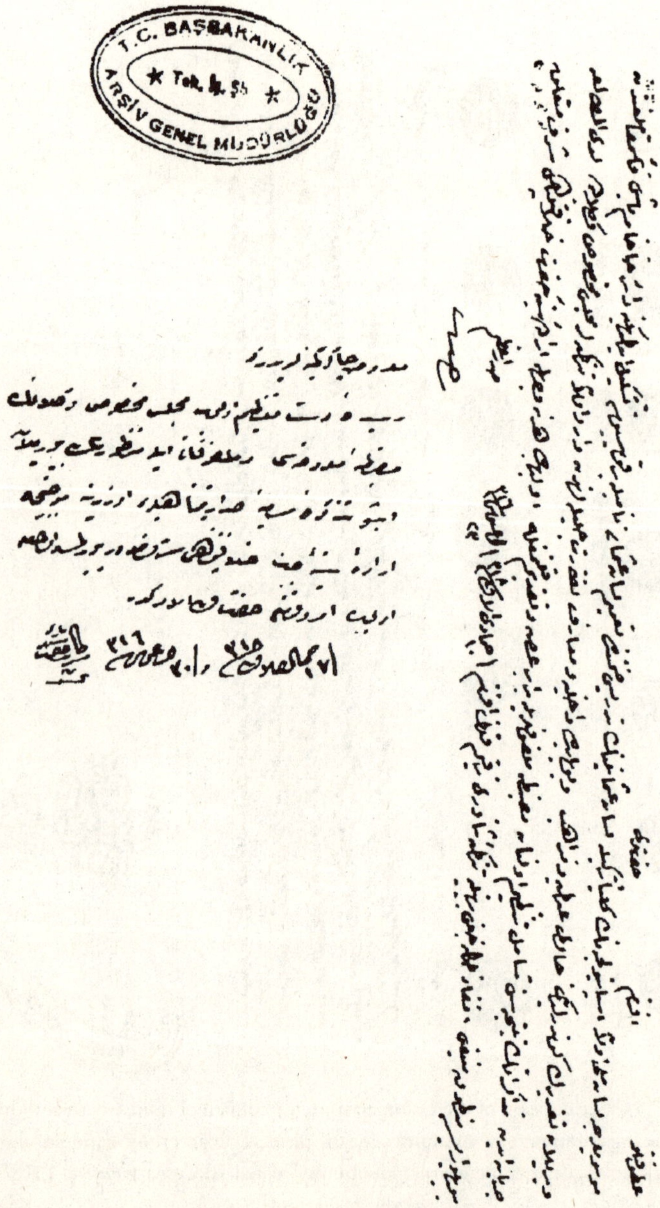

Doc. 4 – The imperial İrade dated 17 Cemaziyelevvel 1318/12 Eylül 1900, ibid.

2

The Ottoman Millet System and it's Social Dimensions

The Ottoman *millet* system forms the historical background of different peoples in the Balkans and Middle East. Even though this system does not exist in modern times, residual traces are still alive and can explain the basic features of contemporary ethnic-religious conflicts in the region.

The Ottoman Empire was a Muslim state and a successor of the Roman empires in this region as well. Historically, it was the last Islamic empire. Its disappearance in historical terms does not mean that its history is dead: history lives forever and the remnants of the Ottoman system continue to inform world events today. It was the last multinational empire in the Balkans and the Middle East, and therefore had to adopt a new way of coexistence between different ethnic and religious groups. The practice of living alongside non-Muslim communities began at Medina before the emergence of the Islamic empire (the period beginning with the conquests under the second caliph Omar) and at the very start of the Islamic state and its history. In the home of Islam (Dar'ul İslam) non-Muslim subjects of monotheistic religions had to pay dues and taxes (*haraç* in agriculture) and a poll tax *(cizye)*. However, various details need to be borne in mind on the subject of these taxes. In the first century of the Islamic empire tax revenues had already dropped because non-Muslim subjects required to pay the *haraç* had converted to Islam; after a time, a new interpretation was therefore developed to the effect that the tax was not levied on the taxpayers themselves, but on their land, and the tax as thereafter classified as a land of *haraç (arazi-i haraciyye)*.*[1]

It is known, however, that a number of non-Muslims served in the army and navy. Not only as officers but as ordinary seamen as well. Occasionally, too, young Muslims would pay a fee and be exempted from military service. During the First World War, however, exemption was largely abolished and young non-Muslim officers among the professional ranks of the army.

The Ottoman Empire also adopted the institutions and customs of the early empires that it considered appropriate. In the Sassanid Empire, for instance, the Christian churches' custom of bell-ringing was frowned upon and the faithful were called to mass by the sound of a wooden mallet. This continued to be thought appropriate, but the ban on bell-ringing was lifted by a reform decree[2] and bell-ringing resumed. The Czar of Russia donated a huge bell for the Holy Sepulchre in Jerusalem. However, Christians must also have identified with the early custom of knocking with a wooden mallet, since even nowadays the ringing of bells before mass is accompanied by the sound of a wooden mallet.

Members of the different religious groups were also required to wear different clothes. Non-Muslim groups went along with obligations such as wearing different clothes and living in different neighbourhoods because these prevented them from mingling with

---

1 (*) Some problems relating to the collection of this tax had been resolved under Halid bin Velid (the conqueror of Iraq) by the appointment of the Sassanid *dikhan* (village notables). A poll tax like the *cizye* was levied in practice under the principles of Islamic law in excange for exemption from military service. Although the term disappeared in the last century of the Ottoman Empire (during the 19th century reforms), the tax continued to be collected from non-Muslim subjects under the name *bedel-i askeri* (military exemption tax).

2 Tanzimat fermanı- BOA (Cabinet Archives of Prime Ministry) ADVNH, no.2251 of 20 Safer 1263/7 February 1847.

Muslims and thus allowed them to preserve their own religion and traditions. This is a very important point. The *millet* system under the Ottoman Empire and the individual's membership in a religious community differ from the status and psychology of minorities in the modern world in both objective and subjective terms.

The difference in status between Muslims and non-Muslims in the Ottoman Empire was both distinct from and similar to the difference between *civis* and *fides* in Rome. The status of *civis* (citizen) in Rome was an institution, a status conferring specific rights on the individual. There were *civis* of all religions and races. The inhabitants of certain regions and towns enjoyed this status. In a well-known incident, St Paul, then a Jewish rabbi, told the centurion who wanted to have him put in chains for his preaching, "Civis Romanus sum" (I am a Roman citizen), and the centurion apologized at once (Acts, XXII, 25-29). A *civis* was not necessarily an administrator, but might even be a poor subject; in fact most *civis* were poor.

In the Ottoman Empire the two corresponding types of status were *askeri* and *reaya*. Anyone, irrespective of race or religion, could hold *askeri* status. It did not confer individual rights on the person concerned, but only privileges, privileges and rights being two different categories. An *askeri* person bore arms and was exempted from tax. A muslim *mufti* or *müderris* (teacher), a Greek Orthodox metropolitan or archimandrite, a Bulgarian *voinuq* (warrior *sipahi*), a Jewish chief rabbi and a Greek Phanariot at the Sublime Porte could all hold the same *askeri* status. But a Muslim peasant and a Greek peasant or craftsman had *reaya* status. However, Muslim and non-Muslim *reaya* paid different taxes, lived in different districts and wore different clothes. Both sides observed these distinctions with great care.

An interesting aspect of the Ottoman Empire is the fact that a person holding *askeri* status was not a "citizen" with rights like the *civis Romanus*, (as mentioned above) with responsibilities under the law. People lived in the community formed by their religious group. The schools where they were educated and the books they read were controlled and censored by the church, where marriages took place and matters of inheritance were dealt with. Where Muslims are concerned, all this was done under Muslim law. An individual could not leave the *millet* (community) system. The *milletbaşı* (the patriarch and his representatives, the chief rabbi and his representatives) was an *exilarch* and an administrator within the community. He collected taxes, shared them out in the community, applied the laws and also inflicted punishment. On the orders of the clerical administrators *(exilarch or ethnarch)*, the Ottoman security forces arrested those who disobeyed orders and established rules.

The term *millet* reflects membership of a religious group. Its present-day use in the sense of "nation" was introduced in Eastern nations by the Ottomans, especially in the 19th century. Individuals lived in the religious section, the *millet*, in which they were born and came under the spiritual, financial and administrative authority of the community concerned. They could change their community only if they converted to Islam. The Islamic state did not allow non-Muslims to convert to a religion other than Islam, nor did this often occur in practice (eg the conversion of Jews to Christianity or that of Christians to Judaism). But Christians sometimes changed denomination within their own community. Examples include the conversion of Gregorian Armenians to Catholicism or Protestantism and the conversion to Catholicism of members of the *Süryani Kadim* community (Jacobites, Monophysites) and even of Copts and some Bulgarians in the 19th century. *Millet* does not denote a nation, (nor an ethnicity) but a form of social organisation, based on religion, a state of mind and the subjects' mutual consideration of one another. The term *ekalliyet* (minority) was introduced into the life of our state and society in the last decades of the Empire.

Members of a *millet* had a number of attitudes and behaviour patterns which were contrary to those of a minority in modern society. Membership of the group gave individuals self-confidence and indeed dignity within the family, the family line and the community. They lived in their own social group with their own traditions and oral culture. There were few links and few conflicts between communities. Unlike members of minority groups in modern society, people did not have to battle with the world around them or fight to demonstrate their identity or resist assimilation. There were none of the groupings or competition, and attitudes promoting rivalry and conflict in the struggle for access to the cosmopolitan elite in society were engendered by nationalisation and modernisation in the Ottoman Empire during the 19th century.

At that time a group of young people from all religions were educated in the Empire's schools with people from all the other communities. This group entered the bureaucracy, were promoted to senior posts and joined the Ottoman elite, while a second group, which remained outside this process, took part in nationalist movements and struggles and a third, larger group pursued its age-old way of life as peasants, craftworkers or small city shopkeepers.

What was the *millet* system? It was a from of organisation and legal status arising from the submission of followers of monotheistic religions (*ehl-i zimmet)* to the authority of Islam after the annexation of a region to the Empire, under an *ahidname* or treaty granting protection. In addition to this definition, there are many different aspects to the legal principle of *millet*. The *ahidname* confered unilateral advantages. As the last Islamic empire in history, the Ottoman Empire gradually improved on these points and on various practical aspects of its legal and administrative structure.

Ottoman expansion took place during the troubled unstable conditions of the 14th and 15th centuries, which were different from those prevailing in the first few centuries of Islam. For purposes of conquest, Ottoman military power and technology had to be combined with policy-making, especially long-term political practice. According to Professor Halil İnalcık, non-Muslims experienced three different periods or phases under Ottoman rule. At the time of the first conquests, peasants, city craftsmen, members of the clergy and landowners in newly conquered territory were granted privileges which sometimes exceeded the bounds of Muslim law for propaganda purposes. They were subject to the rules and institutions that existed prior to the period of conquest. Though conditions under the old system were hard on the people, former groups of dismissed officials and landowners were incorporated into the *askeri* system, under which to ensure their support, they did not pay taxes (H. İnalcık). This policy and systems are known as *istimalet*.[3] As long as there were no pressing reasons for the situation to change after conquest, this status continued to exist. But the Ottoman social order was such that the various religions remained in existence under the *millet* system.

The *millet* system was based on membership of a religious and denominational group, not of an ethnic and linguistic group. The Armenians were not all organized in an Armenian *millet*, but in three with their own accent. The Latin *millet* is directly subject to the Roman Catholic rite; at that time they held mass in Latin in their churches. Eastern Catholics were Armenian, Jacobite and Copt Catholics. They used their own languages in worship and, although under the authority of the Roman Church, protected their own rituals and hierarchies with a form of autonomy. The Lebanese Maronites and the *Melkit* (Greek Catholics) were also included in this group.

The Jewish nation was the most scattered community in the Ottoman Empire, and the one that used the most languages.

3 Halil İnalcık, "Status of the Greek Orthodox Patriarch under the Ottomans", *Turkish Review, Quarterly Digest*, Winter, 1922, p.25 ff.

Those who had come from Spain were known as the Sephardim and spoke Judeo-Spanish (Ladino). Those who had emigrated from central and southern Europe in the 18th and 19th centuries (Ashkenazi Jews) spoke Yiddish. In the Empire and Mesopotamia there were Jews who spoke Aramic, while others in the other Levantine countries spoke Arabic. This nation was not under a central authority like the others, since there is no clergy in the Jewish religion as there is in Islam. Although the term *kefere* (infield, in hebrew *kefarim*) was used under certain circumstances to denote Christians in the Ottoman chancery records of the classical period, it was not used with regard to Jews, who were termed the "Yahud group". Mutual hatred prevailed between Jews and Christians, especially Orthodox Greeks. At every Passover festival the Greeks complained to Ottoman officials and the courts that the Jews had kidnapped and murdered a child. The Sublime Porte consequently issued *firmans* ordering the dismissal of such stupid complaints *(abes dava dinlenmemesi* – may it not accept the appeals of such nonsense and listen to these cases). Similar incidents occured in the 19th century and the Sublime Porte was compelled to protect the Jewish community from such pressures and forbid excesses.[4]

Within the Ottoman system there were two religious groups of a different kind, the *Druzes* and the *Yezidis*. The Islamic *ulama* (theologians) could not consider these two groups as part of the Muslim *umma* and Muslims could not regard them as organic members of the community. Neither could the two groups be defined as a *millet* (nation). The administration opted for saying nothing and the leaders and communities chose to avoid trouble in the matter.

The Ottoman *millet* system was a unique development in history, both as a specific form of organisation and a system that evolved in the specific socio-cultural environment of Ottoman

4 BOA, Irade MV, No.5129, 2 Şaban 1266/June 1850.

society. It cannot be compared to minority nations in colonial empires or to federal structures. It protected the religious, if not cultural, identities of groups living in a geographically determined area and groups scattered across several areas, some of which, like the Jews, lacked linguistic unity. It was so effective that under this system there were instances of reciprocal conversion and some groups assimilated other identities within their religious community. Some Christian Bulgarians and Albanians became hellenised; the Greek-Orthodox people of Anatolia known as *Karamanlı*, who were of Turkish origin and spoke Turkish, had to end their history as Greeks, while some groups that had become Muslim assumed or sided with Turkish identity (like the Pomaks), despite their linguistic differences.

All this cultural geography and history currently lies outside the scope of definitive studies and research. The *millet* system cannot serve as the basis for western-style nationalism, which was able to develop only by opposing the system and bringing about its decline. Obviously, even the terms "nation" and "nationalism" are untranslatable. This discrepancy in terminology also reflects a historical misunderstanding. The *millet* system is one in which the religious community and religious law regulate the subjects' lives and determine their obligations.

The identification of ethnicity with religion brings in this period of history some discrepancies. On the one hand *secularisme (laicisme)* eliminated religious identity based on ethnic origins, whole on the other, religion alone was still the basic element of national identity. However, a process of changing identity role and definitions existed. This is one of the most interesting evolutionary phases of modern history in our part of the world.

3

Ottomanism and Zionism During the Second Constitutional Period, 1908-1915

From several important perspectives the position of Ottoman Jewry presented a unique case in the social and political history of the late Ottoman Empire. When the Second Constitutional Period *(Meşrutiyet)* was inaugurated in 1908, the socio-political situation of the Jewish community was similar, in some respects, to that of the Muslim Turks. Within the community there were some who actively supported the constitutional government. While others were staunch sympathizers on the highest leadership and administrative levels of the community. The most significant and widely known incident reflecting this dichotomy, was the resignation of the Acting Chief Rabbi Moshe Levi (Halevi) upon the deposition of Abdülhamid II, following the 31 March event. It appeared as if the old leadership had opted to relinquish its power to the party which supported the Young Turks, without provoking any kind of incident.

The general situation of Ottoman Jewry during the Second Constitutional Period may be summarized as follows: Geographically the Jews were the most widely spread group in the empire. They lived throughout most of the Arab provinces and in Anatolia. Their presence was particularly noticeable in İzmir and in almost every other urban center in western Anatolia. In the European provinces in addition to the important cities of İstanbul, Salonica, Edirne, and Gallipoli, Jewish communities were found in the urban centers of Bosnia, southern Bulgaria and Macedonia. Ottoman Jewry was also the most culturally diverse ethnic group. In the European and Anatolian provinces the Judeo-Spanish speaking Sephardim predominated. However, with the increased recent immigration of east European Jews, primarily from Russia and Romania, Yiddish-speaking Ashkenazi groups became increasingly noticeable. In addition, in the large port cities of İstanbul, İzmir, and Salonica there existed congregations of Italian Jews. Elsewhere in the empire there were Jews who spoke Arabic, Kurdish and even Aramaic. Indeed there was no other ethnic element as polyglot as the Jews. These two factors, great physical dispersion and cultural and linguistic diversity, could not become easily conducive to the emergence of a nationalist Jewish movement as in the case of other ethnic groups.

It is possible to state that Turks and Jews were two groups within the Empire which were among the least exposed to nationalism. Ottoman Jewry became exposed to European culture only in the second half of the nineteenth century, later than any other non-Muslim minority. For this reason it was slow to accept nationalism as an abstract notion to be applied in practice. On the other hand, the Balkan nations, and especially the Christian elements, had been influenced by, and had supported, each other in their nationalistic aspirations since the end of the eighteenth century. The Greek rebellion owed much to the Serbian; Bulgarian nationalism owed much to the Greek *Hetairia*; and the role played by Bulgarian volunteers in the Greek rebellion is well known. However, it was not possible for the Ottoman Jews, who remained outside the pale of Christian brotherhood and who generally were in economic competition with the Christian elements of the Empire, to feel an interest in, and sympathy for, these movements. In short, at the end of the Empire, the objective conditions which would draw Ottoman Jewry to the intellectual currents of contemporary nationalism appear to have been absent. It would seem that Ottomanism–that is, a modern political theory advocating Ottoman patriotism, which was a product of the nineteenth century–held greater promise for Jewish needs and aspirations.

Ottoman Jewry entered the modernization period under the guidance of western Jewish educational and charitable organizations whose primary concern was to prepare young Jews to become useful and productive members of the general society in which they lived. The most active organizations in the Ottoman Empire were the *Alliance Israélite Universelle* (established in 1860), and the *Hilfsverein der Deutschen Juden* (founded in 1901). The ideology of these organizations was primarily assimilationist and anti-nationalist, although by their structure and curricula they made it easier for young Jews trained in their institutions to assimilate into western, rather than Ottoman society. There are, however, significant numbers of young Jews, especially among the lower classes, who for economic reasons attended Ottoman secondary schools, where a liberal system of financial aid was in existence. A significant number of those later went on to study in Ottoman institutions of higher learning, such as the Faculty of Law and the Medical School. This, in turn, led to the emergence of an Ottomanized Jewish element within the Jewish elite and also within the Ottoman bureaucratic elite. Although no Jew ever attained the office of minister, ambassador, or governor, the number of Jews in the upper levels of the various ministries, and in particular in the financial and medical administration became significant toward the empire's end.[1]

In addition there was a growing number of Jewish intellectuals (as was the case with the other ethnic minorities of the Empire) who were truly bilingual, speaking Turkish as one of their native tongues. Indeed by that time Turkish language instruction had been incorporated into all Jewish schools, which also added

1 Avram Galante, *Türkler ve Yahudiler*, İstanbul, 1928, pp.128-136.

courses on Turkish history and geography. Several Jews began to assume a role in Turkish journalism. Moise Fresco published in İzmir *Ustad*, a Turkish newspaper written in Hebrew characters. Nissim Masliah published the newspaper *İttihad* and Moise Cohen published the *İktisadiyat Mecmuası* from 1915 to 1918. Avram Galante who had attained prominence during this period was also a member of this bilingual group.[2]

Finally there were Jewish political activists who supported the constitutional movement and who had been in contact with the Unionists since the days of Abdülhamid. This group overlapped to some extent with the previous one and included Nissim Masliah, Albert Ferid Asseo, Albert Fua and the *Meşveret* newspaper group in Paris, the famous Emmanuel Carasso, Nissim Russo and Avram Galante. Galante had been a member of the *Mısır Cemiyet-i İsrailiyesi* (the Jewish Society of Egypt) which had been in contact with the Young Turk leader Ahmed Riza and had supported him during the opposition years. These Ottomanized Jewish intellectuals were genuinely staunch supporters of the ideals of the Second Constitutional Period.[3] Their support was not "tactical" and should not be regarded as a national "compromise," as was the case with the position of some of the intellectuals of the Balkan ethnic groups. It was rather a direct result of their Ottoman patriotism. Unlike the Bulgarians, the Greeks and the Armenians who entered the elections with their own nationalist agendas, the Jewish delegates did not exhibit such tendencies. Moreover, unlike the Albanian and the Arab delegates, they did not even establish their own national cultural clubs. In spite of this, in the parliaments of the Second Constitutional Period, the Jewish delegates were represented effectively due to their active support of and participation within the Committee of Union and Progress.

---

2 Idem, *Histoire des Juifs de Turquie* (Editions Isis, İstanbul, 1987), vol.VIII, pp. 89-93.

3 *Ibid.*, vol.VIII, pp.54-59, 187-188.

It should be added, however, that in spite of the lack of "objective" conditions for the rise of a Jewish nationalism, as described above, Esther Benbassa has demonstrated that as of 1908.[4] Zionism became a considerable force within the Jewish community, especially at the grassroots level. Its success derived mainly from the growing politicization of the community and it was able to draw adherents from the camps of its ideological adversaries, both the traditionalist religious groups and the assimilationist Alliancists. It should be pointed out, however, that Ottoman Zionists generally supported the principle of the state's territorial integrity and focused primarily on activities aimed at Jewish cultural revival. Their political activities were conducted almost exclusively within the internal level of the community, aiming at controlling or at least influencing the community leadership.

During the Second Constitutional Period, Ottoman Jewry was represented and governed by the Chief Rabbi Haim Nahum who personified a new type of an Ottomanized Jewish intellectual. Nahum, a native of Manisa, received in his childhood a traditional religious education. He then attended and graduated from a government high school in İzmir and continued to study law at the Faculty of Law in İstanbul. From 1893 to 1897 he studied at the rabbinical seminary in Paris, where he received his ordination as a rabbi. He also studied semitic languages at the Collège de France. While in Paris Nahum established a relationship with Young Turk leaders then in exile.[5] It was this relationship that propelled him to the position of Acting Chief Rabbi, in 1908, and then Chief Rabbi, in 1909. The following appointment decree dated 12 July, 1909 (23 *Cemaziyelahir*, 1327), is noteworthy:

---

4 Hasan Kayalı, "Jewish Representation in the Ottoman Parliament", and Esther Benbassa, "Associational Strategies in Ottoman Jewish Society in the Nineteenth and Twentieth Centuries", in A. Levy, (ed.), *The Jews of the Ottoman Empire*, forthcoming, The Darwin Press, Princeton, N.J.

5 Avram Galante, *Histoire des Juifs d'Anatolie*, vol.II (1939), p.98.

> The Imperial *Nişan* states: I, the Sultan, give this imperial *Berat* (diploma), in which the old provisions concerning the confirment of the Chief Rabbinate are mentioned, to Haim Nahum, leader of the Jewish community, who had been elected by the electorate organized in accordance with the regulation [of the Jewish nation], to the vacant position of the Chief Rabbinate of İstanbul and its dependencies, and whose office has been reported by the Ministry of Justice and Sects and confirmed by the Privy Council of Ministers, and I order that:
>
> The aforesaid Haim Nahum Efendi be the Chief Rabbi of the nation of the Jews of İstanbul and its dependencies, and the Rabbis and community chiefs and all the Jews, of high or low status in my well-protected territories recognize him as their Chief Rabbi, to apply to him for their affairs within the responsibility of the Chief Rabbinate; let them act in cooperation and agreement with him, and not fail in obeying and submitting to him according to their religion and customs...[6]

The government yearbook of the same year (1327/1909),[7] refers to Nahum as *Hahambaşı* and to the other chief rabbis of twenty-seven major urban centers, as *Başhaham*. The term *İstanbul ve tevabii Hahambaşısı* (Chief Rabbi of İstanbul and its dependencies) had been used since the office was first established in 1835 in the reign of Mahmud II.[8] But chief rabbis of other important towns had also been known until then by the title of *Hahambaşı*, and the chief rabbi of

İstanbul was regarded merely as first among equals. Technically there is no difference between the title *hahambaşı* and *başhaham*. Both mean chief rabbi. Nevertheless the distinction now made between the *Hahambaşı* of İstanbul and the *Başhahams* of all other

---

6 *Başbakanlık Arşivi* (Prime Minister's Archives, İstanbul; henceforth: *BA)*, *Gayri Müslim Cemaatlere Ait Defterler* (Henceforth: *GMC*), vol.18 (*Yahudi ve Karai Defterleri)*, pp.38-42.

7 *1327 Salname-i Devlet-i Aliyye-i Osmaniyye*, İstanbul, 1327/1909. No pagination.

8 See the contribution by Avigdor Levy in Levy (ed.) *The Jews of the Ottoman Empire*, op. cit.

cities was intended, no doubt, to further stress the primacy of the former over all other rabbis in the Empire. Indeed following his appointment as Chief Rabbi, Haim Nahum was referred to in semi-official and official documents and in the press, as: "The spiritual head of the Jewish nation of the well-protected Ottoman territories, Chief Rabbi, the exalted Haim Nahum Efendi..."[9] In other words, he was regarded as Chief Rabbi of the Ottoman Empire. This reflects two important tendencies on the part of the Unionists. First it reveals their personal confidence in Haim Nahum. In addition, however, it represents an attempt to establish for Ottoman Jewry a more centralized administrative organization, something which ran counter to the grain of the Unionists' policies regarding other ethnic groups. It is therefore a reflection of the Unionists' confidence in the political loyalties of Ottoman Jewry as a whole. Haim Nahum was awarded the highest Mecidiye order and was held in high esteem in official circles. As a matter of fact, it has his influential position that made him a favourite target of other non-Muslim groups within the Empire.

Zionism, although a national movement, was perceived by Ottoman Turkish intellectuals and officials as something different. In the Ottoman mind the familiar forms of separatist nationalism were those of the Greeks. Bulgarians and Armenians and the ethnic groups in Macedonia, with their underground committees and armed struggle. Due to this, the activities of the Zionist movement, invariably conducted in diplomatic, political and economic terms, did not elicit significant reaction, contrary to what is generally believed. Some Ottomans even viewed Zionism with sympathy as a reaction against European domination and Christian culture. This is how, for example, Dr. Lichtheim, the Zionist representative in İstanbul, had correctly assessed the attitude of Ahmed Ağaoğlu who was sympathetic

9 *BBA, GMC*, vol.18, pp.38-42.

toward the Zionist cause.[10] It is true that among Ottoman bureaucrats and intellectuals there were some who had been affected directly or indirectly by European anti-Semitism. In general, however, it would appear that educated Ottomans did not have a prejudiced atitude vis-à-vis Judaism or Zionism. The policies of the provincial and central Ottoman authorities toward the Zionist settlers have not been studied in adequate depth to render an accurate picture. The few examples which emerge make it impossible to categorically state the position of any official body or forum on the subject of Ottoman policy toward Zionism. Nevertheless, the preliminary general impression is that policies and administrative strategies were neutral vis-à-vis Zionism. This may be due to the basic fact that during the last ten years of the Empire, Zionism had simply not been in a position to aspire to more than some limited administrative and cultural autonomy, as opposed to an independent or even autonomous state within defined boundaries. Hence it did not pose a real threat to the state.

Finally, Ottoman administrators must have been impressed with Zionist support for Ottoman causes during the Tripoli War and the Balkan Wars. The efforts of Zionists to form a group which would join the Ottoman army to offer medical assistance during the Balkan Wars, and to mobilize volunteers to assist Ottoman units during the First World War were also well known. Indeed, it became clear that on the eve of the world war and during its initial stages, Zionist groups viewed the continued existence of the Ottoman state as most desirable for their future plans in Palestine. For this reason the Zionist organization even offered to make a contribution toward the construction of the Hijaz railroad.[11] It appears that for these reasons, some government

10 Richard Lichtheim, *Rückkehr–Lebenserinnerungen aus der Frühzeit des deutschen Zionismus*, Stuttgart, 1970, p.188.

11 *Central Zionist Archive*, Jerusalem (cited as *CZA*), 39-A II a2, 40-A II a3, 41-A II a', "Sympathieaktionen der Zionistischen Organisation der Turkei

circles were less annoyed by the Zionists than they were by some of the other minority groups who sought the protection and intervention of the Great Powers. In spite of all this, relations were too complex to be easily categorized.

It is often repeated that in 1907, the former governor of the district of Jerusalem, Ekrem Bey, convinced the Minister of the Interior, of the necessity to prevent the immigration of Jews, particularly Russian Jews, whom he considered as a "dangerous element" for state security.[12] His successor, Subhi Bey, however, followed an entirely different policy while stationed in Jerusalem, and did not implement the recommended measures. This is one example which demonstrates why Ottoman policy toward Zionism cannot be easily categorized.[13]

Ottoman officials were, generally speaking, xenophobic on the subject of Zionism. Still they recognized the usefulness of the Zionist organization and benefited by maintaining contacts with its representatives. Levontin reported to Herzl on 3 May, 1904: "The governor summoned me in haste and asked me to loan him 3,000 sterlings more, after he received a telegram from the Ministry of Finance." It appears that the governor had regularly received such loans from the Zionist leader when he was in need for his office because of financial crise. Levontin adds: "This year's tax on sheep *(resmi-i ağnam)* will be good. I don't see any hindrance in providing this amount as well."[14] What is interesting here, is that these debtor-creditor relationships between Ottoman officials and the Zionist Organization, which

in türkisch-italienischen Kriege–Entwurf von Dr. M. Nordalu, 5 October, 1911. Same as AII d/z2, donation of the Zionists for the construction of the Hijaz Railway.

12 Cf. Isaiah Friedman, *Germany, Turkey and Zionism, 1897-1918*, Oxford, 1977, p.141; also *CZA*, A 19/7 from Jacobson to Wolfssohn, 10 September, 1908.

13 Friedman, *ibid.*, p.142. Also M. Kemal Öke, *Osmanlı İmparatorluğu, Siyonizm ve Filistin Sorunu*, İstanbul, Üçdal Neşriyat, 1982, pp.92-93.

14 *CZA*, Z1/531 from Levontin to Herzl, Jaffa, 3 May, 1904.

were due to difficulties in the Ministry of Finance, have been represented in the literature on this subject as the fault of only the local officials.[15] During the Second Constitutional Period, we see that various individuals including Talat Pasha and other leaders of the Committee of Union and Progress, observed and recognized that the Zionist colonies were a factor contributing to the development of Palestine and hence to the increase in tax revenues. On the other hand, however, it is this period which also witnesses a deterioration in Arab-Jewish relations and Ottoman attempts to curb the conflict. At this time the Ottomans have also made efforts to prevent the Zionists from obtaining land, fearing increased Great Power intervention. It was particularly for this last reason that Talat Pasha insisted that the Russian Jewish settlers become Ottoman citizens. On another issue, when the request of the Zionist organization for cultural autonomy and participation in local government–which they expressed with the terms *offentlich-rechtlich* (publicly and by law)–was criticized in the Ottoman parliament as a move toward colonization and independence (particularly by Cosmidi Efendi, a Greek-Ottoman deputy), the Grand Vizier Hakkı Pasha stated that preventive measures would be adopted against the Zionist goals. Subsequently, Wolfssohn, one of the Zionist leaders, wrote a letter, dated 10 August, 1911, to Hakkı Pasha who was a jurist. He began by stating: "Your highness does not need lengthy explanations to understand ...the term *offentlich-rechtlich...*" He nevertheless went on to explain that the term did not express a request for more than publicly recognized civil rights.[16]

In the press, Ebüziyya Tevfik had adopted an anti-semitic and anti-Zionist attitude. On the other hand, Ahmed Ağaoğlu and Celal Esad were described by Jacobson, the Zionist representative

15 Cf. Öke, *ibid.*, p.90.

16 *CZA*, Z2/1, pp.401-410, "Türkische Parlamentsangriffe auf der Zionismus," from Dr. Wolfssohn to the Grand Vizier Hakkı Pasha, Cologne. 10 April, 1911.

in İstanbul, as "Friends of Zion." However, his successor Lichtheim who was less effusive in evaluating these matters, wrote that they appeared more prepared to support Jews and Zionists against the British and against other separatist national movements, rather than being true Friends of Zion.[17] Dr. Abdullah Cevdet was a sympathizer of Judaism and the Zionist movement. Rıza Tevfik, an opponent of the Unionists, was an intellectual who was a sympathizer of Zionism. Ali Kemal, the editor of *İkdam*, which was considered an anti-Semitic publication, was apparently not so personally. He had opposed Zionism because it seemed to him that foreign powers were manipulating the movement. In fact, it was common knowledge in İstanbul during this period, that the German embassy, which included several outspoken anti-Semites, among them Ambassador Wangenheim, supported Zionism solely with the expectation that it would advance German interests in Palestine. It was also obvious that Russia, the champion of official anti-Semitism at home, was not opposed to Jewish settlers in Palestine bearing Russian passports.[18] For this reason it appears that support of, or opposition to, Zionism did not reflect a particular political line. For the most part, government officials knew little or nothing about Zionism. Which was a reflection of their general lack of interest in the movement. Arthur Ruppin who was taken to court due to the anti-Zionist measures implemented by Cemal Pasha during the war years, recorded in his memoirs: "The Turkish officers who functioned as judges, did not have the slightest idea of Zionism, and things were not better with the civil judges who prepared the charges..."[19]

17 Lichtheim., *Rückkehr*, p.188.

18 *CZA*, 23/51, 8 February, 1915, Telegram of Wagenheim to Lichtheim. *CZA*, Z3/49, pp.243-244, from Jacobson to Tschlenow, information about a conversation at the Russian Embassy, 21 May, 1914.

19 Arthur Ruppin, *Tagebücher, Briefe, Erinnerungen*, Jüdische Verlag, Athenaum, 1985, p.264.

During the war, Cemal Pasha and his assistant Bahaddin had a hostile attitude toward the Zionist settlers. However, Cemal and Bahaddin followed the same rigid attitude toward the Arabs. This can be explained by a desire to ensure peace in a region not far from the front through the administration of strict measures, avoiding thereby conflicts between Arabs and Jews. Bekir Sami, the governor of Beirut, was a sympathizer of Zionism. In the capital, Talat, Cavid and Hacı Adil were leaders who had implemented policies against Zionist immigration. But their opposition to Zionism was tempered by the latter's economic contribution. Hacı Adil even stated, in January 1912, that "they were friends of Zionism, but opposed to immigration"[20] Moreover, it is well known that the wartime policies of the German Ambassador Wangenheim and the U.S. Ambassador Morgenthau, who were both opposed to the expulsion of Zionists, were not rejected by the government. The leaders of the Committee of Union and Progress accepted a Jewish presence in Palestine stipulating, however, that the settlers become Ottoman subjects.[21]

In this period, we are able to observe among the Ottoman Jews, a cautious attitude toward Zionism. Although, as some authors have demonstrated, the Zionists encountered a groundswell of popular support within the community, their relations with its official representatives and spokesmen were uneasy and even hostile. For example. Judge Hammon, an Ottoman Jewish resident of Jerusalem, had been encouraged by Jacobson to become a candidate for the Parliamentary elections. Jacobson had considered him as someone who could represent the Zionists. On 11 November, 1912, he wrote about Hammon: "Although not a Zionist, he has an understanding in this matter; he is an

20 *CZA*, Z3/43-00186, dated 4 January, 1912.

21 İlber Ortaylı, *Osmanlı İmparatorluğu'nda Alman Nüfuzu* [German Influence in the Ottoman Empire], İstanbul, Kaynak Yayın, 1983, p.127, based on *Archiv des Auswaertigen Amtes*, Türkei 195, bd 5, telegram no.3, February 1915.

honest and well-known young judge."[22] Apparently, Hammon was one of those who believe that "silence is golden" and refused to cooperate. In İstanbul the Zionist representatives were often in disagreement with the eminent Jewish deputies Emmanuel Carasso and Nissim Masliah.

The one individual whom Jacobson and Lichtheim were most disappointed in, and whom they later came to hate, was Chief Rabbi Haim Nahum. Nahum is a historical figure who had been misrepresented in the literature on this subject.[23] Just as Cavid, the Minister of Finance, Talat Pasha, the Unionist leader, and even Musa Kazım Efendi, the Şeyhülislam, were sometimes depicted as Zionist sympathizers, so was Nahum included in this category. On 16 February, 1912, Lichtheim says of Nahum, "Our aim should be to overthrow Nahum and to keep the secular council."[24] In reality, Nahum was a member of the francophile and anti-German group in İstanbul. He continued following this line also after the Ottoman Empire entered the war as Germany's ally. On 14 December, 1914, Jacobson reported from İstanbul on a meeting between Nahum and Wangenheim in the German Embassy. According to this report, Nahum had told the ambassador that while being francophile he was not germanophobe. When Lichtenheim evaluated his own conversation with Nahum following this meeting, he commented that Nahum was not very fond of Zionists and added: "In his stupidity, he told me this himself, that he had somewhat slandered the Zionists on this occasion, because after all he hates us."[25]

22 *CZA*, Z3/43-0014, 11 November, 1912, from Jacobson to Auerbach.

23 Öke, *ibid.*, p.105.

24 *CZA*, Z3/43d, 16 February, 1912, from Lichtheim to Auerbach.

25 *CZA*, Z3/50, 2 December, 1914, Lichtheim's report.

4

The Greeks and Ottoman Administration During the Tanzimat Period

Even though the Greek Revolt was not the first successful national revolt, it had a shock effect on the Ottomans. The Serbian Revolt had paved the way for the other Balkan peoples to revolt and had increased their hopes for national revival; but the Greek Revolt directly accelerated the Balkan nationalist movements. After the foundation of the Kingdom of the Hellenes, the Greek nation all at once faced structural problems and elicited great hope and despair. After the Greek Revolt, the Ottoman Empire developed a consciousness of decline, and immediately tried to change its administrative, educational and military structures. Even though Austria and Russia had favoured Greek Independence for a while they soon gave up their Hellen phile policy out of fear of unrest from their own national minorities, namely, the Hungarians and Poles, who had a rich past.

One of the most striking consequences of the Greek Revolt was that the Ottomans began to eliminate Greeks from important positions in the bureaucratic and social structure of the Empire. As is well known, the Phanariot dragomans in the Sublime Porte were replaced either by converted Christians like Bulgarzade Yahya Efendi or by Armenians such as Sahak Abro Efendi. Some of the Phanariots however, remained faithful and favored subjects of the Empire (with exceptions like Mavrokordato and Ypsilanti.)[1]

1 See for the origin of Phanariot families, M. D. Sturdza, *Grandes Familles de Grèce, d'Albanie et de Constantinople (Dictionnaire historique et généaogique)*, Paris, 1983.

For example, Musurus Pasha was sent as the first ambassador to Athens in 1840 and was hated intensely by Greek nationalists who attempted to assassinate him. As a result of this attempt on his life, he suffered permanent injury to his left hand.[2] Photiadi Bey, his successor too as ambassador to Athens. Kalimaki Bey, the ambassador to Vienna, and Sava Pasha (who compiled a still favoured manual of Islamic law) are other prominent figures in the Ottoman administration. But these men are the exceptions. In fact, Greek supremacy in the Ottoman Empire was in decay. The Ottomans took measures in order to prevent further revolts of Greek subjects in Rumelia and the islands.

In the following decades, the Ottoman administrative apparatus showed two features: reforms and grants of concessions to the Greek communities, on the one hand, and distrust and inspection, on the other hand. One of the most remarkable cases of counter-measures taken to prevent a nationalist revolt was in Samos. The Sublime Porte granted autonomy to this island by a special concessional decree *(imtiyaz fermanı)* issued in 1832, and named it "Sisam Emareti." The islanders almost gained a constitutional structure. The waves of revolt had forced the Ottoman administration to create such a concessional status. A Greek Orthodox subject of the Porte was appointed as the governor of Samos *(Sisam Beyi)*, and elected representatives from among the notables formed a *meclis* which was responsible for taking decisions on matters related to navigation, tax collection, construction, school instruction and even church affairs. The Ottoman army evacuated the island, (except a small corps of gendarmes) and public maintenance and security functions were left basically the islanders. Sisam had to pay a certain annual tax to the Sublime Porte.[3] In 1861, Miltiadi

2 Sinan Kuneralp, "Kostaki Musurus Pasha" in *TTK Belleten*, 1970/3 Ankara, pp.421-35.

3 İsmail Hakkı, *Hukuk-u İdare* first publication 1328 H/1910 Konstantiniye, p. 369-74. A correspondance of Grandvizir of 9 RA 1310 (1 Oct. 1892), clearly describes the limits of the authority of this small corps. B. A. *Y. A. Hus.* Nr.266-53.

Bey Aristarchi was granted a new firman which regulated the functions of the *meclis*, defining the legislative period and matters of tax collection and the budget of the *emaret.* The annual tax was set at 400,000 Ottoman kuruş and had to be paid to the Sublime Porte in two portions. However, the Ottomans retained the right to keep a small body of gendarmerie, consisting of twenty men with their commander. As jurisdictional authority, a judge had to be appointed by the Sublime Porte, who then would have to work with a court whose members were elected from among the local notables. The first provincial newspaper in the Ottoman Empire, *Vilayet cerîdesi,* was probably puslished in Sisam before that of the Danubian province. The issue must have been in two languages: Greek and Ottoman Turkish. However, even though I found and *irade* in the archives,4 I have not yet been able to locate a copy of this issue. The constitutional status of Samos challenged, in a way, the Ottoman Constitution, since it remained in force even after 1878, together with Mount Lebanon, Crete and Eastern Rumelia.

On the other hand, fear of revolutionary activities abroad as well as in the Greek Kingdom caused a certain recession of the Greek element in the Empire, and Greeks were subjected to greater control than in the past.

The affairs of the Patriarchate became a quite controversial issue. This institution was criticized by the Greeks in the Kingdom as too conservative and was suspected by the Sublime Porte of being a spiritual and national center. Russia, on the other hand, had an ambivalent attitude towards the patriarchate, supporting it as it did formerly and yet hesitating because of the conflict with the nationalist demands of the Bulgarian Church movement. In spite of this, Russia spent much effort to keep its representative functions and its protective role of the Greek Orthodox Church in the Empire. For instance, it became customary around this period for members of the Romanov family to visit the Ottoman

4 B. A., *İrade-Meclis-i-Valâ*. Nr.9105 (II L 1268/February 1852).

Empire about every other year, and stop in Constantinople and Jerusalem, kissing the hands of the Patriarch in the presence of the public. Grand Duke Constantine's visit to Jerusalem in 1859 is a striking example of this. Russia continually sponsored the Greek Orthodox schools, defended the rights of Greek subjects, and turned some cases of conversion into a diplomatic issue.[5]

After the draft of the general educational law, Greek schools, like others, were put under the control of the Ministry of Education. The books used in these were subject to scrutiny. Occasionally even some Greek subjects informed the Porte by a petition of the harmful contents of these books. Such a case took place in 1860. This petition stated that some schoolbooks brought from foreign countries to be used in these schools contained harmful material, and was signed by Ottomans belonging to different *millets*,6 including Greeks. They demanded that these books be rewritten and corrected. The decision of the Sublime Porte was that the history books had to contain the lives of the Apostles. These petitioners, mostly, *muallims* (school teachers), asked for twelve years to rewrite these books. They suggested Biblical history for primary schools, and ancient Greek history, general history together with Ottoman history and hagiography for secondary schools.

Others, such as a clerical professor named Filippaki from the Seminary of Halki (Heybeli), informed the Sublime Porte that the professors in the Seminary were teaching the students harmful ideas. Filippaki was sent to Europe with a salary of 300 francs.7 Also, the newly founded Ottoman high schools (like *Mekteb-i*

5 B. A., *İrade-Hariciye*. Nr.4028, 21 S. 1268/December 1851, after the death of a former Christian (named Ali), two of his daughters (who probably kept their faith) took asylum in the Greek consulate in Adrianople.

6 B. A., *İrade-Meclis-Valâ*. Nr.914. The petition is dated 6 Receb 1288/October 1869 where the corresponding *irade* is dated 2 Receb 1288/September 1872. The procedure covered a period of two years.

7 B. A., *İrade-Hariciye*. Nr.10276, 12 Safer 1277/August 1860.

Tıbbiye, Medical School, *Mülkiye Mektebi*, Imperial School of Administration, Veterinary School etc.) granted a quota of 33 percent to non-Muslim students of Ottoman nationality. That quota caused both rumors and a struggle among different non-Muslim communities. In 1857, the Medical School, following a petition from the Armenian community, reduced the number of Greek candidates to 50 from 55, to the benefit of Armenian candidates. That case indicates a general trend in the *Tanzimat* period, when the Greek element in the Empire started to lose its former privileged status among other non-Muslim communities.[8]

Certainly the reaction of the elite Ottoman Greeks indicates of different character. Some of the Phanariots during this era tried to impose a confederative administrative structure, for the safety of the Empire and their own community. One of them, André Coromèles proposed a Turco-Greek empire and suggested that the Sultan should have the title of "Sultan of the Turks and King of Greeks." Another, Stefanos Xenos, emphasized "the common interests of the Turks and Greeks is the Empire" during the days of the Bulgarian revolt and anti-Turkish demonstrations in London. Another, Pitzipios Bey suggested in his book, the adaptation of Byzantine institutions, equality of two religions and the coronation of Sultan Abdülmecid as Emperor of the Byzantines.9 The Church had to fight on the one side against the secularist tendencies of some modern Greeks, and on the other side to oppose the demands of the Bulgarian nationalists, who sought to have a national independent Bulgarian church.

The Ionian Islands, a joint protectorate of the Ottoman and Russian Empires and later of Britain, on the one side, and Crete on the other, were strictly controlled by the Ottomans. Whenever the General of the Ionian Islands *(-Cezaîr-i Sab'a Generali-)*

8 B. A., *İrade-Hariciye*. Nr.7140, 12 N 1273/May 1857.

9 André Coroméles, *Réforme praticable en Turquie*, Athènes 1853, p.30 and Stefanos Xenos, *Union or Dismemberment of Turkey*, London 1876, p.11, and J. G. Pitzipios Bey, *L'Orient, les Réformes de l'Empire Byzantin*, Paris, 1858.

visited citics like Preveza on the continent, the Sublime Porte was informed by agents.10 And the missionary activities of the British Protestants in the islands were stopped by a cooperation of the Sublime Porte, the Greek Patriarchate and Russia. An *irade* of 1839 is a very clear and precise illustration of that.11

A report of the Ottoman ambassador Musurus Pasha in London informed the Sublime Porte that the Greek Kingdom enlisted the local people of Crete for the Greek army (28 March 1861). Musurus Pasha learned about this from his agents in London and net with Lord John Russell, and the Sublime Porte pressured Great Britain to prevent the Greek Kingdom from doing this. Some Cretans, registered in the islands belonging to the Greek Kingdom, had become Greek subjects. Musurus Pasha demanded, however, that they should not be entitled to claim Greek citizenship if they had migrated to one of the Ottoman Dodecanese islands or Anatolia.12 Actually, the small Hellenic Kingdom was in need of population and migration from the Ottoman continent and islands. It was not rare, nevertheless, that many of these immigrants tried to go back to the Ottoman Empire is disappointment. The Ottoman government, favouring this movement, exempted them from the capitation tax or *cîzye* for 8-10 years, and sometimes subsidized them in agriculture. In May 1850 alone, 90 families came from Greece, back to their home.13 During these years even the regulation of tithe *(aşar nizamnamesi)* was translated into Greek language.14

Armenians, Jews and Maronites were favoured to the detriment of Greeks in officialdom. In fact, Greek intellectuals

10 B. A., *İrade-Hariciye.* Nr.4118, 1268 of H/1852, *İrade-Hariciye.* Nr.4697, 6 C 1269/March 1853.

11 B. A., *İrade-Hariciye.* Nr.120,29 Ca 1255/August 1839.

12 B. A., *İrade-Hariciye.* Nr.10214, "Musurus to Ali Pasha" 28 March 1861.

13 B. A., *İrade-Hariciye.* Nr.4000, selh-i Muh. 1268/October 1851, *İrade-Hariciye*, Nr. 3209, selh- i Receb 1266/May 1850.

14 B. A., *İrade-Hariciye.* Nr.10 308, 25 Zilhicce 1277/July 1861.

had been suffering slowly from a brain drain, though in special professional branches of the army, officers and sailors of Greek origin were employed. At Easter the navy had to anchor in certain ports because of the Greek crews.[15] Therefore at the Naval Academy *(Mekteb-i Bahriyye-yi* Şahane*)* the Greek language was instructed to all of the students. In 1858 a certain Kostaki Bey was appointed to the Academy as instructor of Greek.[16]

During these years, it would be hard to claim that the Ottoman political mind could evaluate the essence of Greek nationalism. Nationalist movements and the activity of bands are usually cited as *eşkiya* and *eterya eşkiyasi*, and countermeasures which had to be taken were not achieved on the spot.[17] Both official documents and Ottoman historiography contain little knowledge of the political background and character of this movement and their contacts or position towards other Balkan nationalisms.

The activities of Greek nationalist bands spurred Ottoman authorities to take some drastic countermeasures. In Thessaloniki alone, five leading persons were arrested in 1852. Therefore merchants and priests coming from Greece to Ottoman ports were subjected to investigation. Suspected of subversive activities, some Greek neighbourhoods in İstanbul, such as Tatavla and Pangalti were subjected to military control in January 1854 and Izzet Pasha was appointed as military-commander of Beyoğlu.[18] In the same year even in Beirut, the Greek colony of the town was put under strict control. Nationalist ideas spread widely among the Greeks of the Empire, leading the authorities to control every booklet and newspaper from Greece.

Greeks in the Aegean region and Trebizond enjoyed an economic

15 B. A., *İrade-Hariciye.* Nr.8997 14 R 1264/March 1848.

16 B. A., *I D* Nr.27954-22 C. 1275/January 1859.

17 B. A., *İrade-Hariciye.* Nr.3188, 12 Receb 1266/May 1850. *İrade-Dahiliye.* Nr. 18295 selh-i Ca 1270/January 1854. See also *Yunan Defteri.* Nr. 236.

18 B. A., *Yunan Defteri.* Nr. 238 of the year 1270 H/1854 and *İrade Dahiliye.* Nr. 18295 selh-i Ca 1270/January 1854 for the case of Beirut, *İrade-Dahiliye.* Nr. 18691, 1270 H/1854.

renaissance. Kydonia (Ayvalık) and İzmir were transformed into cultural centers of Hellenism in Asia Minor, and a rich merchant class as well as rich Greek farmers emerged in small towns like Phocea (Foca). Greeks were represented in provincial councils *(Meclis-i İdare-i Vilayet* and *Meclis-i İdare-i Liva)*, but now they had to share this new privilege with other non-Muslim *millets*. At times they were subjected to abuse by Muslim members of these councils, which raised protests from the Patriarchate.[19]

The bureaucracy of the *Tanzimat* period, especially in the provinces of Rumelia, had a cultural fringe. A good number of them had a knowledge of Greek and Bulgarian. As Ahmed Mithat Efendi, a famous writer of the Hamidian era mentions in one of his books, "European children have to learn foreign languages in school, but Ottoman children, Turks, Armenians and Greeks of İstanbul pick up their languages by playing with each other..."[20] A so-called book "Tuhfet'ul Uşşak-A Present for Children" by Fevzî teaches Greek vocabulary in a poetic form to the Turks: Nam-i Hudadir Teos, ademe de antropos Dervişe der asketis, evliya adi ayos (The name of the *God* is *Theos*, and *man is anthropos Dervish* is *askhetis*, and *evliya* is *agios*).[21]

---

19 B. A., *İrade Meclisi-Valâ*. Nr.226, 9 Za 1256/January 1841.

20 Ahmed Midhat, *Ana babanın evlad üzerindeki hukuk ve vezaifi*. Dersaadet 1317/1899, pp.72-4. Ahmed Midhat, *Cocuk melekat-i uzviyye ve ruhiyyesi*, Dersaadet 1317/1899.

21 Fevzî, *Tuhfet'ul Uşşak*, from A. S. Levend, *Divan Edebiyatı*, İstanbul, 1943, p. 637.

5

From the Ottoman Experiment in Local Government to the First Constitutional Parliament of 1876-77

It would be an exaggeration in speak of a rich tradition of local government, reaching deep down into the past, in Turkish history. The ability of urban or rural communities to undertake autonomous action and to sep up their own organs of government was a relatively recent phenomenon in the Ottoman Empire, as indeed in many other countries (with the very limited exception of certain parts of medieval Europe). Nevertheless, some authors have made much of, for example, the say that craft guilds had in urban administration, or the fact that the city of Ankara was run by the *Akhis* until the fifteenth century – to the point of arguing that religious orders like the *Akhis* represented a certain tradition of local government. It is difficult to regard such claims as resting on careful study of the available documentation, which reveal no evidence of any institutionalization nor hence of any continuity in local government. It is not on craft guilds or religious orders but on economic and financial autonomy that local government should be based, and it should be capable of sustaining itself by incorporating local resident as citizens into that institutional framework. But such processes were very late in setting in under Ottoman administration.[1]

Pretty much the same holds true for the non-Muslim *millets*, it is worth noting, for Ottoman society incorporated a number of

1 İ. Ortaylı, *Tanzimattan Cumhuriyete Yerel Yönetim Geleneği*, İstanbul, 1985, p.15-18.

selfenclosed religious communities that were saddled with certain legal, financial and administrative responsibilities, and which organized among themselves to take care of education or social welfare. Consequently, this *millet* system, too, has been regarded as constitutive of a certain tradition of local government, with much attention centering on the autonomy of the Greek or the Armenian patriarchate. On balance, however, the *millet* system represented no more than an organizational model hased on the compartmentalization engendered through the overwhelmingly religious definition of social identity, while local government is a society of free citizens in embryonic form and hence also the beginning of the transition out of *communitas*. Yet in the Ottoman Empire, no Christian ethnicity or region coming under the jurisdiction of the Greek Orthodox patriarchate enjoyed any financial-administrative nor for that matter any cultural autonomy, for from the Christians of the Arab provinces to the Serbian, Bulgarian and Albanian Orthodox Christians of the Balkans, the Patriarchate itself was the only Christian community that was recognized as a community and accorded autonomy. Subordinate groups or communal units did not possess any secular organisations other than the patriarchate; the Eastern Church, moreover, did not leave any scope for the *parish* or *Pfarrtum* to exist as a lower unit of organization.

It was only the administrative reform of the Tanzimat era, therefore, that prepared the ground for the emergence of local government in territories held by the Ottoman Empire. The top bureaucrats of this period did not appear to be interested in fostering political democracy or in institutionalizing mechanisms of popular participation; they were, instead, only concerned about creating an administrative structure and environment that would be based on legality, function well, and induce economic prosperity and development, we have noted elsewhere.[2] And to

2 İ. Ortaylı, "Tanzimat Bürokratları ve Metternich" in *A. Ü. Siyasal Bilg. Fak. Dergisi*, "Fehmi Yavuz'a Armağan", Ankara, 1983, pp.361-367.

that end they took as their model not British parliamentarianism or French republicanism, but probably a more authoritarian system of successful administration, such as that represented by Metternichian Austria.

It is safe to say, hence, that it was only in context of efforts at financial reform that the central bureaucracy embarked upon is first experiments in local government. Thus when İstanbul tried to abolish the *iltizam* system of taxfarming, this initially led them into an attempt to have taxes collected not by the *mültezims*, which were a kind of contractor, but the officials in each *sancak*, who would be helped in this regard by the local people. A decree ordered so-called councils of *muhassıls* (or collection councils) to be set up, composed of an appointed *muhassil* (tax-collector) and his deputies as well as the local judge, *müftü*, top military commander and religious leaders plus six local notables elected by the said notables themselves from among their own ranks. Their method of election was described in the following way in the first paragraph of the regulations drawn up by the *Meclis-i Ahkâm-i Adliye*, the Legal Decisions and Appeals Council, concerning the formation of the collection councils: Candidates would first register at the court, and then stand forth before the gathered electors, who would step to one side or the other depending on whether they were for or against the candidate in question. Candidates who got a majority of the votes would be considered elected, while lots would be drawn among those for whom yeas and nays were split equally. This procedure was clearly not very conducive to ensuring the participation of a broad stratum even in principle,[3] but neither was it implemented properly and everywhere. Those who ended up to the collection councils, contemporary observers noted, were either those appointed by the top local administrator, or those selected by non-Muslim

3 B. A., *Cevdet-Dahiliye*, Nr.16602, 23 Sefer 1256 (26 April 1840) same found Nr. 3269, 17 Safer 1256 (20 April 1840), A. Vefik, *Tekâlif Kavaidi*, vol.II, pp.30-31.

clerics from among their respective congregations, or else local notables who had successfully curried the favour of high officals.[4]

Centralization was the fundamental aspect of the Tanzimat in administration, determined not only by the world-view, objectives and achievements of the bureaucracy but also by technological progress. New centers of urban growth and the changing spatial hierarchy around them, the eclipse of certain provincial seats and the resurgence of others, necessitated modifying the Empire's provincial divisions accordingly.

Furthermore, since Russia and Austria demanded a decentralized status of autonomy for national minorities and subject peoples or regions in the Balkans, the Tanzimat elite reacted to this threat by imposing a centralized model of provincial administration – and it was in this concrete context that our tradition of local government came into being, under the pressure of a sudden international crisis over Lebanon. This whole area (except for Beirut) had been granted an autonomous status, on the basis of congregational representation, through the *Cebel-i Lübnan Nizamnamesi* of 9 June 1861, which was intensely disliked by the Porte since it tended to transform the Empire into a mosaic of autonomous provinces. Ahmet Cevdet Pasha, whose approach to law and administration was one of enlightened despotism, Fuat Pasha and the liberal-minded Midhat Pasha then set about drafting new statutes for the provinces, and the system of provincial organization, revolving around the *sancak* or *liva* as the basic unit, that was sebsequently set up through the Regulations of 7 November 1864 embodied an attitude of "taking the different characteristics of each province into account," in the words of Ahmet Cevdet. Hence, too, these regulations were first put into effect in the Province of the Danube (where Midhat Pasha was governor) as well as in Aleppo, Edirne, North African Tripoli and Bosnia, with encouraging results. The explanation Ahmet Cevdet

4 Halil İnalcık, "Tanzimatın Uygulanması" in *TTK Belleten*, vol.XXVIII, No. 109-112, Ankara, 1964, p.633.

Pasha provided for making elected bodies of local representatives part and parcel of provincial administration echoed paragraph 14 of the Reform *(Islahat)* Edict of 1856 as drafted by Âli Pasha: "Implementing the basic rule about ensuring popular participation in governing the country is designed to relieve the absolutist tendencies of the current practice of centralism."[5] But did they truly and genuinely mean this, one might well wonder. It could have been due in part to a desire to temporize in the face of external pressure, combined with the fundamental determination to achieve administrative rationalization. The regulations of 1864 ostensibly imitated the French system of *départements* while actually going much further along the road to centralization, with the opposite alternative rendered virtually unthinkable by the reformers' prevailing outlook. All in all, between Âli Pasha's centralist inclinations and Cevdet Pasha's cautious conservatism, there was hardly any scope for greater autonomy in provincial administration.

There were, however, some practical problems which transcended such principles or ideological preferences, in that the leading core of the Tanzimat had suffered from a shortage of trained personnel from the very beginning: There simply were not enough administrative, legal and financial cadres to carry through the necessary reforms in central and provincial administration; long after the Tanzimat had been promulgated indeed, provincial governors lacked the staff to handle even routine work. That was why the later *Islahat* generation, too, could not radically reorganize the entire system on the lines of hundred percent centralization, and had to have recourse, *volens nolens*, to more classical methods as well as to local notables in their provincial rearrangements. (All was not well, however, for relations between the members of various congregations were already deteriorating, with the various

5 G. C. Scalieri, *La Décentralisation et la réforme administrative en Turquie*, Constantinople, 1911, p.121, Ortaylı, *Tanzimattan Sonra Mahalli İdareler*, p.41.

Christian *millets* vying for priority with one another, while the Muslim members of the local councils were behaving in an insulting and overbearing manner toward their non-Muslim counterparts – as the Greek patriarch was quick to lodge a complaint about.[6]

Nevertheless, the practical requirements in question led to some partial and hesitant moves towards complementing an essentially centralized framework with a limited degree of local govenment, which however was to prove quite inadequate when it came to undertaking the transition to a modern municipal system. Underneath it all, perhaps, was a different historical tradition from that of Western Europe in the Middle Ages, where some towns, at least, gradually acquired political autonomy from loci of feudal power that were essentially concentrated in the rural areas. In the Near East, in contrast, terms like *belediye* or *şehrdari* were not really equivalent to *commune*, *Rat* or *Gemeinde:* the Near East was where a civilization of towns and cities first arose, but this also meant that states and their ruling elites were always concentrated in, and had a tight grip on, those same cities,[7] so that it would be a mistake to regard the brillant examples of urban administration provided by the history of this region as making up a *communal* tradition of local government. (This was also the case, of course not only outside Europe but in large areas of Central and Eastern Europe.)

In the nineteenth century, on the other hand, Ottoman cities in general, and particularly those ports and coastal towns that served as the hub of developing relations with the outside world, were undergoing major structural transformations, and it was this chain of country-wide economic, social and administrative change that also built up procedure for reforming traditional

---

6 B. A., *İrade Meclis-i Valâ*, 19 ZA 1256/14 Jan. 1841, Nr.226, Ortaylı, *Tanzimattan Sonra Mahalli İdareler*, p.25.

7 As noted by Fuat Köprülü in his "Ortazaman Türk İslam Feodalizmi" in *Belleten*, vol.19, Ankara, 1941, pp.319-34, with references to a number of earlier authors.

urban administration and municipal organization: It was no longer possible for the port cities of the Eastern Mediterranean to cope with the requirements of the vortex of European trade that they were increasingly drawn into without creating a whole new network of infrastructure and services comprising, for example, adequate lodgings as well as harbour and quarantine facilities for commercial navigation, plus public health facilities and more orderly urban transport. For Europeans, Oriental ports were no longer so exotically distant and inaccessible, but a vital area of economic activity and income, which was why they needed to develop new municipalities capable of providing the requisite urban services. Thus it was at the time of the negotiations over the Aydın railroad concessions that British merchants initiated the eventually successful attempt to set up a municipality in İzmir.[8] Without going into its details, let me only note that in İstanbul, too, the first municipal organization set up through government initiative coincided with the Crimean War, and that the European-style Sixth Municipal District *(Altıncı Daire-i Belediyye)* that came into being in Pera (Beyoğlu) was also an embodiment of the objectives of urban sanitation and prosperity necessitated by the advent of urbanization.

This, then, is the basic context for assessing the rise and enracination of Ottoman municipalities which represented neither urban selfgovernment nor an autonomous corporate identity *(personne morale)*. Instead, the municipality *(belediye)* simply meant the sum total of urban tasks and services: it was no more than an organ saddled with responsibility for the physical upkeep of the city, its lighting and its sanitation. That was the way the enlightened bureaucrats of the Empire conceived of municipal organization – as a mere instrument of infrastructural development – and it was an extension of the central administration that they were also taken

8 Orhan Kurmus, *The Role of British Capital in the Economic Development of Western Anatolia*, umpublished PhD Thesis 1974, p.88.

over by the Republic, so that its has taken more than a century to go beyond that original conception, with many politicians still unclear about what a municipality is or should be after nearly fifty years of pluralism. But the real tragic insolubility, of course, derives from the attitude of citizens themselves to municipal life.

Even a partial screening of the period's press, for example, suffices to reveal the sort of public opinion that had already sprung up in the second half of the nineteenth century around municipalities – an atmosphere that was not marked, unfortunately, by any great degree of democratic naturity, nor by any propensity to assume responsibility for popular participation and control. As in all authoritarian societies, citizens have kept demanding urban services from the municipality while showing absolutely no organizational initiative or activity of their own. The other side of the coin was, and has been, that the municipality is the only organ people are willing and not afraid to criticize, even to abuse, at every opportunity. If people are discontent with their material or cultural environment, it is at the door of the mayor's office that they lay their bill – this is another by-product of authoritarianism. It is as if Ottoman municipalities were set up solely for the purpose of providing slim urban services and then getting blamed for everyhing under the sky.[9]

Despite all such drawbacks, however experiment in local government initiated by the Tanzimat era may be said to have played a very important role, eventually in the formation of the first Ottoman parliament. At the very least, it was in the Provinicial Administrative Councils *(Vilayet İdare Meclisleri)* and municipal councils that the deputies who converged on İstanbul from all corners of the Empire on 19 March, 1877 had acquired whatever experience they had in the way of parliamentary work – a learning process that had apparently had its negative as well as positive aspects, since, for example, it was rather in the

9 See for example *Sabah*, 22 Muharrem 1307 and 28 Muharrem 1308 issues.

grand manner of a provincial governor presiding over such local councils that Ahmet Vefik Pasha chaired the sessions of the first parliament. That body itself, moreover, appeared at first sight to be more ethnically colored than social-class-based, and neither did it have any organic connections with a whole constellation of non-parliamentary institutions or mass organizations, as a result of which its debates and deliberations were often left hanging in the air, or tended to revolve not around national but mostly local demands and issues. Although the narrowest kind of parochialism was eventually superseded as the more learned and enlightened deputies from the richest and most populous provinces in particular came to take stock of broader social realities, such progress was both gradual and partial, and on balance the Ottoman parliament was not on a par with other, contemporary multinational empires, including the 1906 Duma in Czarist Russia, from the point of view of struggles waged to realize organized class interests or over problems of an ethnic or national nature. It is not correct to speak of the Ottoman parliament as having witnessed dangerous nationalist rivalries; there is no strong evidence for this claim, while there are a good many more examples of a common Ottoman patriotism rising to the fore. But equally it would be wrong to say that at least with regard to its creation, composition and procedures, this first Ottoman constitutional assembly was a purely artificial and rootless institution: Granted that it was a national assembly brought forth by a non-industrialized country exhibiting a low degree of social integration, it still had behind it some thirty years' familiarity with representative politics and debate at the local level – which was probably why it was able, in its very first act of legislation, to produce a technically perfect text as the Law of Provinces and the Municipality of İstanbul *(Vilayetler ve İstanbul Belediye Kanunu)* after deliberation that also set relatively high standards of learning, maturity and poise.

The deputies to the Assembly of 1877, indeed, had acquired their mandate not through general elections held for the purpose, but by first being confirmed as elected members of provincial councils and then being also accorded parliamentary status. Thus on the negative side, "governors conferred the title of Member of Parliament on their own men, on the civil servants and *âşar* tax-farmers under their wing," comments Engelhardt.[10] Nevertheless, they knew about things like speaking in turn, voting and making points of order –and they even considered themselves superior to members from İstanbul in this regard. Deputies like Salim Efendi (Kastamonu), Nufel Efendi (Syria) and Rasim Bey (Edirne) shone brilliantly in parliamentary debates; "We are from the provinces, we have been voting since the beginning of the Tanzimat. İstanbul, however, has encountered elections only this year," boasted the latter.[11] And the insistence of the Ottoman parliament on confining electoral rights to the propertied classes in proportion to the amount of taxes paid also reflected what such notables had long been accustomed to in the provinces.

They were not entirely alone, though, for the top echelon of imperial bureaucrats had also acquired a certain experience in debate and negotiation at central bodies like the Tanzimat Council, which was why the Senate *(Ayan Meclisi)* was able to claim a certain maturity of its own. But unfortunately, only an incomplete edition of the minutes of the first Ottoman parliament is available (which we owe to the efforts of H. Tarik Us), and we are still in the dark concerning the activities of the provincial councils as well as their members' biographies. It is only through the further development of late Ottoman historiography that such gaps in our knowledge can be disposed of.

10 Engelhardt, *Türkiye ve Tanzimat*, trans. Ali Reşad, İstanbul, 1328, pp.354-55.

11 Hakkı Tarık Us, *Meclis-i Mebusan Zabit Ceridesi*, 17 April 1877 session, pp. 84-85.

HISTORIOGRAPHY

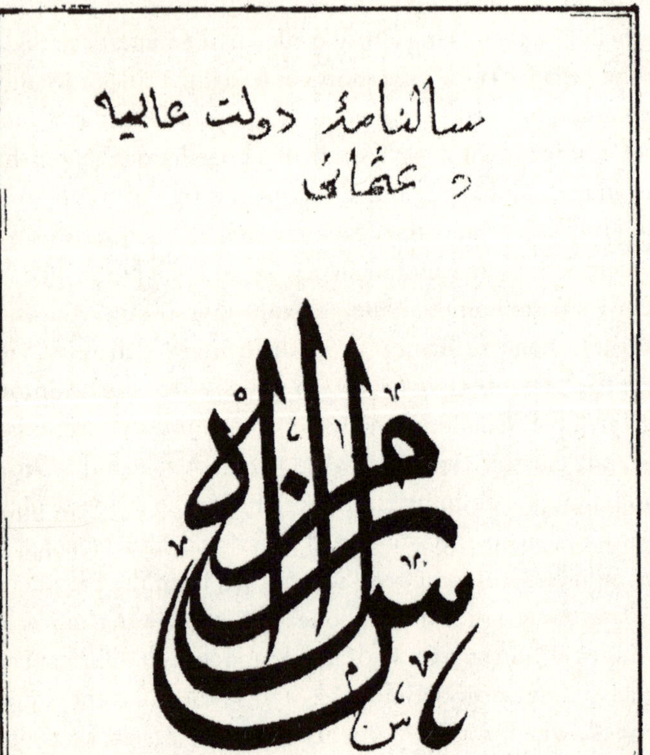

Yearbook of the State (Devlet Sâlnâmesi) 1847.

6

Basic Trends in Ottoman Turkish Historiography

Ottoman chronicles, whether written anonymously or by known authors have a common characteristic. Almost all of the chronicles which describe the 14th century were produced during the second half of the 15th century. Moreover, the contents have many characteristics in common. These chronicles exalt the era of the foundation and the following century and a half of an empire which had reached its zenith by mid 15th century. Further, the chronicles reflect the warrior and romantic spirit of the founding days. This approach, while nurturing the 15th century imperial ideology of consolidating the empire, somewhat misleads both Turkish and foreign modern Ottoman historians. After Paul Wittek's study, it has become very fashionable to account for the foundation and rise of the Ottoman Empire with the *ghaza* (Holy war) factor. At the same time, anonymous Ottoman chroniclers constantly praise the fact that the warriors fought on an equal position and with a spirit of equality. They also emphasize a tribal spirit and the Turcoman tradition whereby even the booty was shared equitably between the warriors. But, was this really the case?

Modern historians who do not consult other sources of the period have also accepted the theory of equally shared booty. Although Professors Fuad Köprülü and Halil İnalcık studied the state traditions of the Seljuk state and approached the issue in a critical manner,[1] these authors, too, have not consulted contemporary Byzantine and Slavic sources of the late 14th century. The early periods of Ottoman history are written in a categorized way, depending on the sources utilized. Two of the earliest Ottoman chroniclers, Aşikpaşazade and Neşri did not witness the events they related. A source which both chroniclers claimed to have consulted, the Yahşi Fakih chronicle, is lost to modern historians. Likewise, the prospect that literary historians may be able to identify the sources or oral traditions that anonymous historians relied on, does not seem promising. One point needs to be emphasized here. Although at a first glance, it looks as if these chronicles differ in their world view (Weltanschaung), they basically utilize the same concepts. All these chronicles favor certain legends and myths in order to justify the legitimacy of the Ottoman dynasty and the charismatic nature of some of the sultans. However, the origins of these myths and legends are debatable. Some have their roots in ancient Persia and the Middle East and some are of Asian Turkic origin. For instance, the conquest of Aydos castle which involves a love story between Abdurrahman Ghazi and Byzantine lord's daughter, is somehow linked with the Ottoman success. The story almost reads like Rapunzel can be seen in Iranian and Seljuk tales. Interestingly enough, such legends and figures are sometimes misleading and are an impediment to a healthy synthesis of Ottoman history.

Aşikpaşazade relates the story of the Ottoman passage through the Dardanelles and its subsequent conquest of Gallipoli as if the process had been accomplished by Süleyman Pasha and the ghazis simply passing across the straits on rafts. This approach remained a historiographical motif until Professor İnalcık corrected the

1 P. Wittek, *The Rise of the Ottoman Empire*, Royal Asiatic Society Monographs, XXIII, London, 1967; see also F. Köprülü, *Les origins de l'empire ottoman*, Paris, 1935 and H. İnalcık, "The question of the emergence of the Ottoman state", *International Journal of Turkish Studies*, IV, pp.71-79.

version with his historical and topographical study of Gallipoli.[2] However, the issue has not yet been definitively resolved, and in this author's opinion, the Italian city state archives and late Byzantine studies may shed further light on the topic.

The context of chronicles which describe the first Ottoman administrative organization is even more interesting. In fact, they have provided sources for speculation in social history research: one example of administrative history being the first taxation in the Ottoman state, and the establishment of a treasury and accounting system. Anonymous chroniclers mention that someone from the Germiyan advised Osman Ghazi to impose a bazaar tax (bac-i bazar), but that the sultan was offended by this advice.[3] Other sources indicate that when Osman Ghazi was convinced that this taxation was necessary, he did not hesitate to impose it. Some historical accounts, especially anonymous chroniclers, claim that the Viziers Çandarli Kara Halil and Karamanli Türk Rüstem Pashás introduced the system of a treasury and tax accounting, and that those two malicious[4] men caused sedition in the society of the time. Obviously, rumors of this kind led certain writers to build up colorful(!) interpretations around concepts such as feudalism, anti-feudalism and tribal democracy. In fact, as Fuad Köprülü and some other historians who were familiar with the Middleeastern state structure observed, the Ottoman tax system was adopted from the Seljuk state. When a treasury was established, it followed that the state would claim a portion of the war boty and, naturally, that the ghazi class would react to such a loss of privilege. However, the fact that this negative attitude and reaction to what happened in the 14th century carried over

---

2 H. İnalcık, "The conquest of Edirne (1361)", *Archivum Ottomanicum*, III, 1971, pp.185-210.

3 Aşıkpaşazade Ahmed Aşık, *Tevarih-i Al Osman (History of the Ottoman House), TOEM*, İstanbul, 1332, p.19.

4 İ. H. Uzunçarşılı, *Osmanli Devletinin Merkezi ve Bahriye Teşkilâti*, Ankara, 1948, p.319.

to the second half of the 15th century is a curious matter and deserves further research. Some of the 15th century histories – poetic sources such as *Düsturname-i Enveri* and İskendername of Ahmedi, and Yahşi Fakih (chronicles written in early 15th century, but known to us only in fragments as related by earlier historians) – do not give us clues to explain these problematic issues. Both in anonymous chronicles and in the Aşikpaşazade, Neşri and Oruç Bey chronicles, there are interpretations which go against the ghaza perspective but at the same time offer unanimous support for the consolidation of the dynasty. In conclusion, the context of the chronicles poses a difficult problem when we try to classify them ideologically.

The chronicles all have another point in common: none of them mention any continuity between Byzantine, Seljuk or Persian civilizations and the Ottoman administration or their effect on it, though modern historiography has captured this linkage. These chronicles offer no clues, for neither Persian kings, Byzantine caesars, or Seljuk sultans are mentioned, let alone glorified. Ottoman chronicles link the state tradition to Oghuz and Turcoman lore, and emphasize this tradition. And yet, these works also belittle the Turcomans and extend this attitude to other Anatolian beyliks such as the Karaman, through they distinguish the Ottoman beylik from other more disparaged Turcomans. Curiously, we come across passages in the chronicles which describe Bayezid I as immature and ambitious during the war between Tamerlane and Bayezid.[5] In short, it is very difficult to interpret the early periods of Ottoman history ideologically, through studying the chronicles. It is mainly because of this that modern historiography makes wrong interpretations.

Both the anonymous 17th century chronicles and those which bear the signature of their author, present some different

5 *Tevarih-i Al Osman (anonymous chronicle)* in *Die Altosmanischen Anoymen Chroniken*, Friedrich Giese ed., Teil I, Breslau, 1922, pp.38-40.

interpretations. For example, as against the works contemporary with Mehmed II – Tursun Beg's *Tarih-i Ebu'lfeth* and Kritovulos' history – there are anonymous folk chronicles such as Mahmud Pasha legendsmenakibnàme, which were compiled during that century and copied over and over again by medrese students in later centuries.[6] In these narratives, Grand Vizier Mahmud Pasha, a Christian recruit who was executed by Mehmed II, is not only praised but miracles are attributed to him, and his knowledge as well as his virtues as a statesman are exalted in a highly exaggerated style. This points to the fact that Mehmed the Conqueror, who is glorified by modern historians, was not that popular among some classes of 15th century society; this dislike stemmed from his despotic militarism, the deportations from Anatolia to newly conquered territories and the confiscation of *waqf* and other properties in the name of the state. Consequently a statesman whom Mehmed had executed was glorified as a saint in the Mahmud Pasha narratives.

This brings us to an important topic. What was the philosophical foundation of Ottoman historiography before the 19th century historian Ahmed Cevdet Pasha? What norm did these earlier historians use? The question appears both complicated and simple. If we compare the Ottoman historians with their western counterparts and Ibn Khaldûn, the great historian of Islam, it seems quite easy to evaluate and judge Ottoman historiography, and a colorful picture emerges when it is aproached from the methodological point of view. Ottoman historiography was established by unusual people, who were different from what would be expected of a traditional society. A 17th century, historian, İbrahim Peçevi had even read the works of the Hungarian

6 Tursun Beg, *Tarih-i Ebu'lfeth* (History of the conqueror), Merdol Tulum ed., İstanbul, 1977, p.35; Kritovoulos, *History of Mehmed the Conqueror*, trans. by Ch. Riggs, Princeton, 1954; İ. Ortaylı, "Menakibname-yi Mahmud Pasha-The Legend of Mahmud Pasha" in *Tahsin B. Balta Armağani*, Ankara, 1974, p.459-481.

historian, İstvanfyvi. Peçevi, who spoke German and Hungarian, refers to the history of Golden Horde and even to that of the Ukrainian cossacks of the Kipchak steppe while discussing the Crimean khans. Ottoman chronicles look like traditional histories because they have a sense of world histories, which start with Adam and Noah. But unlike traditional histories, some of the chronicles are also concerned with the problem of identity when the authors claim that the Turks,[7] originated from Yafeth.

From the viewpoint of language, Hace Saadeddin is one example of a 17th century historian who enriched the Turkish language by using Persian stylistics in his work, *Tac'üttevarih*. Consequently, a neo-Persian style was introduced to Turkish historiography which was almost like the Hellenistic stylistics of Ana Komnene and her 10th century contemporaries. This brings us to the question of the philosophy of history.

In 17th century, Naima and Selaniki discuss the disruption of order in the state structure and society[8] and propose the remedy of restoring the 16th century institutions of Suleiman the Magnificent's era. Generally speaking, Ottoman historians were under the influence of the ancient Persian tradition of writing *nasihatname* (advice to the sultans) and this was the case with the 16th century historian Kinalizade. According to him, a just government is the source of peace and wealth. The concept of predestination in history is non-existent in this case. Besides, no "quod factum est factum est" type of approach or methodology, as it used by one of the early Christian historians such as Kiprianus, is observable.

7 M. Köhbach, "Die Osmanische Fassung von Istvanfy's Bericht über die erste Belagerung Wiens durch die Türken 1529 in der Chronik des Ibrahim Peçevi" in *Wien 1529, die erste Türkenbelagerung*, G. Dürseyl ed., Wien, 1979, pp.93-106. For the identity of the Turks see the Ottoman chronicler İbn Kemal, *Tevarih-i Ali Osman, Fasc. VII* (16th century), Şerafettin Turan ed., Ankara, 1991, pp.LV and 240 and 362, İbn Kemal, despising the nomad Turks (Turkoman) but praises the Turkish identity.

8 Selaniki Mustafa, *Tarih-i Selânikî*, Mehmet İbşirli ed., IUEF, İstanbul, 1989, pp.425-432.

Ottoman historians treat the concept of state as the "eternal state" (devlet-i ebed müddet). In addition, Ottoman historians are not familiar either with Ibn Khaldûn or with a sociological approach to history of the kind Ibn Khaldûn used. In fact, Ibn Khaldûn's was not understood and his methodology was not used or preferred even by a 19th century historian like Ahmed Cevdet Pasha, who translated Ibn Khaldûn's works impeccably into Turkish. Consequently, Ottoman historiography never took into consideration either the duality between theory and practice or the search for bridging the gap between the two. Yet, it is very fortunate that the late Ottoman historians did not adopt a Voltairian or Hegelian teleological methodology as did the 19th century Slavic historians.

One of the major conditions for the development of any historiography is the observation of world history as well as of other peoples and cultures. This has been an accepted fact since Heredotus, but it appears that, until the 19th century, the Ottoman chronicles which fulfill these basic conditions are exceptional and unsatisfactory. And yet, during the age of classical Islam, Arab and Persian historians took world history into consideration. In the 11th century (1068) Sa'îd Ahmad al-Andalusi, classified the peoples who were useful to civilization in his *Kitâb tabagât al-umam* as Egyptians, Persians, Romans, Greeks, Jews, Indians and Arabs.[9] He is aware of the history of cultures in his classification. al-Andalusî qualifies other peoples as undeveloped because of geographical and other conditions. He considers the Chinese and the Turks as possessing practical intelligence, but as two peoples who had no direct impact on the development of civilization. (Civilization, in al-Andalusî's estimation, geographically belonged to the Mediterranean basin). Ibn-Khaldûn, in his *Introduction to his History* (Prologemena-Muqaddima) wrote a rich universal history of the era. In fact he even goes further than rabbinical sources

9 B. Lewis, *The Muslim Discovery of Europe*, London, 1982, p.68; Sa'id b. Ahmad Al Andalusi, *Kitâb tabaqât al-umam*, French trans. R. Blachère, *Livre des catégories des nations*, Paris, 1935, pp.36-37.

which do not mention Flavius Josephus' Iosippon, and he describes the Masada war and the Jewish history of the Roman period. The Persian historian Reşiduddin of the Ilkhanid period consulted very interesting sources to write a world history.[10] During the classical Ottoman period Ottoman historians did not give proof of similar capabilities. In the late 17th century, Hezarfenn Hüseyin Efendi attempted to write a universal history because he knew Latin and Greek and finished the work in 1673. European diplomats such as Antoine Galland and L. F. Marsigli (his contemporaries), speak highly of him.[11] Katib Çelebi, too, was a product of the 17th century Ottoman intelligentsia, and was familiar with universal history, geography, the sciences, besides knowing Greek. But, these examples are exceptions to the rule.

In the 18th century, Ottoman historiography assumed an interesting practical function. The growth of Russia and the loss of a Muslim-Turkic land such as the Crimean Khanate caused the historians to focus on a new motif, i.e. the caliphate. Vasif-i Enderuni claimed that Selim I assumed the caliphate in 1517 from the Mamluks in Egypt. It is difficult to corroborate a historical event of this kind. Though they were the servants and protectors of the Hejaz, the Ottoman sultans rarely resorted to the title of "caliph" until the 19th century. It was only on the late 18th century that the caliphate was introduced to historical writing as a tool of diplomacy to be used in Muslim lands which had been conquered by the Christians. Hence, the caliphate was described as a universal political-religious (Caesero-Papist) institution. The fiction of the 'caliphate-transferred" to the Ottoman-Sultan in

10 Rashid Aldin, *Histoire Universelle l-Histoire des Franks*, ed. and trans. by Karl Jahn, Leiden, 1951, see B. Lewis, *The Jews of Islam*, Princeton, 1984, pp.89-90.

11 F. Babinger, *Geshichtesschreiberder Osmanen und ihre Werke*, Turkish trans. Üçok, Ankara, 1982, p.251, refers to the letter of Marsigli to Baron Rosen, *Remarques sur les mss. orientaux de la collection Marsigli*, Rome 1885, p.8; see also reference concerning the memoirs of Antoine Galland: Ch. Schefer, *Journal d'Antoine Galland pendant son séjour* à *l'Ambassade de France* à *Constantinople (1672-73)*, Paris 1881, p.150.

a ceremony which was developed in the 18th century chronicles continued in the 19th and even the 20th century textbooks. But the conqueror sultans of the 16th century paid no attention to a ceremony and protocol of the kind.

In the 18th century, there was a remarkable change in the Ottoman outlook on Europe and Russia in historiography and in ambassadorial reports. Basically, historiography followed the change in outlook and the new information which came through the ambassadorial reports which described foreign lands. In the Ottoman Empire knowledge about foreign lands was not acquired through geographical, historical or philological studies any more than through military or strategic research. Information was obtained in a pragmatic way, i.e. through the observations of the envoys sent to Europe. And their reports inevitably affected historiography. By the 19th century, Ottoman historians began to discover the histories of Europe through translated works as well as the geography and history of the empire's foremost enemy, Russia. And there are some interesting interpretations of Russian history. Despite some falsifications, 19th century Ottoman historiography offers attractive evaluations of European and Russian history. In the course of one century, Ottoman historiography went through a curious transformation concerning the evaluation of Petrine Russia and its reforms. Conservative official Ottoman historiography changed within one century of Petrine Russia. At the time Peter the Great's death was recorded by Rashid Efendi, the official chronicler (vak'anüvis) of the Ottoman state, in the following words:[12] "The Muscovite Czar Peter being dead, his corpse was left lying in some quiet corner; he had tried to impose crazy new fashions on his people". And Mehmed Agha, an Ottoman ambassador who had visited Petrine Russian at that time, had gone so far as to heap scorn on a parade organized by the Emperor and on the European protocol used there with the expression "The Czar's clownings". Another Ottoman ambassador, Shehdi Efendi, left the following

12 A. Ubicini, *Lettres sur la Turquie*, pt. I, Paris, 1853, p.165.

description of an opera he attended in 1757 at the invitation of Empress Elizabeth: "The singers and instrumentalists stroked their instruments in a strange fashion, shouting according to certain modes in their own language". By 1794 however, the ambassador at the court of Catherine II, Mustafa Rasih Pasha, left us detailed information concerning the way of life and the administrative and military organization of the period, expressing great admiration.[13] Apparently this change in attitude occurred around the time of the signing of the Küçük Kaynarca Treaty. In 19th century Ottoman thought and historiography, Peter was no longer 'the mad' (deli), but 'the Great'.[14] Thus, an official book by an unknown writer (probably a dragoman at the Sublime Porte), with the significant title *Büyük Petro Tarihi* (The History of Peter the Great), was printed right at the outbreak of the Crimean war. Cevdet Pasha, too, spoke of Petrine Russia and Peter's reforms with unmistakable praise in his famous history:[15] "The Russians never had a powerful state of great renown. Now they rule one ninth of the world. The real founder of this state is Peter the Great". While giving insistent credit to the myth of the *Testament of Peter the Great*, or deliberately falsifying this 'testament' to provoke the anti-Russian attitude of Ottoman-Turkish intellectual circles, this same author makes the following interesting comparison between the reforms of Peter and of Mahmud II in his correspondence with Sadullah Pasha, the Ottoman ambassador in Vienna:[16] "The political organization of the two states is essantially similar and parallel". He further believes that:

> in England reforms were initiated by the gentry, that is, the upper class, and it was this that led to the creation of a constitutional monarcihy, whereas in France, the upper class proving incapable of the doing same, the initiative came from below, and the resulted in a republic.

13 F. Reşit Unat, *Osmanli Sefirleri ve Sefaretnameleri*, Ankara, 1968, pp.62, 107, 162.

14 *Büyük Petro Tarihi* (author unknown), İstanbul, 1270/1853-54.

15 *Cevdet Tarihi*, I, İstanbul 1309/1890-91, p.241.

16 Cevdet Pasha, *Tezâkîr*, Cavit Baysun ed., pt 40, Ankara, 1967, pp.217-19.

To this he then adds:

> Ottoman as well as Russian reforms were embarked upon by the Crown (taraf-i saltanat-i seniyyeden). Even the dissolution of the Janissaries resembles the dissolution of the Strelitsy, with the difference that, whereas the Janissaries had been a cancer in the very heart of our Sublime Porte, the Strelitsy had been a tumor on Russia's back (lakin yeniçeri devlet-i aliyyenin kalbinde bir seretan idi. Strelistler ise Rusya'nin sirtinda bir ur idiler). Here, once the Janissaries were dispersed, continuous reforms in every administrative department became inevitable, but there (in Russia) a vacuum became apparent only in the military field and therefore Russian recovery was quickly completed... We do not posses cadres with the necessary courage and will... Peter was very determined and he acquired further learning in Europe. When he removed the Strelitsy, he knew what he was doing and how he was going to replace them. Sultan Mahmud was also a determined ruler, but he had not seen not and would not see Europe. Our statesmen were not endowed with sufficient learning and determination.

It should be pointed out that instead of focusing on the personalities of Ottoman statesmen, Ahmed Cevdet Pasha could have dwelt on the fact that the Ottoman reforms were a full century late in coming. Nevertheless, the comments reveal him to be a serious historian who was able to approach the Russian reforms analytically.

Later Ottoman historiography was both sincere and naive in its interpretation of Islamic history and institutions, with a view to supporting the concept of constitutional monarchy. In the late 19th century historians claimed, by stretching the evidence, that *mashvara* (consultation) in Islamic history equalled parliamentarism. In conclusion, demystification was not only difficult to apply and a late comer to Ottoman-Turkish historiography, but its mission is still incomplete.

7

The Archives of Russia and Ottoman History[1]

There can be little doubt that for Ottoman history today the archives of such centers as London (the Public Record Office), Paris (the Quay d'Orsay), Berlin (the Preussische Geheime Staatsarchiv),[2] Bonn (the Auswärtiges Amt), Potsdam (the old Zentral Archiv DDR), and Vienna (the Haus, Hof und Staatsarchiv), are far surpassed in importance by the archives of Moscow, Besides the Turkish documents in the Moscow archives, the holdings for Russian history itself are important for Turkey. Russia's origins, and her foreign relations, have taken on an increased significance for Turkey. In this sense, every archival collection recording the history of Russia is also important for Turkish history. Here we shall discuss only the archives that are important for the relationship between these two states.

Examination of these archives sometimes seems to yield new information even on the types of material and paper the Ottomans used. From the point of view of diplomatics, issues

1 Originally published as "Rusya Arşivleri ve Osmanlı Tarihi," *Tarih Boyunca Türk Tarihinin Kaynakları Semineri; 6-7 Haziran 1996; Bildiriler* (İstanbul: Edebiyat Fakültesi Basımevi, 1997), pp.145-148. Translated by Douglas A. Howard.

2 Since the contents of the old Merseburg archives on the German Democratic Republic were added to this archive, which was not very well known, it is a rich source for the history of the foreign relations of the Prussian monarchy and Austrian diplomatic history.

such as titulature *(elkab)* can be illumined by striking new evidence. And we can gain a new understanding of the character of the Russian chancery. Thus these archives are essential for the establishment and development of a subfield like Russo-Turkish history, and the immense value of both these two countries' archives for the jaint history of these two empires becomes apparent. Then if we add to the history of these two states a third, the field could be fully expanded and developed. Recently, a slow appreciation has grown of the demonstrable importance of Iranian archives for Ottoman and Russian history, and the Iranian archives have begun publications on the subject.[3]

The archives of Moscow containing documents directly relevant to our subject are the following (remembering that materials relevant to Turkish history are to be found in virtually every archive).

THE ARCHIVES OF RUSSIA AND OTTOMAN HISTORY

1. *Zentralniy Gosudarstvenniy Arhiv Drevnih Aktov*, or ZGADA (Central State Archive of Ancient Documents). The basic holdings for the Muscovite Russian period, prior to the establishment of St. Petersburg, are here. Documents relating to the correspondence between the Ottomans and Muscovy, and between Muscovy and the Crimean Khanate, and the documents of the Crimean Khanate itself, are especially important. Contrary to what we have previously thought, not only the grand vizier but also the second vizier, the fleet admiral and other officals such as the sancakbeyi of Kefe and the Pasha of Azov, carried on correspondence with Moscow. Interesting chancery practices can also be encountered here. For example, a document from Süleyman Pasha, the Sancakbeyi of Azov, was written in Crimean Turkish [Tatar], meaning that scribes of the Crimean Khanate performed chancery services for

3 For example, *Güzide-i İsnad-ı Siyasî-i İran ve Osmanî (devre-i Dacariyye)*, 5 vols. (Tehran: Defter-i Muahedat-i Siyasî ve Beynelmilelî, 1365).

the Pasha of Azov.[4] Collections such as the *Krimskoe Delo* and the *Turetskoe Delo* foreign affairs departments of the ambassadorial secretariat known as the *Posolski Prikaz*, include a letter sent by Second Vizier Receb Pasha to the Russian Czar,[5] a letter from Kapudan-ı Derya Hafız Ali Pasha to Czar Michael Fedorovich,[6] and the like. The contents of these document folders are of utmost importance. Most interestingly, the *Golova Posolskogo Prikaza* was similar to a *Reisülküttab*. Even their attire was similar, as can be observed in the portrait of Afanasity Lavrentiyevich Ordin-Nashochkin–an original portrait of Nashochkin, done in the traditional style, hangs in the Foreign Affairs Archives building. The chancery translators at this time were called the *Talmach* (for Western languages) and the *Dragoman* (for Eastern languages). Translators of these languages were employed by the chancery, just as the Ottoman Empire had people who knew Russian, examples of whom are mentioned below.

Undoubtedly the most important collection for our purposes is the *Krimskoe Delo* (Crimean affairs) section of the archives of the ZGADA, file 89,674 documents from the years 1497-1719. In addition to this, the *Turetskoe Delo* (Turkish affairs) section contains correspondence with İstanbul. One of the least utilized collections in the archives of Moscow is the correspondence between the Moscow Patriarchate and the Phanariot Patriarchate, but it is clearly the most important document series for the history of Orthodoxy.

The titles *(elkab)* used for the Russian czar in the documents are noteworthy. In the letter of the Crimean Khan, the Czar is referred to as *Ak Rusnun penahı ve hükümdar padişahı tahtinişi*

---

4 Found 35, opis 2, delo 39, Name-i mergub ve muhabbet 1079 mah-ı Recebü'l-mürecceb beşinci gününde yazılıp (December 1668), List' k'tzar'yu Aleksiveich'u Mihailomu ot' Azovskogo Pash'i Süleimana.

5 Fond 89, opis' 2, no.3.

6 Dated Evasıt-ı Şevval 1036 (June-July 1627), Fond 89, opis' 2, no.4.

(note that *Ak Rus* is used rather than *Uluğ Rus*). In spite of 1668, the Treaty of Andrusovo and union with Moscow, *Ukrayna* continues to be used rather than *Küçük Rus.*[7] One does encounter, however, *Uluğ Rus'nun padişahı and Cümle Rus'nun padişahı*.

With the year 1701 (after the Treaty of Constantinople), however, the relationship changed: *Moskova vilâyetlerinin Çarı ve Cümle Rus'nun ve ana tabi nice yerlerin ferman ferma (somo derjez) hükümdarı (gosudor) Petro Aleksiyeviç hutîmet avakibehu bi'l-hayr*. It is clear that the most important section of the ZGADA (the Ancient Records) are also the reports called the *Posolskie Knigi* (ambassadorial reports). It is no exaggeration to say that the materials here dealing with Ottoman history have hardly been touched. Those archives dealing with the eighteenth century, that is, the Tolstoy embassy, have been evaluated and used by Oreshkova and Merer. They, however, are obviously not the entire series. As can be seen, before us is an additional resource necessary to the development of Turkey's Russian history experts.

2. *Rosiiskii Gosudarstvenniy* Voenno-Istoricheskiy Arhiv, or RGVID (Russian State Archives of the History of War). Up to now these archives, located on Baumanskaya in Moscow Ulitza, a foreign neighborhood called Nemetskaya Slobada in the eighteenth century and earlier, have not been used by our Russian colleagues. The archival personnel beg us to come, assuring us that they have not spy reports, but rather documents relating to cultural history. The reports of Russian military attachés in Turkey are here, with a wealth of cultural and political information going far beyond mere military details. The rich collections of photographs and maps make this archive especially attractive. We Turkish historians have only scratched the surface of this archive. Collections become the richer as we move forward in the collection from the sixteenth century toward 1918. A case

7 Fond 35, opis' 2, delo 39, 1668.

in point is the *Rosiiskoi Gosudarstvenniy Arhiv Voenno-Morskogo Flotta* (The Russian State Archives of Naval History), in St. Petersburg. Another important collection is the photograph section of the *Rossiski Gosudarstvenniy Istoricheskiy Arhiv* (or RGIA, the Russian State Historical Archives), in the same city.

3. For Turkish history another interesting archive of equal importance to the ZGADA, is the *Arhiv Vneshnoi Politiki Rossiiskoi Imperii* (AVPRI, the Foreign Policy Archives of the Russian Empire), on Bolshoia Serpuhovskaia Avenue. This is the archive of Russian foreign affairs for the period between the reign of Peter the Great and the First World War. All the correspondence in connection with Turkey is here. Probably the most important section are the regular reports, dated 1818-1914, sent by the consuls in Edirne, Alexandria, Aleppo, Beirut, Bucharest, Vidin (Sofia), Galati, Gallipoli, Damietta, Çanakkale, Diyarbakir, Haifa, Jerusalem, Kars, Cyprus, Port Said, Rhodes, Sidon, Samos (Sisam), Samsun, Sinop, İzmir, Selanica, Bayezid, Basra, Bitlis, Vitola (Manastır), Bursa, Burgas, Van, Varna, Damascus, Jiddah, Cairo, Kanan, Giresun, Konya, Mitrivitza, Midilli, Mosul, Mostar, Prizren, Ragusa (Dubrovnik), Rize, Ruse (Ruschuk), Sarajevo, Shkodèr (Scutari), Mersin, Tırnova, Skopje, Suez, Tunis, Trabzon, Trablus, Erzurum, Yannina, Jaffa, Iaşi, Baghdad, and Hama, a total of 58 consulates. Thanks to their linguistic and religious affinities with local Balkan populations, the Russian consular officials were sometimes instigators of events, but most importantly they learned the area well, and wrote interesting, detailed reports. The writing of detailed reports was a long standing Russian bureaucratic tradition, and these are very instructive for historians.

In the foreign policy archives I also saw Ottoman *name* documents, examples of which I had not seen at home. Were these papers perhaps produced especially for Russia?

THE ARCHIVES OF RUSSIA AND OTTOMAN HISTORY

Certainly the most organized and most technically accessible archive is the old Communist Party Archives, where there are various documents concerning contemporary Turkey beginning in 1919. The catalogs are superb, and have even been published–we must get copies of these. In the Communist Party Archives can be found interesting materials on recent Turkish history, even more than on the Turkish Communist Party.

In the shortest possible time we should establish a research center in Moscow and set up an exchange program of archival documents and specialists in Russian history and Turkology between the two countries.

MODERNIZATION

Imperial Military School of Engineering (Mühendishâne-i Berrî-i Hümâyun), one of the first steps of Ottoman modernization.

8

The Ottoman Empire at the end of the Seventeenth Century

The outlook of the Ottoman Empire at the end of the seventeenth century constitutes one of the most difficult topics in historical research. Central and provincial administration, financial-economic affairs, culture and social life were all undergoing rapid change in Europe at that time. Even the presence on stage of great generals in the early eighteenth century Europe is among the consequences of this evolution. The neighbouring Ottoman Empire was also subject to great transformations, and to understand this, it is necessary to have a good grasp of what was happening in Europe in the first place.

Briefly put, in the late seventeenth century the Ottoman Empire was in social and economic chaos, and there is no doubt that practically all its institutions were moving towards collapse. But on the other hand, the rulers of the Empire were able to come up with brilliant and interesting examples of bureaucratic manipulation to cope with this imminent threat. The decline of the state did not mean cultural decline, of course. Ottoman society was in search of a new life-style, and a new art and social cultural was emerging, which would come down through successive changes and evolutions to the present day.

Turkish stories about "grandfathers who took part in the siege of Vienna" are more likely to refer to the first attempt of Suleiman the Magnificent than to the final and abortive one in

1683. The defeat of that year was only the logical consequence of given historical conditions, since the Ottoman Empire had been taken over by anarchy and severe economic shortage for the past century. In fact, how the Ottomans were able to undertake the second siege at all continues to pose a problem for the historians of Turkey to this day. The energy and material resources necessary to carry out a protracted war were probably primarily replenished by the drastic restoration of the Köprülü era, while the general desolation caused by the Thirty Years' War must also have played a part in enabling the still well-organized Ottoman army to invade the heart of the Habsburg Empire.

The final result of the long war, which started with the siege of Vienna in 1683 and ended with the Treaty of Karlowitz in 1699, enabled Austria to spread her commercial activity to the Danubian region and to bring the German principalities under its authority. A new epoch of prosperity symbolized by the famous motto *Austria est imperare orbem universum* and based on flourishing manufactures, navigation and commerce then opened for Vienna, whereas the Ottoman Empire entered a period of rapid loss of its European possessions, of qualitative changes in its system of land tenure, and of upheaval even in the structure of its provincial administration, finances and management of international affairs. Finally the European part of the Empire became the stage for national revivals. Transdanubian Hungary but even more so Transylvanian Hungary, with their autonomous state system and autonomous church based on Hungarian cultural revival, could have been models for Ottoman society in its future modernization, but of course one important clause of the Karlowitz treaty ended all that also.

Economic and social signs of backwardness or decay came to be gradually observed in Anatolia as well as Rumelia during the sixteenth century.

Throughout the sixteenth and seventeenth centuries, the share of Central Europe in international trade was diminishing not because of Ottoman conquest but basically as a side-effect of the rise of Western European manufactures and overseas commerce. In the first stage of the development of the modern world economy (based on long-distance navigation), the progress of industrial activity in Europe and growing demand for agricultural products now marketable on favourable terms as a result of the "Price Revolution" had stimulated the agricultural economies of East Central Europe to increase their food and raw material production for the market.[1] Later, however, the opening of commodity exchange (food and raw material) between Western European countries and their new overseas colonies turned East-Central Europe permanently into a backward region.

In similar fashion, Turkey's Anatolian provinces lost more markets for their handicraft products (textiles and other finished goods) with every passing day. These areas were eventually deprived of their once-primary roles in international trade and reduced to the level of sources of raw materials (Bursa for silk, Angora for mohair, etc.). Export of guild products from Anatolian cities ceded its place to raw material export demanded by developing Western European manufactures. It is worthwhile to mention at this point the illicit traffic of which raw materials such as silk, cotton, metals and corn rapidly became a part. Continuous inflation made it impossible for the ruling class of the Empire to keep serving in the army or in judicial posts with fixed salaries. Bribery, oppression of the people and especially usurpation of each other's estates became common malpractices among timariots throughout the Ottoman domains.

The war economy of the seventeenth century plunged the rural and urban population into poverty and anarchy. Though studies of the seventeenth century have so far concentrated mostly on the Rumelian provinces, the study of court registers, *mühimmes*

1 Zs. P. Pach, "Diminishing Share of East Central Europe in the 17th Century International Trade", *Acta Historica*, XVI (3-4), 1970, pp.301-304.

(chancellery records) and *ahkâm defterleri* can in fact provide rich material for describing both pre-war Anatolia and Anatolia under war conditions. The collapse of the classical Ottoman military system meant a structural change in the economic and social institutions of the Empire. Late seventeenth century Ottoman society was cloaked in an aura of tragedy.

The restorative work of the Köprülü's aimed not to radically modernize the socio-economic and military structure but merely to rehabilitate the classical institutions. The defeat in Vienna then caused the decadence to accelerate. Chaos and anarchy in the provinces as well as in the capital did not escape the observing eyes of foreign diplomats, whose reports reveal the administrative apparatus in a process of dissolution. The scarcity of food and money in

İstanbul and the robbery and oppression in the provinces are described in the reports of the French ambassadors, for example. One of them, Guilleragues, wrote in March 1684 about the continuous shifting and expulsions of high-ranking officals (viziersgovernors, *defterdars* and *kadıs*) who sometimes could not keep their posts for even six months. This strange spoil-system caused the destruction of executive authority throughout the Empire and deepened corruption and bribery, oppression, poverty and local revolts. The decline of the army was also carefully watched by these French diplomats; "le miser et l'ignorance des Turcs sont inconuables, il n'y a point dans l'universe..." wrote ambassador Guilleragues. Ottoman military technology was already obsolete. "The starvation of the inhabitants in İstanbul has almost reached the point of revolt; they protest even the Grand Seigneur" noted ambassador Girardin in July 1686, adding that "the *defterdar* was unable to balance the budget in November 1687 because the revenues could not cover the war expenditures..."[2] The chaos in the Anatolian provinces had also

2 Archives du Ministère des Affaires Etrangères Paris, *C. P. Turquie*, vol.17, Nr.168, p.12, Pera, 28 Mars 1684, *ibid.*, fol 40v-43r. (9 Juin 1684) and fol. 283r (Juillet 1686) and fol. 325v., vol.19 (Nov. 1687).

reached its peak point. The land tenure system of the Empire in both Rumelia and Anatolia was in dissolution. The timariots, the *mutevellis* of pious foundations *(waqfs)* and other officials kept usurping the *miri* (public) land and trying to disposses each other of their fiefs illegally. They were flagrantly steeped in corruption; they neglected their duties and responsibilities of maintaining public order and collecting taxes with respect to due procedure; and they failed to fulfill their military obligations. Some governors who had been expelled from their posts and others, poor timariots, even joined large, roving bands of bandits and rebels as commanders (called *Celalis*).[3] During the long rule of the Köprülüs, internal order was stabilized and anarchy prevented for a few decades through draconian measures. For maintaning public order and ensuring regular taxe collection, the Köprülüs introduced a kind of decentralized provincial administrative system where some of the viziers entitled *muhassils* were endowed with extraordinary financial powers and some local begs called *mütesellims* had to fulfill the duties of governors.

The process of land concentration which had actually started in the sixteenth century must have kept gathering momentum throughout the seventeenth. Various cases might be cited in proof. After the death of a timariot, for example, his land would neither revert to the state nor be given to his orphan(s) but would be occupied illegally by neighbouring *sipahis* or by the *beytülmal emini*. Sometimes even the lands of living *sipahis* who happened to be away at war were exposed to the same sort of usurpation. Land and fields deserted by peasants fleeing before bandits or nomads or during other troubles were also seized and occupied by the same local authorities. Not rarely would a newly appointed *sipahi* holding a *berat (timar beratı)* find the fief that he came to take over already in the hands of such usurpers. The court registers of this period are full of such cases and complaints. A sultanic firman

3 Mustafa Akdağ, *Büyük Celali Karışıklıklarının Başlaması*, Erzurum, 1963.

of the year 1098 H./November 1686 admitted that the lands of many *sipahis* who had fallen on the battlefield or of others who were away for a long time in Hungary had been seized by local authorities and their revenues had been illegally collected by the same usurpers.[4] Even officials like the *beytülmal emini* whose main task was to protect and maintain such fiefs were involved in such plundering. The firman of the year 1686 mentioned above cites one *beytülmal emini* who had not shrunk from usurping the salary of a palace çavuş *(dergâh-i mualla çavuşu)* named Hasan to the tune of 16,000 aktches. Similar infringements were widespread in the Rumelian districts as well. Another firman of 8 Ramazan 1097/July 1686 addressed to the *kadı* of Beograd orders that timariots whose fiefs and salaries had been usurped by others during their absence be compensated and their timars returned to them. Since the data from the overaged land registers had become completely unreliable, the central government gave orders, for new registration, but this move only caused and hastened new usurpations.[5] Such new surveys *(timar yoklaması)* intended to prevent abuses and restore order to land tenure inevitably led to further abuses and usurpations. The landholding system remained a mess for long decades after the war of 1683-1699. A general *firman* issued in early February 1703 mentions the broken-up and usurped timars and orders in vain that they be returned to their legitimate holders after new surveys and registration.[6] Firmans ordering several governors in Bosnia, Cyprus, Ankara and other places to prevent vagabondage and robbery or to put a stop to their own illegal practices of confiscating land and collecting oppressive surtaxes from the people *(reaya)* were also mostly disobeyed.

---

4 Ankara Şer'iyye Sicili, Nr.66, hükm 816 (1598 H/Nov. 1686), *ibid.*, Nr.66 hükm 814, *ibid.*, Nr.68, hükm 514. Kayseri Şer'iyye Sicili Nr.93 fol 229, (Şevval 1095/Dec. 1683).

5 Başb. Arş. Maliyeden Müdevver, Nr.2933 (x Ramazan 1097) and (11 Muharrem 1097).

6 Başb. Arş. Mühimme, Nr.114 (Evail-i Şevval 1114), p.33.

During the long years peasants and townspeople were subjected to surtaxes and compulsory labour. First, the number of taxpaying house-holds *(avariz haneleri)* was increased through new surveys. Second, the amounts of *avariz* charges were generally raised. In 1088/1677, for example, the *avariz* households had just been re-surveyed, but ten years later, in 1099 H./1687, a new survey was introduced and the tax amount increased again. In pre-war times, in Beograd in 1613, for example, every ten households had been asked to pay some lump sum of equipment tax *(bildar bedeli)*; in 1098 H./1686, these same households had to pay an increased amount of the same tax amounting to 50 kuruş. Other taxes such as *nüzul vergisi*, *cerahor*, *kürekçi bedeli* (to pay for naval oarsmen) were also collected in large amounts. The required amount of capitation *(cizye)* was also increased. Pack animals were time and again demanded from every city and region, and skilled construction workers were forcibly mobilized in large numbers by the provincial administration for army service.[7] Greater and greater amounts of corn and other agricultural products were subjected to "compulsory marketing" *(sürsat)* to meet the needs of the army. Now and then authorities compelled local notables and merchants to "donate" large sums towards war expenses. Thus the notables of Kayseri had at one time to give 10,000 kuruş (400 gold pieces) in this manner. On the other hand, firmans often rained threats on local financial authorities and rulers for keeping the collected tax money for themselves and not sending it on to the central treasury.[8] Chronic inflation even in the most autarkic provinces of the Empire reached high levels. In Ankara, the exchange rate for the gold ducat rose from 300 to 600 aktches within two years.[9] The *mühimme* records

---

7 Başb. Arş. Maliyeden Müdevver, Nr.2465 (1100-1101 of H/1688-1689), p.564; see also Ankara şer. sic. Nr.68, hükm 380 "excession of the avariz taxes".

8 Ankara Şer'iyye Sicili, Nr.66, hükm 850 (1098 H/Nov. 1686), *ibid.*, Nr.66 hükm 840, Kayseri Şer'iyye sicili Nr.94, p.109.

9 Ankara Şer'iyye Sicili, Nr.66, hükm 840, Kayseri şer'iyye Nr.97, Ankara şer'iyye Nr.66, hükm 862 (Evail-i Zi'lkaade 1098) "Excession of bildartax".

of the years, include some cases where the illegal and unusual confiscation of the *waqf* revenues reached almost to fifty percent of the legal shares. This illegal confiscation has been repeated later during the First World War and caused the protests and resignation of the Shaikh al-Islam.[10]

Another side of the story was that the members of the provincial timariot army and the janissary garrisons in the towns were using all kinds of excuses to avoid active service–being over-aged or untrained *(acemi)* or engaged in protecting the towns *(sefermande olduk deyu)* were the most common ones–or else they simply deserted to join the ranks of the vagabonds and bandits. The central government had to send specially authorized officers *(sürücü çavus)* in order to try to re-enlist such people, but they were usually bribed, disobeyed, threatened or even killed.[11] As mentioned above, large groups of bandits and rebellious peasants were sometimes headed by timariots and even by ex-governors. Gedik Pasha, ex-governor of Sivas, was one of these viziers. In January 1688, he started to mobilize all the forces under his command against the government. He was subsequently joined by some other officials. The central government took extraordinary measures against rebellious authorities and soldiers and the peasant bands, and appointed some high-ranking viziers with distinguished careers like Ali Pasha, Cafer Pasha and Halil Pasha as *müfettis paşas*[12] empowered to pursue the rebels relentlessly and to resort to extremely severe punitive measures

10 Ankara şer'iyye Sicili, Nr.66 hükm 840 (1103 of H.) Kayseri Şer'iyye Nr.97 p.81 the exchange rates of the year 1101 of H/1689-1691; for the confiscation of waqf revenues, see: Başb. Arş. Mühimme Nr.98, p.67, see also H. Sahillioglu, "Sıvış Year Crises", *Studies in the Econ. Hist. of the Middle East.* (ed.) M. A. Cook, p.245, *Silahdar* II, p.273, *Raşid*, I, p.496.

11 Ankara Şer'iyye Sicili, Nr.66, hükm 814 (Evail-i RA 1098 of H.) hükm 827, 862 hükm 830, *ibid.*, (1095-1098 of H/1684-86) Kayseri Şer'iyye sicili Nr.93 (Şevval 1096/Oct. 1684), p.229.

12 Ankara Şer'iyye Sicili, Nr.65, hükm 16, Kayseri Şer'iyye, Nr.93, p.132, Muharrem 1096 (January 1685).

against them. From this time onwards, *müfettiş paşas* became a Turkish administrative measure always resorted to in times of emergency. Even in the Republican period, military commanders with extraordinary (judicial, military, administrative) powers were designated as *müfettiş* charged with suppressing eastern revolts.

For the first time in its history, the Ottoman Empire was forced to fight simultaneously on fronts as widely scattered as the Mediterranean, the Danube, and the Crimea, and to have to overwhelm the revolt in the Caucasus besides. This greatly extended war created for the Ottomans unpredictible problems of military technology and logistics. Ottoman war technology was no longer adequate, and an old-fashioned, inefficient bureaucracy proved itself unable to regularly provide the necessary supplies for operations. This incapacity was most manifest when it came to restoring and consolidating several fortresses along the Danube, in the Crimean and Caucasian zones, in Crete and in Morea. In order to have a stronghold repaired, the commander *(dizdar)* of the fortress had first to ask the central government for permission; then, the central treasury and the grand vizier's office had to send an inspector-architect *(bina ilmîne vukuf ve şuuri olan bigarez kimseler ve usta neccarlar)* to the place concerned; after an on-the-spot inspection and some calculations, this official had to submit a report to the Supreme Imperial Council *(Divan-i Hümayun)* specifying the necessary amounts of money, number of artisans and workers, etc. The local officers were left with no initative in all this. If discrepancies arose between the calculations of the inspector and the real cost, the whole thing had to be done over again. Only after the confirmation of this report were the money and the artisans sent to the place cited. This long and complicated procedure sometimes took several months. Comparison with information given by Pal Fodor concerning procedures for fortress repairs in Hungary in the seventeenth century, suggests a significant deterioration in the operations of the bureaucracy with local commanders rendered passive, even powerless.[13]

During the war years of 1683-1700, many fortresses from Comnits (Kamaniçe) to Saloniki, from Smyrna to Caffa in the Crimea kept asking for urgent repairs and the central government could not meet their needs. At one point, the initial sum allocated on the basis of calculations by the inspector for repairs in Janina could not cover the actual expenses, while Siyavuş Pasha, the vizier governing Bosnia, pleaded continuously and in vain for repairs on several fortresses in his province.[14]

Quite often, the salaries *(mevacib)* of the soldiers guarding distant fortresses were not paid in time or even not sent at all because of simple neglect.[15] Distribution of material and supplies to the fortresses was based on an inefficient spatial and bureaucratic organization. The ammunition required by Cretan castles had to be supplied by the military manufacturing centers in the Balkans. For example, it fell to the factory in Banje-luka in Bosnia to provide the cannon balls needed by the cast of Candia and Resmo.[16] On the other hand, some ship captains and merchants practised smuggling, selling gunpowder and guns to rebellions led by local feudal rulers in the district of Abhazia in Georgia in the Caucasus. Such illicit trade involved not only guns but also other strategic material and corn, which were transferred to French, English and Dutch ships for delivery.

The war after 1686 was carried to large extend by auxiliary forces of the autonomous provinces *(eyalet-i mümtaze)*. Not rarely

---

13 Pal Fodor, "Die Bauarbeiten der Türken in Ungarn im 16-17. Jahrhundert", *Acta Orientalia* XXXV/1 p.55-88.

14 Başb. Arş. Maliyeden Müdevver, Nr.2933 (7 Sefer 1097/Dec. 1685) also, *ibid.* (13 Şaban 1097/July 1686), p.166 the request of Siyavuş Pasha from Bosnia, Maliyeden Müdevver Ahkâm ve Şikâyet Defteri, Nr.2933, p.18 fortress of Varna, Maliyeden Müdevver-Tamirat Defteri, Nr.3922, p.532.

15 Başb. Arş. Maliyeden Müdevver, Nr.2933, p.37 (Sefer 1097/Jan. 1686) the complaints of soldiers in the fortress of Neve-i Cedid.

16 Başb. Arş. Ahkâm Defteri, Nr.9860 (25 Receb 1095/July 1684) firman to the factory in Banje Luke.

firmans had been sent, ordering the equipment and mobilization of the eyalet soldiers or some tribes in Anatolia. Firmans were sent to mobilize the Egyptian forces *(Mısır kulları)* or the navy of the Maghreb or *eskinci yürekler* or Turcoman and Kurdish tribes of Kilis *(Türkmen ve Ekrad aşâirinden sefere memur olan süvari asker)*. This was a new and chaotic aspect of Ottoman military history.[17]

In some corners of the Empire, some peasants *(reaya taifesi)* began to wear janissary uniform and were actually employed illegally by fortress commanders in Bosnia, for example. In this way, many peasants who kept living in their own villages posed as janissaries and this was tolerated by corrupt commanders.[18] One consequence of this development was a strong tendency towards decentralization, since some towns and fortresses decided to look after their own defence. Chaos in Rumelian towns forced local people and notables to take the task of establishing public order in their own hands as the central government completely failed to do so. The local notables *(ayan)* and the local rulers who were now appointed as *mütesellims* began to carry out financial and administrative organizations and functions through their own efforts. In this way the towns acquired a kind of autonomy which their commercial activities and wealth would later consolidate. This administrative and financial decentralization was an adjustment on the part of the Empire to the new siege conditions.[19] Urban notables and clerics often met with Ottoman officials to solve financial and administrative problems, and this led to the existence of some local councils in practice. The eighteenth century can be described as the age of administrative

---

17 Başb. Arş. Mühimme, Nr.98, p.29 (Muharrem 1100/first decade).

18 Başb. Arş. Mühimme, Nr.114 (first decade Şevval 1114/1703) to the qadi of Bosna and the governor.

19 H. İnalcık, "Saray-Bosna Şer'iyye Sicillerine Göre Viyana Bozgunundan Sonraki Harb Yıllarında Bosna", *Türk Tarih Vesikaları*, Nr.2, Ankara, 1943 (ii), pp.1-3; see also, Avdo Suceska, "Die Rechtsstellung der Bevölkerung in den Staedten Bosniens und Herzegovina", *Südosteuropa Jahrbuch*, München, 1968/8, p.84-99.

decentralization in the Empire, which was trying to survive through prodigious bureaucratic manipulations.

Ottoman society and culture entered an era of renovation. In the *Enderun* (palace school) where previously *devşirme* children had been recruited and trained and had gone on to take up the reins of central rule, this role was from the eighteenth century onward to fall more and more frequently to the Anatolians, those who in Ottoman terms had always been regarded as "crude Turks". The tastes and views of the new ruling elite led to an increase in the share and influence of the Turkish element and language in Ottoman life. As famous poets Sadi and Nabî put it poetic language had to be purified of Arabic and Persian vocabulary.[20] Ottoman architecture, decorative arts, daily life and attire were more and more influenced by European baroque. No wonder that the era after the second siege of Vienna is described as the Ottoman baroque age. The existence of a slow modernization or Europeanization process in Ottoman society became gradually visible.

In this newly beginning age of Ottoman modernization, Transylvanian and Transdanubian Hungary, which had come into contact with Renaissance culture early in the fifteenth century, could have served as effective models. But these lands were annexed by the Habsburgs, and later, the constant revolts against their rule and the consequent Habsburg repression and colonization by German peasants further severed the links between Hungary and the Ottoman lands. Seventeenth century Transylvania (Erdel), was going through a national cultural and economic revival. In comparison with that part of Hungary which was in Habsburg hands even before the treaty of Karlowitz, the clerics and laymen of Transylvanian and Transdanubian Hungary had enjoyed perfect religious freedom.[21] The Ottomans had not only

20 A. Sirri Levend, *Türk Dilinde Gelişme ve Sadeleşme Safhaları*, Türk Dili Kurumu, Ankara, 1949, pp.94-95.

21 Katalin Peter, "La vie de la société transylvanne dans la première moitié du XVle siècle", *Acta Historica*, XXVII (1-2), 1981, pp.7-9 and 22-25, see also, Andras Székely, *Illustrierte Kulturgeschichte Ungarns*, Budapest, Corvina, 1978, pp.89-106.

tolerated Hungarian Protestantism but had also actually tried to manipulate it against the Catholic Habsburgs. Protestantism and autonomy had facilitated the development of Hungarian national culture, and this would later be a base for national revival under the Habsburgs. Agricultural improvements in seventeenth century Transylvania had led to a rise in living standards in both urban and rural areas. Many young Hungarians studied in England, Germany, Italy and other European countries. In 1622 Bethlen Gabor, Prince of Erdel, founded the Communal Academy. Prince Rakoczy I Goyrgy is another ruler who introduced and spread modern educational institutions from which even talented serf and peasant children could benefit.[22]

The Ottoman Empire had from its very beginnings been influenced by Hungarian culture, engineering, military technology and even cooking. Hungarian converts could be found in every section of Ottoman society. One example only: familiarity with the Hungarian language was an important element in the original style and deep learning of the famous historian İbrahim Peçevi, who had read some history books in Hungarian. Another one was Cafer Iyanî from Pecs, who wrote an history about Hungary *(Tarih-i Cedid-i Ungarus)*. On the other hand, the Ottoman conquest bequeathed to Hungary wellknown monuments, customs and other imprints in every aspect of socio-cultural life. Thanks of the studies of Hungarian turcologists, we are quite well informed about the influence of both languages upon each other.[23] Although after the treaty of Karlowitz this cultural integration was interrupted for a few decades, Hungarian emigrants continued to contribute much to the modernization of Ottoman society and state and to the improvement of Turkish culture up to the mideighteenth century and then again especially in the nineteenth.

22 L. Benczédi, "Historischer Hintergrund der Preadigerprozesse in Ungarn in den Jahren 1673-74", *Acta Historica*, XXXI (3-4), 1976.

23 S. Kakuk, "Les mots d'emprunt Turcs-Osmanli dans le Hongrois et les recherches...", *Acta Orientalia*, 1955/V, p.181-194 see also, J. Németh, *Die türkische Sprache in Ungarn im siebzehnten Jahrhundert*, Budapest, 1970.

9

The Problem of Nationalities in the Ottoman Empire Following the Second Siege of Vienna

I.

One unquestioned development in the Ottoman Empire following the second siege of Vienna is the clear-cut emergence of the problem of nationalities. Doubtless the causes of this go back to before the rout in which the siege ended; but it is also true that here at the end of the seventeenth century, it was demonstrated not only to the powers of Europe but also to the Balkan peoples living under the Sultan that the Ottoman might was capable of defeat and even debacle. This was a stimulus to them in organizing national movements; Ottoman Rumelia of the later seventeenth century was host to a very different dynamism than had existed before. Meanwhile thanks to the hastening – induced by the rout at Vienna – of the process of administrative change, the Turkish element within the Empire's Muslim population acquired a greater role in matters of government. Thus, though the overriding culture and the process of ruling were still Ottoman, Turkish Anatolia began definitely to come to the fore; with the net result that the traditionally structured Empire, until then "Ottoman" in character because cosmopolitan, as ancient Rome and medieval Byzantium had been cosmopolitan, was in actual fact ceasing to be Ottoman. By the time we reach the eighteenth and nineteenth centuries, the Ottoman state has assumed all the earmarks of a political and social system in which the problem of disruptive nationalism is the predominant factor.

Ottoman conquests in the Balkans during the fourteenth century in a way brought stability to the region. The throes of social change that tossed the Balkans throughout the fourteenth and fifteenth centuries were quelled with the restoration of stability and a feudal system. But inevitably, as Ottoman power reached its zenith in the sixteenth century, the beginnings of economic and social unrest began to make themselves felt, not only in Rumelia but, more particularly, in Anatolia as well. Coming up to the seventeenth century, we see an empire that has lost its former might and, carried inexorably forward by the stream of time, finds itself unable to adapt in a modern world of changing conditions; so much so, that it is still an unresolved question of historiography how the Ottoman armies managed, in 1683, ever to reach the gates of Vienna at all. The State's land tenure and bureaucratic structuring, and most significantly the military chain of command, were rocked by one upheaval after another. In all likelihood, the fact that the siege actually took place, and even achieved initial success, is owing partly to the turmoil caused in Central Europe by the Thirty Years' War, partly to the waning but still felt superiority of the Ottoman troops, and in some measure to the failure of the Austrian lands to develop.

We know that among the various religious and linguistic groups which came under the Ottoman sway, certain movements, or at least stirrings, that could be described in some cases as cultural, in others as national, began to make their presence felt in the sixteenth century. To call the events of 1789 the cause for national awakening in the Balkans cannot be an entirely prudent course for the historian to take. The national consciousness of the Balkan peoples was a feature of their medieval heritage that survived the Ottoman period, with every community having its own schools, and its own guilds helping to regulate economic life. Thus national identity or, if one prefers, early nationalism has its roots, for the peoples of the Balkans, as far back as the

Renaissance. It is no mere coincidence that the ideas put forward by Machiavelli in *The Prince* were greatly in vogue at the end of the sixteenth century and the beginning of the seventeenth, among the intelligentsia in certain south Slavic communities. Furthermore the spontaneous peasant uprisings that occurred in the sixteenth century, or the *hayduk* movements[1] opposing local Ottoman authority, show that, to some extent at any rate, national identity in the Balkans had not completely disappeared.

The nationalist movements of the Balkan peoples, and the way in which these movements developed, were quite different from those to be found in the various countries of western Europe. They are also different–I am speaking of the eighteenth and nineteenth century Balkans–from the nationalist movements of today's world. Under the socio-economic and legal order imposed by the Ottomans, the hereditary aristocracy in the Balkans ceased to develop, and native aristocracy in existence before the fourteenth century had all but died out. So it was that the nationalist movement of the Balkan Slavs developed, first and foremost, with the participation of the Church, to which starting in the eighteenth century was allied a rising commercial bourgeoisie and, in time, the peasantry. In opposition to nationalism stood "Ottoman-ness" (but not Ottomanism), a way of life and a social order, but not yet an ideology. Only after the eighteenth century would Ottoman-ness begin to evolve into an ideology, which in turn was to be altered by the influence of Balkan nationalism(s), until finally the Empire's Muslims too were caught up in the wave, clamoring for their own national existences. The Church conducted a campaign in which Christianity and nationalist ideology were at the very least conjoined, and in doing so played

1 B. A. Cvetkova, "Problems on the Bulgarian Nationality and the National Consciousness in the XV-XVIII century", Étude*s Historiques* 6 (1973) pp.57-80; M. Janov, "Die Ereignisse in Südosteuropa am Ende des 16. Jahrhunderts und die politische Tätigkeit der Anführer der Befreiungbewegungen in Bulgarien", Étude*s Historiques* 8 (1978) pp.158-177.

a highly active ideological role in the national movements of liberation. The very existence of the Church, and the process of its evolution, bore within them the seeds of dispute between the Ottoman rulers and the Orthodox believers; disputes which were naturally to affect the nationalist movement.

II.

From the moment of its inception in the 14th century, and all through its spectacular rise for the following two centuries, the Ottoman Empire was in fact a Balkan empire. The Ottoman culture and way of life had, it would seem, long since received the stamp of the Balkan and Mediterranean cultures; with the corollary that an understanding of Ottoman society is hardly possible without a previous knowledge of medieval Byzantium and the structure of the Balkan states.

In the middle of the 15th century, the peoples who owed allegiance to the Eastern Orthodox Church lived under Ottoman rule; the second Orthodox state was Czarist Russia. Mehmed II (the Conquerer) followed a deliberate policy of favoring unilateral rule in the Church. He appointed as Patriarch Gennadios, virulent enemy of Rome, and displayed towards him a consideration greater than he had enjoyed during Byzantine times. The Patriarchs of Constantinople now enjoyed a position in the official protocol.[2] In addition, the Bulgarian and Serbian Churches had been deprived of their autocephaly, with spiritual, administrative, financial and judicial authority over all Balkan Orthodoxy devolving on the Patriarch in Constantinople. In these circumstances, Greeks living in the Ottoman lands enjoyed prerogatives and a general prominence; for just as the Orthodox Church had autonomy and privilege, the Greek tongue under the empire, and Greek education, were able to go their way unhindered. To a certain extent, even Byzantine legal heritage continued to exist and be

2 F. Babinger, *Mehmed der Eroberer und seine Zeit*, München, 1959, pp.110-111.

applied. At *Bab-ı alî* (the Sublime Porte) edicts were drawn up in Greek, which thrived as a semi-official language. Over and beyond these distinctions, the Greeks were the sole non-muslim group to be employed in the bureaucracy and in chancellary service. In this respect the Greeks were better off than any other ethnic group, the Turks included. For until the 18th and 19th centuries the Turks, usually thought of as the heart of the empire, took only a limited part in governing, and the very name of "Turks" was used to mean "uncouth peasant lout". Authors of Ottoman times are insistent in saying that Turkish element must not be allowed to meddle in the business of government.[3] "Turk" was an insulting epithet not only among the Ottoman meritocracy, but also among the İstanbul populace at large; for example, "Baba Himmet", the most idiotic, unlovable figure in all of *Karagöz* (the Turkish shadow theater), is constantly referred to as "the Turk".

The Greeks were a sea-faring people, they had had relations with Italy and Central Europe since the Renaissance, and they were viewed with feelings of kinship by Europe as a whole. It was then only natural that they would have nationalist sentiments from a very early date, but this under European patronage. Meanwhile Ottoman supremacy was making it possible for the Greek Patriarchate to exert monolithic control over Orthodox Slavs in the Balkans, which in turn encouraged the strengthening of resistance and nationalist feelings in the latter. In the eighteenth and nineteenth centuries, the Patriarchate was as unwelcome to the Bulgarians as was the Sublime Porte. The Bulgarian national movement strove from the outset to establish an independent church, and succeeded in doing so during the second half of the nineteenth century.

Ottoman rule was never a threat to the survival of Greek education and culture. From the seventeenth century on, schools

3 See, B. Lewis, *The Emergence of Modern Turkey*, Oxford 1968), pp.1-2; C. Cahen, In: *Unity and Variety in Muslim Civilization*, ed. G. E. v. Grunebaum (1955), p.330; also J. Hammer, *Geschichte des Osmanischen Reiches* I, Pest, 1827.

were opened by wealthy Greek merchants not only in the Peloponnese and Epirus, but also in western Anatolia and on the Black Sea coast. This process continued in Cyprus and Crete after they fell to the Ottomans. The positive contribution of Europe to the Greek enlightenment came not only in these schools, but also thanks to the children of the commercial bourgeoisie who early on began receiving their education in Europe. Another point was that the Ionian islands were not beholden to the Sultan, and therefore came under Italian and French cultural influence, on account of which the local Greeks were more exposed to classical Greek culture and modern humanism. These islands in turn exerted their cultural influence on all the Ottoman Greeks. On them there was wide-spread learning of French, Italian and English and classical Greek in its choicest form was a medium of instruction. In the early eighteenth century, when Austria became commercially and politically more influential along the shores both of the Adriatic and the Danube, a sizable number of Greeks, having in view political, commercial or cultural aims, migrated to major Austrian cities from Epirus, Macedonia and the Ionian islands, and there established their own churches and their own schools. Having been the first to establish contact with Europe, the Greeks wasted no time in exerting a cultural and ideological influence over the other Balkan peoples.

Undeniably, Bulgarian monks in their monasteries on Mount Athos made contact with the newly enlightened Greek culture,[4] and in the Balkans this culture just as undeniably became institutionalized. In 1694 Prince Constantin Brinceveanu set up for the Romanians the "Saint Savas Academy" where instruction was given in Greek.[5] Before long the Balkans had established direct cultural ties with Western Europe.

---

4 G. Nesev, "Les Monastères Bulgares du Mont Athos", Étude*s Historiques*, 6 (1973), pp.97-115.

5 A. Dascalakis, "Le Rôle de la Civilisation grecque dans les Balkans", *Actes du premier Congrès International des* Étude*s Balkaniques*, Sofia, 1969, pp.109-110.

In fact, it would be a mistake to explain the emergence of the national problem in the Balkans entirely by the Greek Enlightenment or, as we said, by the French Revolution. A certain idea of irredentism or Slav unity can be seen among the Balkan Slavs as early as the sixteenth century. When Ottoman rule led to the bestowing of all spiritual authority on the Patriarch in Constantinople, the Balkan Slavs found themselves deprived of independence not only in religious matters, but equally in questions of language, law and education. Pushed by those adverse circumstances the Balkan Slavs turned early on to Russia, a sovereign power. It is possible that the first glimmerings of Slav irredentism were born from the ideas of Machiavelli; engaged as they were in intense cultural and commercial relations with Renaissance Italy, it cannot be coincidence that Ragusan and Croatian thinkers make mention in their writings of a kind of Slavic unity and liberation. In 1626 the Ragusan poet Ivan Gundulic, in his lyric poem "Osman", speaks of liberation and the unity of the Slavs in a style reminiscent of Tasso's. It was Gundulic's belief that this historic mission could only be accomplished under the aegis of the Polish king.[6] One of the most striking instances of this phenomenon is the Croatian priest, philosopher and historian Juraj Krizanic (1618-1683). Having settled in Russia, he proposed that all Slavs unite under the leadership of the Czar and a church of Catholic tendency to break away from the Ottomans. To accomplish this historic task, he recommended the modernization of Russia, a build-up of its might, and reform of its church and social system. Needless to say, his views were highly unpopular with clerics and conservatives, and were quickly forgotten.[7]

---

6 A. Fischel, *Der Panslawismus bis zum Weltkrieg*, Berlin, 1919, pp.19-20.

7 Fischel, *Panslawismus*, p.20; H. Kohn, *Panslavism–It's History,* Notre Dame Indiana, 1953, p.4; M. Petrovich, "Juraj Krizanic a Precursor of Panslavism", *The American Slavonic and East European Review*, 6 (1947), pp.75-92.

An active role for Russia was one recurrent theme in the discussion of national awakening among the Balkan Slavs. Balkan historians, no less than those in Turkey, at one period laid great emphasis on the expansion of this Russian role; and nineteenth century European thought tended also to see Russia as the most active element in the "eastern question".[8]

Now, although there is no arguing with the fact that this role increased following the Treaty of Küçük Kaynarca (1774), it would nevertheless be wrong to consider the Russian role as the most dominant factor in seventeenth and eighteenth century Balkan nationalism. In fact, as can be seen in the example of Krizanic, ideologically the Balkan Slavs were ahead of Russia. Russia's role became more influential as she developed and modernized. The westernizing process in Muscovite Russia began after the sixteenth century. The period of the Romanov Dynasty in particular saw the establishment of permanent ambassadorial relations with the whole of Western Europe, and Russian merchants were familiar with cities in Scandinavia, Germany and Poland. These improving political and commercial relations could not but introduce into Russia, however slowly, a western style of living. A number of noblemen began furnishing their homes in European fashion, at the same time adopting Renaissance and Baroque ways along with German customs. Russian culture at this period began to be acquainted, through translation, with European literature and science. One such europeanized noble was Knez Golitzin, favourite of the Regent Sophia.

Russia had long ago set her sights on becoming the successor to Byzantium, and there were now many Balkan Slavs and Greek intellectuals and members of the church within her marches. These arrivals worked in libraries or in the palace printhouse, did

8 F. Engels mentions in one of his articles in 1853, the maladroitness and ignorance of European diplomats, whereas he stresses the successful activities of Russian diplomats among Balkan-Slav circles, *New York Daily Tribune*, Nr. 3748 (April 21, 1853).

translation from Greek and Old Church Slavonic, or tutored the children of wealthy families; on their visits back to the Balkans they took with them numerous books of a religious, literary or political nature. About the middle of the seventeenth century we see in the Balkans the beginnings of a certain Russian political influence. One instance of this is the first printing press in the Moldavian city of lasi, which went into operation in 1640 thanks to the good offices of Pjotr Mogila, Metropolitan at Kiev.[9] As time went by, Balkan Slavs were to follow more and more closely cultural developments in Russia.

Russia's relations with the Balkan Slavs, unlike those of Western Europe, came not through the channels of trade but through the Church. From the seventeenth century on, Serbian, Montenegrin, Romanian and later Bulgarian priests were in contact with Russia. Between 1557 and 1766, the Ipek (Pec) Patriarchate in Serbia, which performed its function autonomously, experienced financial and administrative difficulties which meant that the survival of Serbian monasteries and churches was to some extent only possible with the help of Russia. Each year Serbian priests carried to Russia a number of manuscripts and icons. These priests, some of them admitted into Moscow, others turned back at the border with a gift of alms, began in the eighteenth century to bring with them lay publications as well.[10] The Russian Church made extensive use of Balkan priests and the manuscripts in Balkan monasteries, starting in the seventeenth century. As C. Rogel points out, "during the period of Russian church reforms in the mid-seventeenth century, requests for manuscripts and books were frequently sent to Serbian monasteries. In 1655, for example, three Hilander monks carried to Moscow eleven handwritten books (seven Old Slavonic,

9 *Vsemirnaja Istorija* [World history], red. Zutis, Vejnstejn, Pavlenko, ed. Akad. Nauk SSSR 5, Moskva, 1958, p.182.

10 C. Rogel, "The Wandering Monk and Balkan National awakening", in: *Nationalism in a nonnational state*, ed. W. Haddad, Ohio-Columbus, 1977, p.90.

four Greek) which had been specifically requested by the Russian patriarch Arsenii Sukhanov; they were to be used according to the official request to correct Russian religious books."[11]

It was nevertheless true that compared to Montenegro, Walachia-Moldavia and Bulgaria, serbian monastic life after 1690 was to a certain extent culturally influenced by the Habsburg Empire. This was behind the choice made by D. Obradovic (1742-1811), best known of all Serbian clerics, to substitute secular for religious learning. After 1804 Obradovic became Karageorgi's secretary and superintendant of Serbian schools. The one most important factor in the persistence of church leadership in the Balkan national awakening was the ability of the clerics to adopt secular education and secular views. They were the first to pen popular works on subjects such as history and geography. Foremost among such priests were the Serbians Jovan Rajic (1726-1801) and the Romanians G. Sincai, Petru Maior, and Samuel Clain. Finally, Paissij Hilandersky, justly considered the father of Bulgar nationalism for his writing at the Hilander monastery on Mount Athos in 1762 of the first popularized Slavgan-Bulgarian history; and after him Sofronij Vracansky are two typical examples of Balkan Slav church clerics contributing to the development of Bulgarian national feeling, Throughout the eighteenth century such men were busy translating works from ancient Greek and Old Church Slavonic into contemporary tongues, and were thus instrumental in transforming the vernacular into a polished literary language. In this matter they were very different from the Greek priests, who persisted in the use of a language remote from the colloquial.[12] It is true that Balkan Slavs always had a xenophobic attitude towards the Roman church, but they were impelled by the presence of the Constantinople Patriarchate–which they viewed as

11 Rogel, "The Wandering Monk", pp.85-86.

12 N. Danova-Z. Markova, "Ideja zerkovnogo reformatorstva i balkanskoe proşvescenie (XVIII-XIX vv)" [The idea of church-reform and Balkan enlightenment], Étude*s Historiques* 7 (1975) pp.161-174.

more oppressive than their Ottoman rulers–into entertaining the idea of an alliance with the Catholic Church in order to obtain cultural and spiritual autonomy for the Slavic peoples. To some extent this idea was put into action. We know of active centers for Catholic propaganda in Bulgaria and Romania, not very successful enterprises which date back almost to the beginning of Ottoman rule in the region. The French envoy to İstanbul, Girardin, writes in his report of 13 February 1686 that a Bulgarian orthodox priest had approached him with a petition directed to the French king, in which the Bulgarians are declared ready to convert to Catholicism and to seek the protection and intervention of the king.[13] It should not come as a great surprise to meet with such a bid in the years immediately following the rout at Vienna.

The Bulgarian historian B. Cvetkova says that during the war year there was an increase in the hayduk movements along the banks of the Danube.[14] The petition sent in 1688 to Czar Ivan IV and to Peter I by the Vlachian ruler Serban Cantacuzen is well known. It contained a declaration of intent of the part of the Serbians, Bulgarians and Moldavians to aid the Russians if they advanced to Akkerman. The rout at Vienna, in the third century of Ottoman sway, had an accelerating effect upon this reaction.

III.

One of the most important outcomes of the second siege of Vienna was the strengthening of the Habsburg Empire's politico-military power in central Europe, the Balkans and the eastern Mediterranean, and the improvement of its commercial position. The spreading commercial influence went hand in hand with increased cultural influence, while internally Ottoman Europe

---

13 Archives du Ministre des Affaires étrangères, Quai D'Orsay, Paris. C. P. Turquie, vol.18, Ambas. Girardin, Pera 13 février 1686, fol.102 v.

14 B. A. Cvetkova, "To the History of the Resistance Against the Ottoman Feudal Domination in the Danube Region of Bulgaria", Étude*s Historiques* 4 (1968), pp.221-223.

entered a time of crisis, brought on by the defeat, in which prolonged deficiencies in the military, administrative and economic mechanisms led inevitably to a process of decentralization in the provinces. This process was witnessed not only in the Balkans but in Anatolia as well, and it meant the beginning of momentous structural changes.

Until the end of the seventeenth century, Austrian trade, whether foreign or domestic, was not at a level to enhance tax revenues. Because of her lack of control over the territories along the Danube, Austria's river-based commerce had also failed to develop. Another barrier to the flourishing of trade on Austrian soil was the paucity of trade relations among the German states belonging to the Holy Roman Empire. Having almost no access to the Mediterranean, Austria had not taken to the seaways to project her power abroad. (The "Orientalische Handelskompagnie" set up by Becker in 1667 declared bankruptcy after a brief struggle.[15]) Nor was it any help that roads in the country were terribly primitive, compared to those of Western Europe. One primary factor in the Ottoman defeat in 1683 was the deteriorated state of the road system in Niederösterreich. Following the treaties of Karlowitz and Passarowitz however (1699) and (1718), the Habsburg Empire moved into the Danubian basin, making possible inroads into Balkan commerce. The Balkans became a market and a source of raw materials. When in 1719 Karl VI opened Trieste as a major port to rival Venise, it meant the launching of Austria's career in the Mediterranean. During the eighteenth century she signed navigation acts with the Ottomans to secure safety of passage in their waters.[16] And thus, legal or illegal, trade was carried on

---

15 H. Hassinger, "Die erste Wiener Orientalische Handelskompagnie 1667-1683", *Vierteljahresschrift für Sozial-und Wirtschaftgeschichte* 35 (1942), pp. 1-53; F. Tremel, *Wirtschafts-und Sozialgeschichte Österreichs*, Graz, 1969, pp. 232-235, 255 and 261-262.

16 İ. Ortaylı, "1727-Osmanlı-Avusturya Sözleşmesi" [Handelsvertrag zwischen Österreich und Osmanenreich in Jahre 1727], *Ankara Üniversitesi Siyasal Bilgiler Fakültesi Dergisi*, 28/3-4 (1975) pp.97-109.

throughout the Mediterranean and the Balkans. In the vanguard, with a fleet of 600 ships, came the Greeks. This burgeoning of commerce and Austrian manufactures faciliated the emergence in the Balkans of a commercial bourgeoisie. In the eighteenth century the growth of raw material and semi-manufactured goods oriented towards the demands of industry wrought changes in the cities of the Balkans.[17]

To the Ottoman Empire's senior commercial people, the Greeks, were now added the Serbo-Croatians and Bulgarians. During the eighteenth century, cultural renovation at the national level developed parallel to the emergence of the commercial bourgeoisie among all the Balkan peoples. In the European cities of Livorno, Naples, Trieste, Venice and Vienna, and in certain cities of Russia, there appeared sizeable groups of merchants, religious clerics and students, as churches and cultural centers sprang up.

It was in the wake of these events that the effects of the European enlightenment truly began to make themselves felt. Eighteenth century philosophers such as Voltaire, Diderot, Herder and Lessing became known to the Balkan intelligentsia. Albanians in southern Italy, Serbs in the cities of central Europe, Bulgarians in Romania, all these groups enjoyed a culture and an education that was western in orientation.[18]

Austrian influence in the Balkans was particularly great during the eighteenth and nineteenth centuries. On factor in this was the cultural flourishing of the western Slaves within the Habsburg Empire. There is increasing recognition of the

17 N. Todorov, *Balkanski GorodXV-XIX vekov* [Balkan city in the XV-XIX centuries], Moskva, 1976, pp.194-222; V. Paskaleva, "Die Wirtschaftsbeziehungen der bulgarischen Gebiete mit Mitteleuropa im 18. und 19. Jahrhundert", In: *Wirtschaftswege, Festschrift für H. Kellenbenz*, Stuttgart, 1978, p.169.

18 V. Traikov, *Ideologiceski teceniya i programi v nazionalno-osvoboditelnite dvizenija na Balkanite do 1878 godina* [Ideological tendencies and programs during the national-liberation movements of Balkan countries until 1878], Sofia, 1978, p.169.

importance on Balkan cultural development of Austrian and Hungarian baroque culture, literature, theatre and plastics arts.[19]

Following the second siege of Vienna the Ottoman Empire's Balkan provinces were immediately thrown into turmoil, lawlessness and economic collapse. The heavy taxation necessitated by war and the attempt to enforce order brought on a similar collapse in Anatolia. The rout of the army, the attrition of garrisons assigned to enforce order in the cities, the crumbling of the economy, the disappearance of safety on the highways, and the fighting of wars that never seemed to be over, all spelled a virtual end to central government control in the Balkans. The citizenry of Bosnia, for example, made repeated appeals to İstanbul for funds and military assistance, appeals which the central governments was unable to answer. As a result people in the cities had recourse to law-enforcement on their own.[20] From the beginning of the eighteenth century problems of security and finance in the Rumelian cities began to be sloved by the people in concert with local notables. The *ayans* who were local landowners and administrators of pious foundations (known as *waqf*), assumed surrogate authority in the cities. Peter Sugar has described in detail this coming to the fore of local authority in the cities and provinces of Rumelia. The Muslim *beys*, who were the descendants of minor Bosnian aristocrats who converted to Islam immediately after the Ottoman conquest, had, through the viziers and sandjak beys that they produced throughout the Ottoman reign, always managed to stay on good terms with the central administration. Now, although remaining loyal to the Sultan, they were impelled

19 V. Paskaleva, "Sredna Evropa i kulturno-prosvetnoto razvitie na Bulgarite prez vazrazdaneto" [Central Europe and cultural enlightenment and development in Bulgaria before the Renaissance], *Istoriceski Pregled* 3-4 (1977) pp.116-117 and 136.

20 H. İnalcık, "Saray Bosna Şer'iyye Siciline Göre Viyana Bozgunundan Sonra Bosna" [Bosnia after the siege of Vienna according to the Cadi-records of Sarajevo], *Tarih Vesikaları*, 2/2, Ankara, 1943, pp.1-3.

by the anarchy that follows long wars to take over the reins of local government. In the face of peasant uprisings and the specter of roving hayduk hands, İstanbul looked upon this new decentralization and shift of authority with benevolence. The local population of course prefered these new rulers, who, by language and tradition were Bosnian; and the governor was often nothing than and honored guest. It was the local lords who ran the province as they pleased.[21] The same conditions could be said to have prevailed in the Albania-Epirus region.

The situation in the Anatolian peninsula was different only by nuance. The process of land concentration that had continued since the sixteenth century had led to the emergence of a new class of local landlords. The timariot system of military enfiefment had broken down, and troops could no longer be summoned to battle as in the past. The keeping of order in Anatolian towns and provinces at this period had been largely left to local power groups and representatives.[22] The people by now habitually sought protection with the local rulers, in the face of heavy taxation and the depredations of the everpresent hayduk. Decentralization had become a fact of life. From the eighteenth century onward, the presence of this new governing class would lead to profound changes in the social and political structure of the Empire.

IV.

In the year 1685, the sultan bestowed upon the bandit chieftain Yegen Osman the title of *beylerbeyi* or governor general. The decision to do so was hardly an outpouring of generosity, for

21 P. F. Sugar, "Southeastern Europe under Ottoman Rule (1354-1804)", In: *A History of East Central Europe 5*, London, 1977, pp.233-236.

22 İ. Ortaylı, "17. Yüzyıl Sonlarında Orta Anadolu Vilâyetlerinin Toplumsal Ekonomik Durumu Üzerine" [On the Socio-economic conditions of central Anatolian provinces at the end of the 17th century], *Toplum ve Bilim*, 1981, Nr.15-16.

Osman had gathered around him a powerful force of rebellious peasants, stoic souls who had finally had enough of being plundered whenever their villages became the target of tax agents or imperial soldiers who had deserted. The central Ottoman power was weary, depleted by constant war with Venice, Poland and the Czar. There seemed no choice but to distribute titles, rank and honour to bandit chieftains in the hope of pitting them against robber bands and rebels.[23] A report drawn up by the French envoy Guilleragues in March of 1684 depicts a country in total disarray. "Highly placed commanders and functionaries are constantly being replaced, administrative authority, is stricken with paralysis."[24] During the war years the timariots had raided and appropriated each other's holdings, thus increasing land concentration. There was more frequent seizure of land and local power in a fashion that simply bypassed the central government, as repeatedly shown by the official records of the time and in the edicts issued by the Sultan.[25] Meanwhile armies of bandits, deserting troops and timariots heedless of their fealty added another dimension to the growing anarchy.[26] In these circumstances, with the central government unable to wield authority, responsibility was assumed by local notables called *ayans* who became, in place of the pasha's, administrators both in matters of government and in the originally cosmopolitan *devşirme* (recruitment). During the long decades of turbulence, the government was to appoint to positions of responsibility army officers who had distinguished themselves in Anatolia, and local

---

23 M. Akdağ, "Genel Çizgileriyle XVII. Yüzyıl Türkiye Tarihi", [Central features of the history of Turkey in the 17th century], *Ankara Üniversitesi Dil Tarih Coğrafya Fakültesi Dergisi*, 416-7, Ankara, 1968, pp.236-238.

24 Archives du Ministre des Affaires Étrangères (Paris). C. P. Turquie, vol.17, Nr.168, p.12. Pera, 28 Mars 1684.

25 Ankara Şer'iyye Sicili [Cadi-records of Ankara] Register 66, Hükm: 816 from year 1098 H/November 1686.

26 Ankara Şer'iyye, Hükm: 862 (Zilhicce 1098-October 1687).

figures who had proven themselves capable of preserving order in their own territory. Replacing the *valis*, these local lords (known as *mütesellims*) represent an important change. For, where before one had *devşirme* children recruited and trained in the *Enderun* (palace school), who went on to take up the reins of central rule, now, from the eighteenth century onward, this role was to fall more and more frequently upon the Anatolians, those who in Ottoman terms had always been regarded as "crude Turks".[27]

So it is that the renowned grand viziers and military commanders of the eighteenth century are mostly of Turkish extraction. İbrahim Pasha and Halil Hamid Pasha, both reform-instituting grand viziers in the Tulip Age *(Lâle Devri)*, are typical examples of this new administrative class. This increase of the Turkish presence in administration lost little time in making itself felt in art and culture as well. In a feudal society the tastes and demands of the ruling class are bound to be carefully considered by artists of every stamp. The poets of the eighteenth century, when *Divan* poetry was the literature of the highest class, to some extent abandoned the tortuous locutions of an Arabic-and Persian-laden style in favour or purer Turkish. The language of poets such as Nabî and Nedîm is far closer to the Turkish of the ordinary people of İstanbul than had been that of earlier poets. What is more, the content too of poetry became livelier and closer to reality, Sadî in particular, of the poets of this time, openly pleaded for the written word to reflect the spoken language.[28] As he put it:

> *Nice Türkî dinür ol şi'rekim her lâfzunun halli lûgatler bakmaya muhtac ide mecliste yaranı*
>
> (If the audience for a poem has to look everything up in the dictionary, how can you call it a Turkish poem?)

---

27 Akdağ, "Genel Çizgileriyle", p.238.

28 A. Levend, *Türk Dilinde Gelişme ve Sadeleşme Safhaları* [The development and purification phases of the Turkish Language], ed. Türk Dil Kurumu Nr.031, Ankara, 1949, pp.94-95.

On the military plane, the rout at Vienna made speedy and efficacious reform a necessity. When imperial schools of military engineering were opened (Mühendishane-i Bahri-yi Hümayun and Mühendishane-i Berri-yi Hümayun) the very first piece of business was to translate texbooks for foreign languages. In doing so, every effort was made to see that the vocabulary was Turkish rather than Arabic or Persian, since most of the students were Turks of humble origin. Such scholars as Şanizade and Hoça İshak, although active in the fields of geography, medicine, chemistry and mathematics took their terminology from Latin, also did their best to find purely Turkish equivalents.[29] Eighteenth century Turkish is still virgin terrain for the researcher, but one thing is clear: the language of bureaucracy, education and literature was brought closer to the spoken tongue, as the "Arabate" and "Persified" jargon of Ottoman began to give way to a more Turkish idiom.

The dominance of the Turkish ethnic element in government and culture was a platform from which Turkish nationalism could rise in the centuries to come, but for a time no more than that. In the eighteenth century it is still too early to speak of the emergence, within the Ottoman Empire, of a Turkish nationalism rooted in the Turkish ethnic element. The first unmistakeable examples of Turkish nationalism came in the 1860's, with a book *(Les Turcs anciens et modernes)* by Mustafa Celaleddin Pasha, a Pole who had come to Turkey in 1849 as a refugee; and with the admonition directed by Ahmed Vefik Pasha to a Syrian Christian member of the first Ottoman parliament (1877-1878): "If you know what is good for you", he said, "you will learn Turkish".[30] Always the official language, Turkish was first proclaimed as such in the Constitution of 1876; and it would take until the end of the nineteenth and beginning of the twentieth century for Turkishness to become the seed of a nationalism. Throughout

29 Levend, *Türk Dilinde*, pp.89-91.

30 *Meclis-i Mebusan Zabıt Ceridesi* [Protocol-book of the Ottoman parliament 1877-1878-1878], ed. H. T. Us [40th session, May 18, 1877), p.313.

the eighteenth century, nationalism in the Ottoman Empire was confined to the Balkans, as Anatolia witnessed no more than a strong process of purification. Because of this process, however, the Empire in the eighteenth century rapidly began to lose its centuries-old cosmopolitan character. With the loss of the central European *eyalet*s (provinces) through the treaties of Karlowitz and Passarowitz, national developments all through the Balkans, and the beginnings of intervention by the European powers, a new Islamic ideology began to emerge in the Empire during the eighteenth century. For the first time in Ottoman history, fanaticism wound its way into religious life and thought. The institutions and title of caliphate took on a far greater importance. At the same time, of course, the threat posed to the Empire by Europe made it vital to modernize and become acquainted with developments in the West.

At this period the report drawn up by the Sultan's ambassador to Berlin, Azmi Efendi, speaks in glowing terms of Prussia both as state and social order. It goes on to make various suggestions for Ottoman reform. Self-encomium, so long a hallmark of the Ottoman's, had clearly become a thing of the past.[31] In architecture, central European influence had brought a new baroque style, visible in the *eyalets* as it is in the mosques, barracks and palaces of the epoch in İstanbul. In Ottoman painting as well, European influence was not restricted to İstanbul. The new style appeared also throughout Anatolia and the Balkans. There are grounds for the claim that this eighteenth century style was less refined then the classical Ottoman, but on the other hand there is a welcome infusion of movement and variety after the set, static forms of the centuries that preceded. Contributions of the West to eighteenth century Ottoman painting include perspective, landscape, and the depiction of the human form.[32] There was no aspect of daily life

31 B. Lewis, *The Muslim Discovery of Europe*, London, 1982, 208.

32 G. Renda, *Batılılaşma Döneminde Türk Resim Sanatı 1700-1850* [Turkish painting in the era of westernization 1700-1850], Ankara, 1977.

not touched in some manner by the wave of modernization and westernization. That this would hasten the process of turcification is only natural, if we consider that printing presses began at this period turning out works in Turkish, thus making science and art available to a broader range of the people.

There is an eighteenth century canvas, an instance of Austrian folk art that depicts by means of stereotypes the nations of Europe. Beside the Spaniard, the Frenchman, the Swede and the Muscovite, we find the most antipathetic, evil personage to be a turbaned figure wearing a caftan. Curiously, he is labeled *Turk* or *Greek.*[33] But this European ignorance of Turkish affairs would soon give way to an interest that led to serious research. In the first half of the eighteenth century, a number of students at the Lycée Louis-le-Grand in Paris began receiving instruction in Turkish, while in Vienna eastern languages were introduced into the curriculum of the Maria Theresia Academy. By the end of the century Europe could boast of such famous Turcologues as Joseph von Hammer. As Turcology came into its own in Europe, a source of future inspiration for Turkish nationalism developed, in the form of linguistic and historical inquires. In the central European countries, the eighteenth century marked the beginning of Balkanistic as well as Turcological studies, the effects of which were seen among both peoples. During that century all the nations of Europe were busy studying one another's history, language and ways; a pursuit that went hand in hand with the long war, with its consequent loss of territories, was in some sense the beginning of a historical process that would result in the birth and further growth of a belated nationalism among the Turks.

33 Österreichisches Museum für Völkerkunde, Inv. Nr.30905.

10

Ottoman-Habsburg Relations 1740-1770, and Structural Changes in the International Affairs of the Ottoman State

I.

Although it witnessed changes so important as to herald a new era, the Ottoman eighteenth century cannot be said to have received due attention in research. Source guides for this period surveying available documents and summarizing archival acquisitions and classifications are rare, and not even the initial, indispensable paleographical and diplomatic studies have yet been undertaken. Work on the eighteenth century, of course, should be based not only on the Turkish but also on Balkanic and European archives as well as those of the monasteries and the Phanariot Greek Orthodox patriarchate, all of which can be combed only through teamwork. In this context, examinations of Austro-Ottoman commercial relations of the eighteenth century, for example, is obviously central for economic history but also and less obviously so for the political, diplomatic, administrative and cultural history of the two empires, while the events and transformations which have shaped the recent history of the Balkan nations may also be considered to have commenced in these hundred years. Balkan historians such as N. Todorov, N. G. Svoronos, B. Cvetkova, V. Paskaleva, A. Suceska, T. Stoianovich therefore naturally dominate this field, and we must cite their work with gratitude. In Turkey, H.

İnalcık and C. Orhonlu have led the way in creating interest in this area. Although among Austrian writers themselves, Hans

Halm for one, has also contributed some valuable monographs to the study of Austro-Ottoman trade, it cannot be said that all in all, enough comparative and critical spadework has been done in the Ottoman archives in this respect. In the İstanbul archives of the Prime Ministry, for example, the 'Düvel-i Ecnebiyye Defterleri' as well as the 'Nemçe Ahkâm Defterleri' and 'Ahidname Mecmuaları' in the same series are important sources, while the 'Şeriyye Sicilleri' of the major ports should not be omitted. Ottoman foreign trade was undergoing structural change in the eighteenth century: despite what some maintain, the integration of the Empire into international trade was not the sudden product of the Anglo-Ottoman commercial treaty of 1838 but the outcome of a slow development with its roots further in the past.

II.

After the Treaty of Belgrade of 1739, the Ottoman Empire entered a period of relatively lasting peace vis-à-vis Austria, Russia and Persia, its immediate neighbours. Prevailing until the Russo-Ottoman war of 1768, this phase of tranquillity left its mark on political, cultural and economic life. It was a time when the growing strength of the Habsburg monarchy began during the reign of Maria Theresia to turn its attention from Western Europe towards Ottoman territories in the Balkans, initially following there a moderate policy.

The Ottoman Empire of the sixteenth century had lived not so much through peace treaties as through armistices; its foreign affairs were not marked by institutions of the European type. In the eighteenth century, however, the Empire may be considered to have already joined the system of the period before the Congress of Vienna with respect to its diplomatic relations and international legal institutions; among the latter adopted in those days, commercial and consular ties, free choice of residence for missionaries, security of navigation, etc., stand out immediately. There is no need here to dwell on the transformations of the landholding and military system of the Empire and the decentralization of its urban and provincial administration in any greater detail. In Austria, on the other hand, the eighteenth century was the epoch of Maria Theresia during which the monarchy underwent an important revolution in transportation and commerce in the eastern Mediterranean, the Maghreb, and especially along the Danube. By the mid-century, Theresian Austria was already a merchant state active in the Balkans and the Mediterranean, and an entire series of social, cultural and political changes in the Ottoman Empire bears the stamp of this ascendancy. The supplementary conventions following the Treaty of Passarowitz in 1718 and those after the Treaty of Belgrade in 1739 opened a new era for practices such as security of navigation, flag and cargo rights in Ottoman waters, determination of consular status and tariffs, protection for merchants, exchange of prisoners, etc. Just how the Ottoman bureaucracy and administration managed to adapt to these new developments constitutes an interesting topic for research. The sixteenth century system would not change immediately and thoroughly simply because a few treaties and supplementary conventions had been signed – that much is evident. Austria had relatively quickly sezied the initiative in the Mediterranean and along the Danube, but just how was her activity carried out? The archive materials we have examined reflect through innumerable examples that adjustment was slow and hard to come by.

III.

Eighteenth century Europe, despite occasional wars, may on the whole be aptly called the continent of peace and prosperity. The monarchs, deputed by God to take care of order on earth, were the very images of wealth and splendour. The opulence of these states and their wordly outlook found expression in the magnificence and liveliness of baroque art. Europeans of the time were really becoming Europeans; the French, German and English intelligentsias were merging with one another. Although it was of course somewhat outside the general atmosphere, the Ottoman Empire also entered a phase of increasing European influence.

Baroque art and the new, luxurious style of living began to manifest themselves not only in the Ottoman capital but even in the villas of the gentry *(âyân)* and the merchants of the wealthier towns of the provinces. European manufactures found widening channels to Ottoman markets, and ambassadors at the Sublime Porte sought out the grand vizier and the *reis-ül-küttab* not just for peace talks but also to demand protection and concessions for merchants of their nationality. Gaining in importance and undergoing a functional transformation, the *reis-ül-küttab* became in this process a full-fledged foreign minister responsible for listening to foreign diplomats; remonstrations concerning trade, consular activity etc., and taking the necessary measures, and a high rate of turnover in this post may indicate an inability on the part of Ottoman bureaucrats to fulfill their new tasks. Provincial bureaucrats such as customs officials, of course, were also forced to change their ancient habits concerning navigation and supervision of trade which were holdovers from the "classical" period.

Austrian trade in the area stretching from the Danube to the Mediterranean was carried out not so much by German and Bohemian merchants as those of northern Italy and Crotia. Traders and sailors of such newly conquered territories had by the fact of Habsburg annexation become "*Nemçe* subjects" and passed into their service. This suddenly acquired patronage of the ancient Mediterranean trade, the Habsburg Empire would cede first to France and then to England only in the early nineteenth century; meanwhile, the resurgent Austrian domination gave a new lease of life to some old hands like Tuscan, Lombard and Livornian sailors, merchants of the Levant, Croatian traders and seamen who once more obtained commercial security under the Habsburg flag and whose activities in the eastern Mediterranean therefore witnessed a second renaissance.

IV.

That the Ottoman bureaucracy lost its efficiency of the fifteenth and sixteenth centuries during the eighteenth has become something of a commonplace; although this is not really a very meaningful phrase behind the observation would seem to lurk the problems faced by the bureaucracy in adapting to the new order. But the new treaties and their supplementary conventions on transportation and trade had rendered this adaptation inevitable. The status of "most favoured nation" acquired by the Habsburg Empire (Nemçe)[1] placed Austrian vessels and merchants (as well as, theoretically, their Ottoman counterparts) under the sort of mutual protection that had already become common practice in other polities of the Early Modern era. The supplements to the Treaty of Passarowitz, which in legal form were not commercial treaties but simply conventions of navigation, granted the subjects of the Caesar of "Nemçe" (or Roma Çesarı) the right to engage freely in trade on Ottoman soil, seas and rivers. In 1718 Charles VI declared Trieste and Fiume to be "open ports"[2] (both, however subsequently became part of the Austrian customs union under Maria Theresia). The Ottoman-Habsburg commercial treaty of

1 Başb. Arş. *Düvel-i Ecnebiyye Defterleri - Nemçe Ahkâm Defteri*, Nr.58 (Evail-i Shevval, 1154, Evasit Safer, 1158) *ve devlet-i Aliyyemde bulunan saîr mustemen taîfesine, bahusus Françe ve İngiltere ve Nederlande milletlerine olan müsaade Nemçe tüccarına mebzul ve merî olub bigûna munakîd ve emniyet ile müntefi ve emin olalar deyu ahidname-yi humayunum mestur olub...*

2 E. Zöllner, *Geschichte* Österreichs, Wien, 1970, p.287.

27 July 1718 settled questions of consular status, navigation, overland trade and customs duties.[3]

Another navigation convention of 1727 sought to guarantee Habsburg vessels against the official piracy from the Maghreb,[4] but this did not include formal rights of free trade in Maghreb ports, although the security of navigation it involved obviously made some commercial activity possible – this was mostly illicit traffic of the type carried out by England and the Netherlands in Spanish colonies. The following expressions from certain firmans clearly indicate that Habsburg ships thereby also obtained flag and cargo rights and began to carry passengers from one Ottoman port to another: *Kraliçeye tâbi vilâyetlerin tüccar ve reayaları memalik-i mahrusama kendü hallerinde gidip alış ve veriş edib, bugünedegin virilegelen günrüklerin verdiklerinden sonra bir dürlü rencide verilmeye...*[5] Another firman dated April 1763 and addressed to the vizier and *kad*ıs of the Morea also dealt with Austrian passenger and cargo service between Ottoman ports in these terms: *Devlet-i aliyyeme tabi olan tüccar taifesi, devlet-i çasariyyeye tâbi tüccar sefinelerine süvar olup, eşya tahmil ederlerse, İngiltere ve Françe ve Nederlande sefinelerine süvar olanların virdükleri rüsumu vireler.* Local authorities must obviously have attempted to interfere in this traffic, but it was the policy of the center to prevent such interference. That this was in fact the attitude of provincial officials is also revealed by a *firman* of Evail-i Safer 1177/1764 addressed to the governor of Damascus

3 Baron I. Testa, *Recueil de Traités de la Porte Ottomane avec les puissances étrangères*, tome 9e (Autriche), Paris, 1898 (28 Shaban 1130, 27 July 1718), pp. 82-89 (16 Zi'lkaade 1130-10 Nov. 1718), p. 89 (26 C 1137-12 March 1725), convention for the exchange of prisoners, pp. 89-100, treaty of Belgrade (14 C. 1152-18 September 1739), p. 90.

4 İ. Ortaylı, "1727 Tarihli Osmanlı-Avusturya Seyrüsefaîn Sözleşmesi", *SBF Dergisi*, vol.XXVI-II/3-4, pp.97-110.

5 *Nemçe Ahkâm Defteri*, Nr. 60, p. 167 (Evail-i Shevval, 1176), Nr. 60, p. 117 (Evail-i Safer, 1177).

and the *kadı* of Jerusalem:[6] the customs official *(gümrük emini)* of Yafa had demanded *two* gold liras for each Greek, Armenian, Jewish and Ottoman pilgrim boarding "Nemçe" ships, whereupon the captain–one Hanna Damiano–complained, in answer to which it was written that: *Yafa gümrügi emini olanlar ez kadim avaîd-i külliye virilegeleni almaya kanaat etmeyib, Nemçe sefaîni kapudanlarına: sefinenize irkâb olunan ziyaretçilerden adem başına ikişer altın sizden alırız, siz dahi onlardan alınız- Vallah ziyaretçileri sefâininize irkâbden men ederiz deyu, hilâf-ı ahidnamem akçe taleb...* Let us only add that Austrian vessels quickly came to seize the major portion of the passenger traffic between Ottoman ports and kept this position until the end of the nineteenth century.

Those hit hardest by this right of navigation were the so-called *Garb Ocakları*, Algeria, Tunis and Tripoli. The Maghreb, raking in the profits of official piracy throughout the eighteenth century while participating in Mediterranean navigation at the same time, stood to lose the most from the concessions to Austria. This was in fact why the new regime of free navigation, faced with continuous violation of treaties and conventions, could not be immediately and fully implemented. Algeria and Tunis kept seizing some "Nemçe" ships to confiscate their cargoes and capture those on board. Two *firman*s of July 1744 (Evail-i C.1157) and 1741, on the other hand, the first sent to the *beylerbeyi* of Algeria and the second to that of Tunis, testify to the continuous efforts made by İstanbul to put things to rights. But apart from this, it would seem that foreign captains and merchants also strove to obtain special charters (*berat*s) from the Sultan to additionally guarantee their safety on trips within Ottoman waters, as witnessed by four such *berat*s granted to Graf Oelfeld at one time. Another *firman* of the year 1745 (Evail-i Safer 1158)[7] orders the *beylerbeyi* of Tripoli to release

6 *Ibid.*, Nr.60, p.117 (1177 Evail-i Safer).

7 *Ibid.*, Nr.60, p.156, and Nr.58 (Safer 1158), Nr.58 (Evail C, 1157) to the Beylerbeyi of Cezairi-i Gharb).

two nobles of "Nemçe" named Leopold and Strausold and a priest called Lorenco Custinyo (Giustinio) who had been aboard a sezied Dubrovnik vessel. A similar example from later years is the *firman* which orders that Covani (Johann) of Praga and three others be released; apparently they had been captured by one Ahmed Farac Reis (captain) near the port of Draç (Durazzo).

As we have already noted, another original feature of the treaties and conventions of this period is the provisions thereby made for (a) securing borders, (b) preventing mutual raids and banditry, and (c) returning those criminals and rebels who sought to take refuge in each other's teritory. We find these three themes reiterated in two *firman*s of 1755 and 1769 addressed to the governor of Bosnia, and one of January 1768 to the governor of Belgrad;[8] this implies that border security and tranquillity was still only imperfectly achieved in Transylvania and Transdanubia. A large collection of the documents in the Ottoman archives *(Maliyeden Müdevver Defterler)* includes a further convention, concerning the above mentioned situation of Bosnia and Durazzo, saying "... though a treaty between the Ottoman-Porte and the Habsburg Empire has been signed, the merchants around the frontiers of Bosnia and Durazzo, are still not able to travel under secure conditions", *devlet-i âliyye-yi Osmaniye ile Çesariyye devleti arasında dostluk muahadesi mevcud olduğu halde, Bosna hududunda ve Draç cihetinde emniyet ve asayişin temin edilmemiş ve tarafeyn tüccarının selâmet-i mürur ve uburu ifa kılınmamış olduğundan şikâyetle...* This convention was signed between Ottoman authorities, namely Ahmed and İbrahim and dragoman Osman efendis, the vizier of Belgrad Serasker Kıbtî Ali Pasha and on the other part the commander of Tameshwar Veskid (?) in order to restore the maintenance and order within these areas,[9]

8 *Ibid.*, Nr.58 (Evasit-i C. 1168) to Bosnia, Nr.66 (Evail-i Şaban, 1181) to Beograd, p.212, Nr.66 (Evasit-i Ramadan, 1182) to Bosnia, pp.232-34.

9 Başb. Arş., *Maliyeden Müdevver*, Nr.4997, p.92 (15 R. 1122/June 1710), *Mükâleme muhaberatı mektub suretidir.*

in the year of 1708-1709 (1120). This convention of 1708 and above-mentioned *firman*s of 1755 and 1769 indicate to us the continuous disorder and insecurity in these provinces. On the other hand, a *firman* of 1760 (1174), drawn up at the request of the Austrian ambassador, reminded the voivodas of Wallachia and Bessarabia that in accordance with the peace treaty an amnesty had been granted to boyars and commoners previously rebellious against the Ottomans; they should therefore be allowed to return to their lands.[10] But all these measures notwithstanding, with the onset of national revivals guerilla warfare had entered a colourful period in the Balkans, even while the eighteenth century peace could hardly cope with the entire heritage of past wars all at once. Hence, for more than twenty years İstanbul had to keep sending countless *firman*s to all corners of Rumelia and Anatolia ordering captives to be released in exchange for moderate ransoms.

V.

One characteristic of eighteenth century Ottoman-Habsburg trade was that it no longer encompassed only luxury goods but gradually came to include manufactures, semi-manufactures and raw materials as well. In these, Balkan merchants who were Ottoman subjects secured the cooperation of Austrian customs officials and Austrian merchants that of Ottoman customs officials to carry on an illicit traffic, either paying less than the normal duties or engaging in direct smuggling.[11] The silk and cotton, either raw or in yarn form, demanded by Austrian industries were in large part supplied by Ottoman territories; the same was true of mohair. Around the middle of the century, Austrian manufactures began to flow through Venice to Egypt

10 *Ibid.*, Nr.60, p.75 (Evasit-i Z. 1174) to the voivodas of Wallachia and Bessarabia.

11 *Ibid.*, Nr.58 (Evasit-i CA, 1155) and (Evail-i C, 1155) Firmans to Rumelia and Hüdavendigar livası; 20 years later, to Karaman (Evasit-i CA, 1176).

and other Ottoman markets. Austria was also the chief buyer and treater of Balkan tobacco, while Viennese and Bohemian chinaware for a long while remained unrivalled in the Turkish Empire. Products of other Germanic countries also came in over Austria and the Danube, with Slavic merchants of the Balkan serving as middlemen.[12]

Once more provincial governors and *kadı*s from Rumelia to Syria had to be warned time and again not to hinder merchants' free passage or to extract illegal payments from them, and the existence of numerous such *firman*s would seem to indicate that these abuses were in fact quite common. The official ruling was that "Nemçe" traders *(Nemçeli tüccar)* should pay a customs duty of 3 % once only; no doubt, Ottoman merchants operating on Habsburg territory were subject to the same status. It was hard to get Turkish governors and other provincial administrators to forego their accustomed revenues, from the internal tolls; *firman*s announce that to other fee should be demanded of *müstamen* (coming in from the 'Darülharb' under under the grace of the Sultan) merchants and their servants who may come and go as they please by land, sea or river *(bahren, berren ve nehren)*, but local authorities did persist in trying to impose multiple duties, and sometimes even claimed that *müstamen* merchants should pay the polltax, *cizye*, (for which religious law actually made only non-muslim subjects of the Sultan liable), such malpractices being most flagrant in the Danubian principalities and especially at the hands of the voivodas of Wallachia. Hence the *firman* ordering the *kadı* of Yerköy to refrain from collecting *cizye* from *müstamen* merchants, and that ordering the *kadı* of Aleppo to prevent the local customs official *(gümrük emini)* from imposing

12 F. Tremel, *Wirtschaft and Sozialgeschichte* Österreichs, Graz, 1969, pp.270-71; H. Halm, *Habsburgischer Osthandel im 18. Jahrhundert*, München, 1954, p.177, V. Paskaleva, "Die Wirtschaftsbeziehungen der bulgarischen Gebiete mit Mitteleuropa im 18. und 19. Jahrhundert", *Wirtschaftswege: Hermann Kellenbenz Festschrift*, Klett-Cotta 1978, p.169.

on the gold earned by the same a second duty of 3 %.[13] Faced with such violations, foreign traders usually called on their ambassador who then obtained for them passes of safe-conduct *(geçiş tezkiresi)* and special guarantees *(berat)* of security.

Names of foreign merchants that occur in the registers of complaints and decisions *(Ahkâm ve* Şikâyet *defterleri)* indicate that among the subjects of the Queen of the Magyars and the Czechs (or later, of the Roman Emperor) who came to Ottoman territory to trade, Czech, Hungarian or German merchants were not yet common; Serbians, Croatians or Bulgarians were in the majority. These Habsburg subjects were mostly those who had emigrated from the Ottoman Empire in the first place, who therefore had good connections there and were familiar with its ways and customs. Those who operated in the eastern Mediterranean and Syria, on the other hand, were generally Italians from Tuscany and Genoa who had already settled and were doing business there when they came under Viennese sovereignty. To come back to Slavic merchants in Transylvania, they probably got wealthier and wealthier with time, and a few Bulgarians and Armenians among them even bought their way into the nobility during the seventeenth and eighteenth centuries,[14] and some at least of their successors after receiving a protestant, secular education, would become harbingers of Slav nationalism in the future. Among the many tricks invented by merchants to evade customs, bribery, packing more than the declared amount, or smuggling in/out contraband material together with legal goods ranked high. Habsburg imports from the Ottoman Empire came to include even foodstuffs towards the end of the century; this new demand led to capital

13 *Nemçe Ahkâm Defteri*, Nr.60, p.62 (Evail-i Zilhicce, 1173, and 1181 Evasit-i CA) p.206, firman to Aleppo (Evahir RA, 1177).

14 Zs. Trocsanyi, "Das Schicksal der geadelten bulgarischen Familien in Siebenbürgen im 18-19. Jh." *Bulgarian Historical Review*, 1981/1-2, pp.125-134.

accumulation and the rise of large farms *(çiftliks)* in Rumelia. To the increased commercial traffic in agricultural products, the food oils "exported" in 1800-1801 (1215) by only three towns in Romania (Kalas, Ibrail, Ismail) bears eloquent testimony. These districts were basically responsible for supplying İstanbul, but only one-third of their deliveries actually reached the capital. In a typical month of 1800, for example, although 107,074 *qantar*s sunflower oil and animal fat went out from these three cities in just one week, only one-third of this shipment arrived at the Galata customs.[15] It seems quite clear where all the rest went. In two months of 1783, on the other hand, the cotton, raw silk and *sahtiyan* (polished leather) that was exported to Austria through the Belgrade Pass was valued at 12,000 *kuruş*, but of course this was only the legally registered amount, and it is no coincidence that in Anatolia as well as in Rumelia and along the Danube many towns became rich through silk and leather production in the eighteenth and nineteenth centuries.

By this time, Habsburg trade had spread over the entire area from Syria and Lebanon to Baghdad and Basra, as evidenced by the existence in circulation of the Maria Theresian *thaler* along the entire coast of the Gulf until recent times. An Imperial Charter *(berat)* orders that one Martino Masterelli be allowed free,[16] unmolested passage all the way from Aleppo to Baghdad and Basra.[17] This also confirms by the way what we have said above concerning activities of Italian merchants already settled in the Levant and now under Habsburg flag.

15 Başb. Arş., -Kepeci tasnifi- Nr.814 (1215 of H) and Nr.789 (1198 of H).

16 *Kraliçeye tabi Tuskana reayası tüccarlarından Martino Mesterelli'nin Haleb'den Bagdad ve Basraya varın'a vakî kadı ve naîblere tenbih edilerek; cizye, gümrük bac gibi bahenelerle ahidnameye muğaîr zulmedilmemesi.*

17 *Nemçe Ahkâm.*, Nr.60 (Evahir-i CA, 1169) to the vizier of Baghdad and Basra, Nr.58 (Evail-i Receb, 1167), Nr.60 (Evahir-i RA, 1177) to the qadi of Aleppo; *"lakab Velozef Pinyero nam Tuskana tüccarından Nemçelulardan usulsüz gümrük alındığı..."*

VI.

Early in the reign of Maria Theresia, Habsburg consular services in the eastern Mediterranean used to be delegated to consuls of other European states already established in the region.[18] In 1741 the viceconsulate of Aleppo, for example, was left in the care of the British consul there, and that of Paleopatras *(Balyebadre)* in the Morea was entrusted to the local Dutch representative. Elsewhere, notably in Egypt, Tuscan and Livornian merchants who were Austrian subjects were given consular power; thus, at one point, Giovanni Aitone of Alikorno (Livorno) was ordered to replace Gianni Francesco Marbone of Tuscany as the Habsburg consul in Alexandria. The Sublime Porte, on the other hand, did not officially appoint consuls to serve in Austrian territory: it was left to Ottoman merchants (of Slavic descent), operating there to elect one of themselves to serve in this capacity.[19] Under Maria Theresia, Austrian ambassadors and consuls generally employed local Christians and Jews as interpreters; when his first interpreter Jacob son of Karabet died, for example, the ambassador Baron Nepker, obtained permission to replace him with one Jacob Franz (son of Isaac Franz) who was a Jew of Salonica. These interpreters did not formally enjoy diplomatic immunity, but Austrian officials frequently attempted to extend their own legal privileges to try to cover the natives in their service also. A case in point is that of Argiropulo, the *dragoman* of the Habsburg consul in Salonica, who borrowed a certain sum from Hacı Ianni in 1765 (1179). When the creditor then died, his widow was unable to make Argiropulo pay,[20] and the local authorities having been rendered powerless or unwilling to

18 *Ibid.*, Nr.60 (Evahir-i Safer, 1161) and (Evahir-i C, 1161) appointment of vice-consul to Aleppo and Paleopatras...

19 T. Stoianovich, "The conquering Balkan-orthodox merchants", *Journ. of Econ. Hist.* 1960 (20/2), pp.243-313.

20 *Nemçe Ahkâm*, Nr.60 (Evail-i Shavval, 1179) to the qadi of Saloniki.

act as a result of the *dragoman*'s claim of immunity, the Porte had to interfere and order the governor-pasha *(mutasarrıf)* and the *kadı* of Salonica to collect the loan from Argiropulo. Privileges and numbers of interpreters *(dragomans)* nevertheless continued to be abased by European diplomats throughout the eighteenth century. Transferred to *müstemen* status, these *dragomans* were exempted from certain taxes and services, and this motivated many merchants to bribe their ambassadors and consuls to have themselves registered as *dragomans*, thus swelling the ranks of the latter considerably.[21]

Here the Habsburg Empire constitutes something of an exception in that its distrust of the Levantines and the non-Muslim Ottomans compelled it to train its own interpreters and achieve considerable success in this field, compared with, say Great Britain. The Academy of Oriental Languages founded in Vienna quickly supplied the Habsburgs not only with skilled interpreters but also some excellent Orientalists, enabling the Austrian Chancellery to post competent representatives in Egypt and other Ottoman lands capable of thoroughly familiarizing themselves with their surroundings to obtain important information; until World War I, the most extensive and successful consular network on Turkish soil belonged to the Habsburg monarchy.

After the Treaty of Passarowitz, Austrian representatives as well as those of other European states obtained full diplomatic immunities and exemptions in the Ottoman Empire. This immunity and exemption included consuls as well. Up to the Congress of Vienna (1815), the outlines of the system of diplomatic exemptions were as follows: the ambassador, for example, would be allowed to procure considerable amounts of meat, grain and vegatables from the region around İstanbul (extending as far

21 C. Orhonlu, "Tercüman", *İslam Ans.*, pp.177-181. A. İ. Bağış, *Osmanlı Ticaretinde Gayrimüslimler*, Ankara, 1983, pp.19, 26-28.

as Filibe/Plovdiv) without paying any tolls or taxes. Thus a *firman* of October 1744 (Şaban I. 1154) ordered the Janissary commander *(ağa)* Hasan Pasha and the *Bostancıbaşı* to remind the voivoda of Galata also that no duties should be collected from Ambassador Nepker for the extensive purchases of grain, livestock, pigs and wine that he was making at the time.[22] The ambassadorial residence also benefited from a certain immunity, but permission was required for both the initial construction and later extension work.

Despite their better training in Oriental languages and history, however, Habsburg diplomats were certainly lacking in general efficiency compared with their French, English and Dutch colleagues. Certain buildings including the houses of priests belonging to the church and colony in Galata which the Ottoman chancellery registered as *Padertrinite* were burned down in December 1768 (I CA 1176).[23] The ambassador applied for permission for repairs only in early May. What a hard winter it must have been for the poor clergymen! Such bureaucratic lethargy was peculiar to the Austrian foreign service whose degree of activity at the time can hardly be compared with that of its French counterpart. Treaties clearly permitted, for example, clerics to provide religious services for Habsburg subjects in the Ottoman Empire. There were complaints that the Franciscan monks in Chios were prevented from giving Mass to *müstemen* merchants visiting the island by the local Ottoman *muhassıl* and *kadı*s. The real reason, however, was probably that these monks clumsily engaged in religious propaganda vis-à-vis the natives beyond the services for their own co-religious nationals defined in the treaty, thus enraging the Greek-Orthodox population. While Catholic missionaries under French protection operated smoothly, the Austrian ones ran into trouble at every turn.

22 *Nemçe Ahkâm*, Nr.58 (Şaban 1154 and Evahir-i CA, 1156).

23 *Ibid*, Nr.60 (Evail-i CA, 1176) to the *kadı* of Galata (Evail-i Muh., 1182).

A *firman* of February 1744 (1157) drew the attention of Ottoman authorities in Chios to the fact that in accordance with a treaty of 1095 (1649) and a previous imperial *firman* of 1718 (1131) Christian clergymen could serve travellers and consuls of their own nationality,[24] but the situation probably did not improve because six months later new *firmans* had to be sent to Chios reiterating the same theme. With the success achieved by the French in spreading Catholicism in the East ever since the era of Colbert, the efforts made and results obtained in the same respect by the ambassadors and consuls of Her Apostolic Majesty stand poorly in comparison.

24 *Ibid.*, Nr. 58 (Evasit-i Muh. 1157) and (Evail-i CA, 1157) to the *naîb* and *muhassıl* of Chios.

PROVINCES

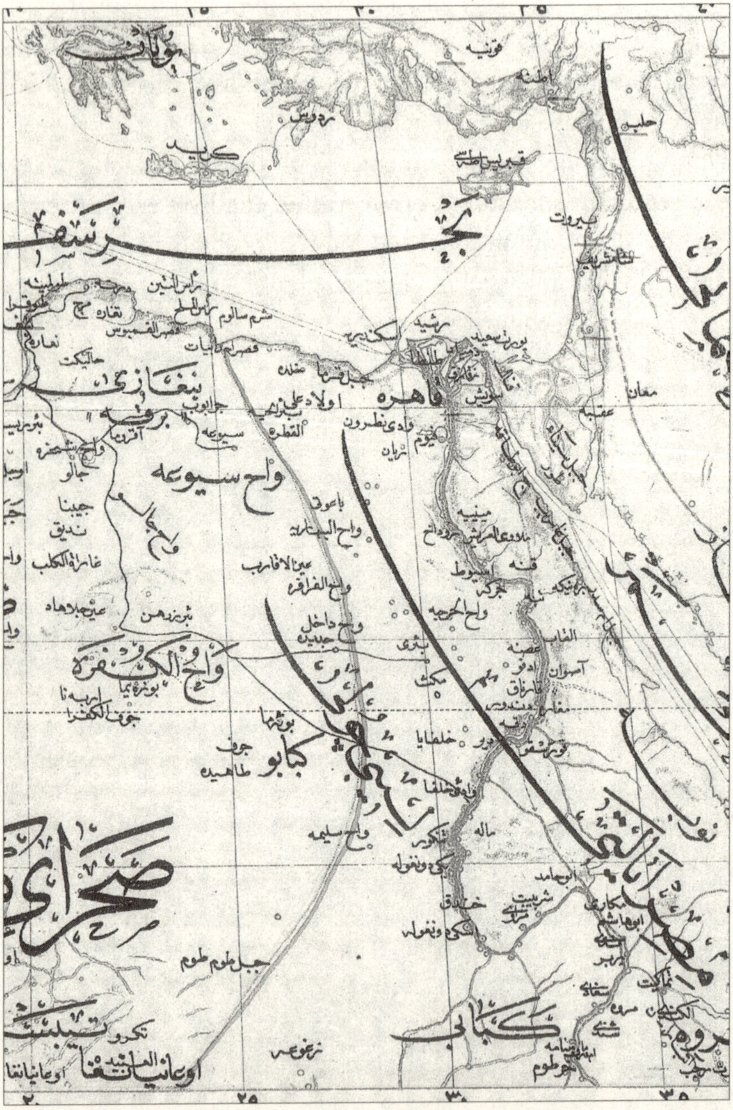

A map showing the provinces in the Ottoman Africa
(By Major M. Nasrullah, Lieutenant Commander M. Rüşdü, Lieutenant M. Eşref).

11

The Port Cities in the Arab Provinces of the Ottoman Empire

(A study of the disintegration of the Arab World in the nineteenth century, with special reference to Basra)

INTRODUCTION

In the nineteenth century important developments occurred in some port cities of the Ottoman Empire. Thessaloniki, Smyrna, Beyrouth and Basra were the first among these ones. The one which we will study here is Basra which connected Mesopotamia with the outside world. Likewise Alexandria, Beyrouth and Basra depended like Smyrna and Thessaloniki first of all on the transition from traditional to monocultural agriculture in the hinterlands of these cities, which aimed at providing the necessities of Western European industry.

Alexandria, which is one of these three port cities of the Arab World, was under British rule. Beyrouth was under the influence of the French and British; and finally all of the European great powers had concentrated their economic and cultural activities there. In the course of the nineteenth century Basra was to become the scene of conflicting interests of the German and British.

BASRA IN THE NINETEENTH CENTURY

The province of Basra is exposed to important alterations in the last century of Ottoman rule. This area was completely conquered by the Ottomans in 1534 and Basra was thus made a part of the Baghdad province. However, the Ottomans have not been very successful in definitely domineering over this area, so the uproars caused by the Bedouin tribes and local dynasties continued. The central government was therefore forced to allow these local dynasties to rule the area. For example, in the seventeenth century, Ali Pasha (1624) and his grandson Hüseyin Pasha (1650) who where descendants of Afrasiyab and his sons were recognized as rulers of this place. This local autonomy facilitated the access of Europeans and Portuguese, British, Dutch merchant fleets were very active in the commerce of the Persian Golf to Basra and its waterways. This autonomy succeeded in surviving in the long range, even though there were some interruptions caused by the efforts of the governors of Baghdad.[1] However, the centralized organization and reform activities that started in the 1830's could also be felt in the same region. Basra had primitive harbor facilities, was frequently plagued with diseases, especially malaria. Its importance in eastern commerce continued against the demonstrations of Bedouins like the Muntefika tribe which interrupted public security.

It is stated by some historians that in H. 1267/A. D. 1850 Basra was bound directly to İstanbul as a province.[2] But this status changed from time to time. There were periods when Basra was left sometimes to autonomous administration or sometimes became a Sandjak of Baghdad. At this stage an increase in commerce with Europe and America and commercial establishments can easily be observed.[3] The harbor was restored to some extent. A deep channel at the mouth of Shattal

1 R. Hartmann, B. Darkot, T. Gökbilgin, "Basra", *Islam Ansiklopedisi*, Maarif Matb., İstanbul, 1943, pp.320-327.

2 Longrigg, "Basra", *Ency. of Islam*, N. E. vol.1 pp.1086-87 see also L. Bouvat, "Le Vilayet Baghdad et son Organisation Administrative", *Revue du Monde Musulman*, 23 (1913), pp.240-267.

3 Hasan Muhammed Salman, "The Role of Foreign Trade in the Economic Development of Iraq 1864-1964", *Studies in the Economic History of the Middle East*, ed. by M. A. Cook, 1970, pp.346-372. The author states that the "Iraq economy was since the 1860s a foreign-trade oriented and dependent economy."

Arab was dredged.[4] It must be pointed out that this visible modernization of the city was realized at the era of Midhat Pasha's governorship in Iraq. The city was thus transformed into an assembly center which could be considered an intermediary between Mesopotamia and the external world.

In the nineteenth century, the Basra province was composed of three subdivisions (sandjak). The central Basra Sandjak, Muntefika (or Nasırîyye) and Necid.[5]

The Administrative Divisions of Basra in the Nineteenth Century.

Province	Provincial Center	Sandjak	Kaza	Nevahi (District)
Basra	Basra		Basra	
			Kurna	
			Kuwait	
		Muntefika	Sukh'-ulsuyuk	
		(Nasriyye)	Shatara	
			Hîye	
			Hamar	
		Necid	Katar	
			Hûfuf	
			Katîf	

After the 1870's Amare was also organized as a Sandjak. Some of the townships were governed by officials elected from among the local chieftains. However, with the new organization systems and reforms that followed the "Provincial Regulation" *(Vilayet Nizamnamesi)* established in 1869, new officials were appointed from the center to replace these local feudal rulers. We know for a fact that Midhat Pasha was the pioneer of such an arrangement during his governorship in Iraq (1869-1872). For

4 Longrigg, *ibid.*, pp.1087.

5 Hüseyin, *Memalik-i Osmaniyye'nin Ziraat Coğrafyası*, İstanbul, Mihran Matbaası, 1303 (1886, A.D.), pp.15.

example, the kaimakam of the Katif district (Nedjid Sandjak) Faysal, his family, and officers followed a policy of great restraint towards the Shiites of this region and asked for excessive taxes, but Midhat Pasha chastised and expelled this independent family through military force.[6]

POPULATION AND CITIES

It is not possible to give an exact total population figure as related to this era of the Basra Province. Obviously this difficulty is due to the disorganization of the Ottoman land survey and census registrations. The population groups were classified and estimated according to religious congregations, rather than ethnic, sexual and age distinctions. Household *(hane)* was the basis of census. The census registrations pertaining to rural areas are old and not realistic. The written surveys that may have aided us in obtaining gross estimates on the figures of rural areas have not been subjected to research or publication. The population figures that exist in relation to the nineteenth century mostly concern urban centers.

The Ottoman Almanac, of H. 1307 (A.D. 1880-1889 *Salname-i Vilayet-i Basra*) states that the population of Central Basra Sandjak was over 10.000.[7] The region that rated second in population gathering was Amare with a figure of 7.000. 30 % of the population of Basra was Sunni, 50 % Shiite, the remainder being either Christian or Jewish.

The city of Basra reflects the functions of a developing harbour. There are official buildings such as the Municipality Office, Governor's Residence, Post-Office in the city; soldiers barracks in Dub, naval barracks in Menavî. Other than these, we can mention the printing house, iron foundry, customs offices and docks,

6 Y. Halaçoğlu, "Midhat Paşa'nın Necid ve Havalisi ile İlgili Birkaç Layihası", *İst. Üniv. Edeb., Fak. Tarih Enst. Dergisi*, sayı 3, Ekim 1972, pp.160-162 see also, Moosa Matti, "The Land Policy of Midhat Pasha in Iraq 1869-1872", *Islamic Quarterly* (1968), pp.146-159.

7 *Salname-i Vilayet-i Basra*, Vilayet Matbaası, 1307 of H. (1889-1890), pp.175.

hospital, one *mekteb-i rüşdîyye* (junior high school), 4 *ibtidaîyye* (primary school), 13 mosques, medrese and quite a vast number of shops (apprx, 1500).

The Supreme Council of the Province *(Meclis-i İdare-i Vilâyet)* was composed of the Vali, *Defterdar* (Financial Authority), *Mektubçu* (Chief Secretary), Mufti and *Nakib*. Apart from these members, there were two Muslim representatives elected from among the local dwellers and two other representatives who were non-Muslim; this ratio of representation demonstrates the economical and social influence that the non-Muslem groups have.

There were British, French, German, American, Austro-Hungarian and Belgian vice consulates in the city. Commercial relationship increased the integration with the external world. Director Ali Bey's (who was the local manager of the Ottoman Debts Administration) trip to this province coincides with the same period. According to his statements, there were ships that sailed directly to Suez when the date crop was gathered. However, as we are going to see later, most of Basra's communications with the Western World was carried out over the Indian subcontinent. This moist place was overflowing with malaria.[8] The disease, mostly seen among the military troops, was one of the biggest problems of the Ottoman administration. A cholera epidemic was added to this in Basra and its surroundings due to the increase in international naval traffic in the nineteenth century and the beginning of the twentieth century.

The Baghdad vice consul of the U.S.A. reports the cases of death in Kerbela, Nedjef, Hilla, Küfe, Divaniye, Amman, Hosrabad and Samara through a period of 15 days, as of June 30th, 1904 (74 in Kerbela, 156 in Nedjef, 146 in Hilla).[9] The

8 Ali Bey (Director in the Duyun-u Umumiye), *Seyahat Jurnalı (İstanbul'dan Bağdad'a ve Hindistan'a min sene 1300 – ila sene 1304)*, İstanbul, 1314, pp.97, 98, 99.

9 *National Archives and Record Service of U.S. Foreign Service - Post Record*; 84, "American Consulate Baghdad", Nr.220.

cholera epidemic could not be prevented in spite of the quarantine measures. This could be attributed to the Ottoman disorganization where sanitation was concerned and also to the indifferent and non-cooperating attitude of Britain who was the ruler of the most active transportation.

TRANSPORTATION

The Ottoman railway system was both under-developed and late in being established as compared to Europe and Russia. Thus at the end of the nineteenth century Basra was not only connected to İstanbul over Baghdad, but also had a cable system set up over the area named Far that reached India and Europe. A perfect mail system was also established between Basra-Kurna-Amare and Kut-ul Amare-Baghdad. However, this service was very frequently interrupted between Basra-Nedjid and Basra-Muntefika where the Bedouins dominated and there was no public security. Here, only letters could be delivered under police supervision (money orders were not accepted).[10]

Due to the flow of the tides in the rivers, the Basra harbour became accessible for the big ocean ships once every 15 days. In addition to this, transportation over the rivers from Basra to Shatr, Amare, Kut-ul Amare and Baghdad was possible; this transportation started to be carried on by modern ships in the nineteenth century. 5 ships belonging to the Ottoman Imperial Navigation Company named Musul, Rıfat, Rasafe, Baghdad, Meskene and two from Britain, Lynch and Halife, operated on this line in 1307 of H. (1889 A.D) The local inhabitants participated in this river transportation using over 250 sailing boats. The riverside quays were connected to the inland centers with caravans of mules, camels and horses. This situation resembles the completion of the İzmir-Aydın railway network by camel caravans.[11]

10 *Salname-i Vilayet-i Basra (sene 1307)*, pp.95-97.

11 Mübeccel B. Kıray, *Örgütleşemeyen Kent – İzmir*, Sosyal İlimler Derneği Yay., A-I, Ankara, 1972, pp.14-15.

International trade already was interested in Basra since the fifteenth century. A branch of the East Indian Company was established in Basra since 1666. Practically the India-Basra cruise was under British monopoly. There were attempts made by the U.S.A. to participate in the Mesopotamian river transportation.[12] A direct ship connection was requested between America and Basra. In the meantime, another U.S. project concerning the building of a bridge on the Tigris river by the Pennsylvania Steel Company was cancelled due to financial disagreements.

In general, it can be concluded that river transport and caravan systems were quite sufficient, whereas the Mesopotamian railway has always been an international problem of rivalry. It has not been possible to solve this problem even until the end of the Ottoman rule over the area.

The unefficient Baghdad railway project suggested by the Germans was aimed at reaching Basra. However, the obstacle for the realization of this project was not only the resistance shown by Britain as a result of her own benefits in the Basra Harbour. First of all, the German capital was insufficient and the ambitions of the German General-Staff were not relevant to the attitudes of the German businessmen and rational technicians team. Thus, the Baghdad railway syndicate was placed in a very difficult position owing to the withdrawal of the British support from the scheme. The German capital required an accomplice for this project, so Siemens and its group did not with hold from partaking in a partnership with the British business circles.[13]

---

12 *U.S. National Archives, Dept. of State*, "Correspondence of American Vice-Consul in Baghdad", Nr.47 4/2/1897 and May 12, 1900, pp.159.

13 *Report from U.S. Legation in Constantinople to Mr. Leishman, Secretary of State*, June 2nd 1903, Nr.431: Nat. Arch. of Unit. Stat. Turkey Koll 69 "The Syndicate placed in a difficult position owing to withdrawal of British support to the scheme..." German documents also refer to same subject: – "Archiv des Auswaertigen Amtes" Bonn; *Türkei* Bd. 2/3 134 adh "kaiserlich Deuts. Konsulat in Baghdad" Report of Richarz of 23 Mai 1899, A 7371: stating that "the

THE REVENUES OF THE VİLAYET BASRA

According to Salman,[14] by the 1860's, there existed approximately 150.000 *dönüms* of agricultural and cultivated land in Iraq. After the 1860's, cultivated lands have been extended. However, there is no indication that shows any change in technology. In the nineteenth century the region was a typical agricultural area. Revenues have been obtained in a large amount from agricultural productions.

TABLE 1

Expenditures of the Vilayet 1307 H. (1890 A.D.)

		Kuruş	**Para**
Religious affairs	Şer'iye	186.716	—
Home dept.	Dahiliyye	1.361.006	20
Justice	Adliyye	377.140	—
Finance	Maliye	799.037	20
Salaries	Maaşat-ı zatiyye	160.380	—
Gendarmery	Zabtiyye	338.531	—
Police	Polis	945	
Various	Müteferrik	32.802	
Total		6.229.567	

In 1307 H. (1890 A.D.) the revenues of the Vilayet Basra, totalled 17.844.373 Ottoman *kuruş* (or 178.443 Ottoman liras).[15] The bulk of this amount consisted of *ushr*, followed by *resm-i agnam* (sheep tax). The main occupations of the population were agriculture and husbandry. Date, wheat, sesame and some citrus

---

Turkish officials are in favor of Baghdad project to avoid the British influence in Mesopotamia"; see also for the atitude of Siemens groups for a collaboration with English businessmen: Bekir Sıtkı (Baykal) *Das Baghdad-Bahn Problem 1890-1903*, Druck Rudolf Goldschlag, Freiburg, 1935, pp.81-86.

14 Mohammed Salman Hassan, "The Role of Foreign Trade in the Economic Development of Iraq", p.359.

15 *Salname-i Vilayet-i Basra*, sene 1307, p.102.

fruits were the main products, which also constituted the bulk of the exports.[16]

TABLE 2
Revenues of the Vilayet 1307 H. (1890 A.D.)

		Kuruş	**Para**
Ushr	(Aşar vergüsü)	438.881	22
Exemption tax from military service	(Bedel-i askerî)	11.788	25
Sheep tax	(Ağnam resmi)	1.792.153	—
Bull tax	(Camus resmi)	187.350	—
Camel tax		194.704	—
Ushr (collected in advance)	(Aşar maktuu)	10.399.333	10
Forestry tax timber, stamps	(Orman kereste, pul)	1.400	—
Tax revenues from private possessions	(Emlâk ve tapu)	23.227	—
Court revenues	(Mehakim borçları)	54.200	—
Various dues	(Rusum-u mütenevvie)	1.338.955	—
Revenues from autonomous fiefs*	(Hasılat-ı müteferrika)	118.138	—
Total		17.844.373	

The main components of the total expenditures of the Vilayet in 1890 were *dahiliyye* and *zaptiyye* (police and home affairs). Expenditures involving investment expenditures such as *nafia* (construction) and *maarif* (public instruction) were only negligible amounts. The Ottoman state could be said to act as gendarmes for such countries as Britain, France and Belgium which were exploiting the Vilayet's resources. The remaining portion of the general income of the Vilayet (approximately 50 per cent) went to the central government. These revenues were, however, earmarked for the repayment of the Ottoman debts. In addition, customs duties and tobacco dues were directly collected

* These fiefs were not subject to local authorities.

16 *Salname-i Vilayet-i Basra*, 1320 sene (1903 A.D.), Vilayet Mtb.

by the Ottoman Debt Administration *(Duyun-u Umumiye)* and the Tobacco Regie, and are not, therefore, included in the list. Basra was a region of exploitation of the Atlantic economic system, not of the central Ottoman government.

Measures to ensure technological modernization in agriculture could not be taken. It was only after the 1860's that the hevay *ushr* (i.e. 1/2 and 1/3) which was collected by the local feudal lords were decreased.[17] A certain degree of welfare must have been thus ensured. El Ucma-El Murre Urban (Bedouins), the Bedouins of the sandjaks of Necid and Muntefika did not pay their taxes regularly. In fact, the Ottoman government always failed in collecting taxes regularly. Among the factors affecting the local uprisings which broke out under the British mandate, after 1918, one may interalia cite regular collection by financially well-organized Britain of the taxes which constituted a heavy burden on the shoulders of the people.

GERMAN-BRITISH RIVALRY IN BASRA

The Basra Gulf was a subject of rivalry during the second half of the nineteenth century. Until the German Empire became one of the big powers it was as if this part of the world was left to British influence. As a matter of fact the Ottomans could not be said not to have any claims on Bahreyn and the Sheikhdoms of the Basra Gulf. It is clear, however, that the Ottoman Empire, which was on the brink of bankruptcy, was incapable of effectively competing with Britain. The emergence of Germany as a big power brought Britain a serious rival. Besides, from now on the Ottoman Empire would begin to pursue an active policy in the region parallel to that of Germany.

The Ottoman Empire claimed that Basra and Baghdad were within its frontiers, and it thus had sovereign rights over the Gulf Sheikhdoms and the Bahrein islands. In fact, a memorandum

17 See Matti I. Moosa, "The Land Policy of Midhad Pasha in Iraq 1869-1872", *Islamic Quarterly*, 12 (1968), pp.149-159 and I. E. Fadayeva, *Midhat Pasha - Jızn-i Deyatelnost*, Akad, Nauk, SSSR Moskva, 1977, pp.45-66.

presented to Lord Granville by the Ottoman ambassador on 16 July 1872 called for the recognition of the Ottoman sovereign rights.[18] However, these attempts failed to bring about an effective result.

The British government saw the Basra Gulf as an inevitable component of its domination over the Indian subcontinent, Egypt and the Suez Canal and desired to bring the region under its influence. The Ottoman government, on the other hand, failed even to collect taxes and could only control surplus products, which barely sufficed to keep the province alive. In these circumstances, Germany's inclination was to bring the Basra Gulf under its control not by way of the sea, but by means of the Baghdad railway project, as a continuation of the Berlin-Basra corridor. Although the Basra railroad did not materialize, Germany attempted at establishing an influence by means of the Ottoman administration. The Baghdad railway project was among the plans of the conservative Disraeli Government.

Layard, the British ambassador in İstanbul who suggested a reform project to Sultan Abdülhamid II, had also pointed out to some measures which could be taken for the development of the Crown lands. These measures consisted mainly of building water canals and highways around Basra, plus a railway that reached the province (The conservative Disraeli governments have preferred to support the Ottomans as opposed to the liberal and anti-Turkish policy of the Gladstone era).[19]

The British domination over this area had long been established. In 1871, Midhat Pasha, the Governor of Baghdad had joined Kuwait as a district *(kaza)* to the Sandjak of Basra and appointed Sheikh Abdullah el'Sabah to this kaza as kaimakam. However, at the end of the nineteenth century when Britain made her first attempts to rule Kuwait, Sheikh Muhammed ibnus Sabah

---

18 İsmail Hakkı Tevfik, *Basra Körfezi Meselesi*, Hariciye Vekâleti Matb., Nr.15, Ankara, 1931, pp.9.

19 Report of the British Amb. Layard: *Başbakanlık Arşivi, Yıldız Esas*, Nr.7-94.

of the same family recognized by British protectorate. At the end of the century Germany made her appearance and selected Kuwait as the end-point of the Baghdad railway.[20] As a result, the Ottoman Sultan announced his supreme rights over Kuwait with great emphasis. However, Sheikh Mubarek preferred to lead a two-sided policy between Britain and the Ottomans. The end of 1898 and beginning of 1899 was the period of military intervention at the area by the Turks and the Germans, but the result was the allowance of British protectorate on the region. However, even this solution could not prevent the disagreement that occured between the great powers such as Russia, Germany, Britain and the Ottoman Empire. It did not seem possible for Britain and the Ottoman Empire. It did not seem possible for Britain to be the one and only ruler over the area at the beginning of the twentieth century.

The beginning of the twentieth century was also the period when the U.S.A. started more planned efforts of gaining influence over the area without getting too involved in the fights that were going on. An educational service and naturalization policy was directed towards the Christian minority in the area for this purpose. The vice-consul of the U.S.A. in Baghdad has left written statements on how lots of individuals applied to the State Department with the request of consular protection carrying genuine of false credentials and how this procedure continued for days until it reached serious dimensions.[21]

20 H. J. Philiby, *Arabia*, London, 1936, pp.25-156-169 and see also G. L. Bondarevski, *Baghdadskaya Doroga i Proniknoveniye Germanskogo Imperializma Na Blijni Vostok 1888-1903*, G. I. Uzb. SSR, Taşkent, 1955, p.156-199.

21 *U.S. National Archives, Foreign Serv. Post Rec. 84*, "Correspondence American Consulate Baghdad," – Dec. 1892 to Febr. 1900", pp.115, "To State Dept. February 10.1899", "The attention of the Department has been called, to the fact that there are more or less permanently domiciled in various cities of Turkey many natives of the country who claim American citizenship and frequently call upon our Consuls for protection. Some of these persons, it is alleged, come to the U.S. for a short time and by means of false affidavits

As a result, we must say that the Mesopotamian area and Basra harbour were under the nominal dominance of the Ottomans at the end of the nineteenth century and beginning of the twentieth century. Economic goods were passed over to the western markets through Basra, a collecting center.[22] The Ottoman Empire served the purpose of a gendarme government that secured the benefits and economic advantages due to disagrements among the major states. In reality, the financial status of the Empire was barely sufficient to carry on this fiction. Other sources of income were either provided by exterior financial groups or controlled through international organizations such as the Public Debt, and their representative.

CONCLUSION

The Arab World in the nineteenth century was in the process of disintegration like the whole of the Ottoman Empire. The Arab World which could conserve its administrative and cultural union within the *Pax Ottomana* till the beginning of the nineteenth century, entered during this era a disintegration process, since the Western powers divided this area into several influence spheres. Beyrouth and Basra were becoming two separate and important controlling centers of these divided areas. This disintegration of economic space prepared in the twentieth century the platform of political division. The falling of Syria and the Lebanon under the French and, Egypt and Mesopotamia under the British economic and finally political influences, caused the emergence of these areas as independent political units after the fall of the Ottoman Empire. These areas came under the rule of the British and the French and until our present times a reunification of the eastern Arab World could not be effected.

---

obtain certificates of naturalization, while others without even visiting this country secure certificates of naturalization and passports by inducing friends to personate them." Rudolph Hurner Vice Consul of U.S. Baghdad-Turkey.

22 M. Salman Hasan, *ibid.*, pp.348, "The export trade of Iraq rose between 1864-71 from 147.000 to 2.960.000."

12

Ioanina and its Port-Town Preveza in the Late Ottoman Empire (1864-1895)

The province of Ioanina during the last decades of Ottoman domination shows both a peripheral character in the Empire on the one hand and an international fringe point on the other. Ioanina and its port-towns Preveza and Arta (Ottoman Narda) were two crosspoints in the eastern Mediterranean. Preveza, which had Venetian and Ottoman periods in its long history, is a good example of evolution in this area until the beginning of the Balkan wars it 1912.

The sandjak Preveza has witnessed some of the most characteristic developments of the Tanzimat period. It had remained outside of the boundaries of the Hellenic Kingdom as it was established in 1829, but still was the closest contact point of the Ottoman Empire with Greece both from commercial and geographical aspects.

Until 1912 the Preveza sandjak was part of the Ioanina province (Yanya *vilayeti*). Between 1864 and 1912 it included 3 subdistricts *(kaza)*; namels Preveza, Loros and Marğılıç (today Margariti). Parga was at first a *kaza* center and later remained as a *nahiye* (commune) within the *kaza* of Marğılıç, Parga was largely dominated by Muslim-Albanian land owners (agha) and kept this economic social feature till the end of the Second World War. 36 villages and two communes *(nahiye)* completed the administrative structure of the Preveza sandjak.[1] The *nahiye* had been established

1 *Salname-i Vilâyet-i Yanya* 1892, Nr.6, p.211-214-216.

on the lines of the French "commune" model; but owing to its autonomous administrative status, specially in the Balkans, it was not favoured by the Ottoman administration. Population figures quoted by Ottoman sources usually repeat the figures of the official yearbook *(salname)*. As the census was not conducted in a very precise manner, these figures are only an approximation of the reality and they should be used to work out population estimates for nineteenth century Ottoman Europe. Population figures for 1895 based on an Ottoman source are as follows:[2]

	Male	**Female**
Greek-orthodox	5.168	4.840
Muslim	3.512	3.097

Another Ottoman source gives the following figures for the same year, (1894) but based this time on households.[3]

	Households	**Male**	**Female**	**(Estimated) Total population**
Preveza	2.306	5.556	4.504	10.060
Lorus	2.780	6.137	6.507	13.654
(Margariti)	5.224	12.576	11.379	23.955

It appears that Muslims were in minority both in the sandjak overall and in the main town. 25 years earlier (1871) the British Consul Barker mentions 4.318 Christians, 1.724 Turks (meaning Muslims) and 58 Gypsies.[4] Either through lack of information or because perhaps a community had not yet been established, Consul Barker does not refer to a Jewish presence in Preveza. 8 years later, another British consul, Blakeney gives conflicting

2 Ali Cevad, *Memalik-i Osmaniyenin Cografya Lugatı*, Constantinople, 1892 (1313 H), p.238, 240.

3 *Salname-i Vilâyet-i Yanya*, Nr.7, 1894 (1311 of H), p.37.

4 *Parliamentary papers and accounts* report of vice-consul Barker Prevesa 1872, 28 January, pp.1353-1355.

figures; 1.200 Muslims to 11.200 Christians, without providing a break-down on ethnical lines.[5]

But on the other hand consular reports provide valuable information on trade and agriculture. In 1864 a new provincial structure had been established in the Rumeli *vilayet*s and this year the center of sandjak was transferred from Arta to Preveza. This new administrative set up had brought along an increase in the number of provincial functionaries and in infrastructural expenditures. In 1864 Preveza was connected to Ioanina through telegraph. Similarly cables were laid between Preveza on the one hand and Parga and on the other during 1878.[6] Public security in the area which had, earlier, been problematic also improved and by 1884 the British consul could write that it was becoming more satisfactory every year, although acts of brigandage were occasionaly heard of. Even in 1864, the British consul at Ioanina, Stuart reports that "brigandage, that used to be so rife here, has for some time been quite repressed, and individual crime in certainly below the average of other years."[7] On the other hand the central government also took measures to prevent the malpractices of security organs and local civil servants, and tried to impose a legal rule and avoid oppression.[8]

The increase in the number of provincial civil servants introduced changes into everyday life in Preveza, which was till then a small sleepy backwater. This numerous group of highly-paid civil servants created a consuming class and new consuming patterns which in turn led to increased demands for imported goods. Since local products started to be exported, Preveza overtook Arta as the

5 *Ibid.*, (vice consul Blakeney) Prevesa, February 13, 1880, p.1032. However he mentions that "I am not aware that a census has over been taken, but the population of the gaza of Preveza cannot exceed 10.000 souls."

6 *Ibid.*, (Vice-consul Blakeney) Prevesa, February 22, 1878, p.886.

7 *Ibid.* (Vice-consul Blakeney), Prevesa, March 1, 1884, p.577, Consul Stuart, *ibid.*, Janina, May 10, 1865, p.462.

8 B. A., *İrade-Dahiliye 1270*, Nr.18726.

main trading center of the area. British consular reports for 1862-63 give the following data for commercial activities in Arta;

	Imp.	Exp.
1862	38.000	14.000
1863	64.000	16.000

In the following year (1863-64) shipping to Preveza reached the following figures.

	Vessels	Value of cargoes in
British	1	—
Ionian	173	8.559
Greek	347	2.667
Ottoman	84	2.000
Austrian	8	1.445
Italian	1	—
Ditto steamers Value of imports reached 29.750	26	5.049

Sixteen years later in 1880 the exports of Preveza reached 104.903 and imports 234.025.[9] The shipping activities in the harbour of Preveza in the same year was such as below:[10]

	Steam	Sail
Austrian	60	5
British Greek	2 —	— 3.252
Italian	—	17
Ottoman	—	1.108
Total	62	4.382

9 *Parl. Accounts and papers* (Great Britain), 1863-64; vol.70, p.111.

10 *Ibid.*, (Vice-consul Blakeney), Prevesa, February 19, 1881, p.579.

Preveza still remained as a relatively small port in comparison to other Ionian and Thracian ports. Especially the annexation of Arta by Greece in 1881 caused a deterioration of the life of Preveza, since it remained a boundary town of the Empire. Certainly, there was no local industry worth mentioning in Preveza. In 1871 vice-consul Barker noted that "Preveza is a very small place and its commerce is limited and comparatively insignificant. The value of imports exceed three-fold that of exports, rendering these countries always indebted to Europe while it proves that the system of government in Turkey as yet does not encourage native industry". But on the other hand Barker mentions that Preveza had the lowest mortality rate and was the most healthy place in the region, free from epidemics and contagious diseases.[11] Industry was limited to a few small workshops, processing local agricultural products (see the list in Appendix 1). In the 1880s there were 24 olive oil presses, 5 flourmills and 3 soap factories. Tax returns indicate the presence of 104.000 olive trees and 5000 fruit trees. Basic export products in 1884 was consisting of wheat, barley, fish, tobacco and soap. But as Consul Stuart mentions "in this country neither machinery, nor the wheeled carriage is employed in aid of labour. The ox is used for ploughing and the pack-horse for transport. Both are falling off as well in quality as in numbers. During the British protectorate over the Ionian islands, the farmers here used to obtain supplies of large Vallachian oxen through the commissariat contractors. This they can no longer do. The Vallachian ox has almost completely disappeared from Epirus; and all the ploughing is now done with the country ox, which is small, light, and of feeble draught power. But even of these the breed is declining." Worse than that for the demands occasioned by the Crimean War, some good amount of horses were exported. The deficiency this created has

11 *Ibid.*, (Vice-consul Barker) Prevesa, January 28, 1872, p.1355 gives a mortality rate of 43 per 2000.

never been supplied; and from that time dated the deterioration of the breed, which every year becomes more observable..."[12]

	Quantity	Value in £
Wheat (kilo)	20.000	4.181
Barley (kilo)	15.000	4.163
Oats (kilo)	19.800	1.080
Wool (kilo)	20.000	1.090
Fish (okkas)	120.000	5.454
Cheese (in skins)	31.000	1.536
Tobacco	15.000	2.045
Butter	3.000	272
Soap	100.000	3.181
Sheep and goat-skins/piece	40.000	2.209
Olive-oil (barrels)	8.600 (in 1880)	626

The value and approximate quantity of main crops given by Consul Blakeney for the year of 1883 is listed below.[13]

In this very same year, Blakeney still reports the existence of some bands of brigands. But these events have been concentrated mostly in the internal districts of Epirus and the international trade of Preveza has not been much affected by it. However in 1882 he had reported a recession of the economic activities following the Russo-Turkish war of 1877-78 and the transfer of Arta to Greece: "the cession of Arta to Greece has produced a great convulsion in the trade of this port and that of Salabora; but this is not the case, for the fertile plain of Arta still remains to Turkey, so that only the imports to Arta from foreign countries no longer pass through Preveza. The prices of the various commodities of life have since the late Russo-Turkish war risen about 50 percent."[14]

12 *Parliamentary Accounts and Papers* (Reports by Consul Stuart on the present state of Epirus), Janina, April, 24, 1871, p.816.

13 *Ibid.* (Blakeney), Prevesa, March 1, 1884, p.571.

14 Prevesa, February 16, 1882, p.1161.

In town there were eleven Greek Orthodox churches, one Roman-Catholic church, two mosques, (Ali Pasha and Ahmed Agha Dino) and two *türbe*. These figures, give a fair image of the religious life of the town. As the town and sandjak of Preveza had a cosmopolitan composition, the administrative council of the sandjak *(Liva idare meclisi)* was composed by the clerical heads of the different communities and besides two elected Christians and two Muslim members.

Ottoman administrators (*mutasarrıf* of Preveza) of the Tanzimat era were usually enthusiastic builders and were instrumental in developing the provinces. However the governors *(vali)* and subgovernors *(mutasarrıf)* of the Danubian region (Bulgaria) were more successful in comparison to those of Morea. After the independence of the Kingdom of the Hellens, Morea could not enjoy a development similar to western Anatolia, western Thrace and the Danubian province. Taking the example of Preveza, the *mutasarrıfs* required long tenures to develop their sandjak and instruct some reforms, but this was not the case. They often had to change their posts. The relatively high turnover of local administrators prevented continuity in policies and slowed down construction activities. The official Ottoman yearbook of Ioanina vilayet for the year 1311 H. (1894) gives the list of the sub-governors *(mutasarrıf)* of Preveza since 1864.[15] The first *mutasarrıf* appointed after the promulgation of the famous "decree of provincial administration" in 1864 *(İdare-i umumiye-yi vilayet nizamnamesi)* was Hasan Şevki Pasha (1 March 1864), followed by Selim Pasha and later by Timur Edhem Pasha. Timur Edhem Pasha, was again appointed to Preveza after Reshid Pasha, İzzeddin Sir Pasha, and Fikri Efendi for a second time. He then was followed by Selahaddin Bey, Kazım Bey, Abdülrefi Efendi and Hadi Ahmed Ferid Pasha (a total of eleven mutasarrıfs within a period of 30 years).

15 *Salname-i Vilâyet-i Yanya*, 1894 (1311 of H), p.78.

It would appear that part of the local population was opposed to cession of the region to Greece. Local notables informed the Palace, that if Preveza, Narda and Ioanina should be ceded to Greece, they would oppose such a move by rising in arms. In February 1881 (1298 H) the King of the Hellens toured Preveza and Narda, which caused some protests of the local Muslims.[16] A similar event in the past also indicates the sensitivity of the local Muslims, namely a short visit of the General of the Ionian Republic (Cezayir-i Seba cenerali) to Preveza and Parga which was a subject for careful observation by the Ottoman authorities.[17] Formerly in March 1879 telegrams to Yıldız Palace claimed that the cession of Preveza, Arta and Ioanina to Greece would spell disaster for the Albanians.[18] In fact it seems that Albanian nationalism was rampant among local Albanians. A new *mutasarrıf* was appointed to Preveza from Argiri (Ergiri) to curb the agitation caused by one Abdul Bey and his confederate, in Ioanina.[19] Albanian elements in those years seem to be deeply anxious.

However, even a study of the issues of the provincial newspaper *Yanya* in these years, indicates that some economic and social changes are intervening; estates are put on sale, bankruptcies and distraints were fairly frequent. Some sets of documents in the Turkish archives also are a proof of this evolution.[20] However the highest percentage of the agricultural tithes, such as *aşar* and *aghnam* (sheep and husbandry tax) in provincial budgets, indicates that the economic structure of the sandjak Preveza remained based for a long time on agricultural activities (see Appendix 2).

16 B. A., *Yıldız-Hususi-165/145*, 15-2-1297 of H (1880 A.D.).

17 B. A., *İrade-Hariciye*, Nr.4118, 29 CA 1268 of H (1851-52 A.D.).

18 B. A., *Yıldız 16 9/2* (15-11-1297 of H [1880]).

19 B. A., *Yıldız-160/72*, 25 Receb 1298 of H (1881 A.D.).

20 B. A., *Yıldız-Its ns: 25-5-1296*, Nr.161/26 see the collection of the newspaper *Yanya* of the year 1873.

APPENDIX 1

Report by Vice-Consul Barker on the Trade of Prevesa for the year 1871, (Prevesa January 22 1872) *Parliamentary accounts and papers*, pp.1355-56.

Habitations, houses and huts	**1.163**
Shops	**283 (total)**
Drapers	14
Cooking-shops	7
Butters	6
Fishmongers	5
Coffee-shops	9
Greengrocers	7
Ship-chandlers and grocers	235
Stores	88
Caravanserailles	6
Flour-mills	5
Military hospitals	2
Soap manufactories (about 127.000 lbs. of this article is fabricated during the year)	3
Gil-presses, wood-screw pressure (the approximate value or cost of one press is 220 £)	21
Schools (two for males, two for females, 3 being public schools supported by private contributions)	
Court of Justice (building)	
Government civil offices (building where the Police-station is held, 42 men engaged for police service in town)	
Metropolitan house	1
Churches (Greek Orthodox)	10
Cathedral (ditto)	1
Chapel (Roman Catholic)	1
Mosques (Mohammedan)	2
Mohammedan Monasteries (probably *tekke*)	2
Vapour bath	
Quarantine office (Building 7 persons employed)	
Forts (Usual garrison, Artillery 260, Infantry 680 men)	
Drinking Fountains (Turkish *çeşme*)	5
2 Harbours (one inner harbour, where the Venetians had their Arsenal)	

APPENDIX 2

Population of the Sandjak of Preveza in the year of 1893 *Salname-i Vilâyet-i Yanya* 1311, p.37.

	Male	Female	Total
Preveza district household: 2.306	5.556	4.504	10.060
Loros district household: 2.780	6.137	6.507	12.644
Marguliç district (Margariti) household: 5.224	12.576	11.379	23.955

Financial Portrait of the Sandjak of Preveza in the year of 1894 (same source, p.310-11)

Incomes (in Ottoman kuruş)	
Emlâk temettü (property and profit tax)	732.344
Bedel-i askeri (military tax)	666.118
Aşar (agricultural tithes)	1.948.376
Ağnam ve canavar (sheep and husbandry tax)	1.172.459
Varîdat-ı saîre (other revenues)	782.355
Public Expenditures (in Ottoman kuruş)	
Şer'iyye (religious courts and bureaucracy)	56.544
Dahiliyye (home-office)	280.960
Adliyye (Justice dept.)	163.324
Maliye (finance office)	210.704
Maaşat-ı zatiyye (salaries)	22.602
Zabtiyye (police)	26.122

FAMILY

An Ottoman Family in 19th Century.

13

The Family in Ottoman Society

Afew words are called for in order to explain why our title is "The Family in Ottoman Society" rather than one such as, "The Ottoman Family". Closely related to this point, is the impossibility of basing the study of the family and marriage in Ottoman society on explanations derived from textbooks of Islamic law *(fıkıh)*. Both these approaches, namely the use of the concept of Ottoman family and interpretations based on textbooks of Islamic law, have been quite commonly utilized by those who have already written on the subject. This does not mean, however, that they have any explanatory value. Whichever sociological classification one adopts, it does not seem possible to specify an "Ottoman family" as a separate category. And evaluating or defining this family in the light of the fundamentals of Islamic *fıkıh* and the information contained in the books of jurisprudence just does not seem feasible, given the nature of Islamic law. The basic sources for investigating problems such as the family and women in Ottoman society should be the *kadı* registers *(şer'iyye sicilleri)* belonging to the various periods and regions of the Empire. Travelogues rank second in importance; finally, we may also utilize the accounts found in certain chronicles.

As in all traditional societies in which the family is the basic economic unit, the extended family was also the predominant type in Ottoman society. This extended family was imbedded within a still larger collective social unit in which three generations coexisted and which included the families of brothers and other close relatives. This was the case for both Muslims and non-Muslim Ottomans. According to the Ottoman tax registers *(tahrir defterleri)*, the unit called *hane* (household) consists of five persons on the average, but it would be erroneous to suppose that the household corresponds to an independent family in each case. More commonly, households belonging to the three different generations of the same family lived as one socioeconomic unit in homes arranged around a courtyard. Again, this entity would usually be complemented by close relatives living in the same quarter. This is why a quarter in a typical Ottoman city was not just an administrative unit but also a close-knit community composed of relatives who always stood up for each other. Together, the individual members of the extended family comprised a unit of production. This was true for urban artisans as well as for peasants who made up to vast majority of society. In all cities in which impersonal institutions have not yet emerged, members of the family and near relatives form the basic matrix of social relationships which surround the individual from birth to death. Security rests with the kinship group to which the individual is connected, and he lives for his family. As with all traditional societies, nepotism also defined the sum total of human relationships into which Ottomans of all classes were born and in which they existed to the end.

Thus, childbirth is an event which is celebrated throughout the entire quarter as well as within the family and which interests everyone living there. This new addition to the community is welcomed through a specific rite called *lohusa hamamı*; another rite, the *amin alayı*, is effected when the small child is starting school. When the same child has successfully mastered reading, he is paraded through the quarter and applauded. Weddings, becoming a parent, etc., are all occasions of great interest, first for the family, and then for the quarter. The extended family produces and consumes jointly. Nurturing all members of three generations, its women sew together, prepare and store winter food in common, visit together and entertain themselves as a group. The men of the family buy food together, build and do repairs for the extended family as a whole. The nuclear family usually does not live as an independent unit. Husband, wife and children do not have the time and energy to devote to their own narrow family. Time and urbanization, of course, inevitably contributed to transforming this kind of family and relationships in Ottoman society as elsewhere. The İstanbul family of the nineteenth century, for example, with which we are quite familiar through literature, although still different from the modern family, clearly reflects a basic transformation of the old family structure.

Residential districts of Ottoman cities were demarcated and moulded not along economic but religious lines. Non-Muslims settled in a narrow belt on the fringes of the town would carry on their lives in much the same fashion within the framework of relationships structured by their own extended families and community. As in many other traditional societies, inter-denominational marriages were very rare. Although religious law allowed Muslim men to marry non-Muslim women, it should be borne in mind that non-Muslim congregations also strove very hard to prevent such marriages. In certain regions the Muslim officials or merchants posted there did marry Christian women temporarily *(muta nikâhı)*, but this also was quite uncommon.[1] Contrary to what is usually supposed, polygamy was not very widespread in Ottoman society. Even some European travelers noticed as much. Salomon Schweigger, for example, a German Protestant priest who passed through Turkey towards the end of the sixteenth century, noted that "Turks rule cantries and their

1 Marie Alexandrescu-Dersca, "Sur le Mariage entre Turcs Ottoman et Roumaines-XVIe-XIXe siècles": *Interventions et Rapports*, XVe Congrès Int. des Etudes Historiques, Bucarest, 1980, pp.15-17.

wives rule them. Turkish women go around and enjoy themselves much more than any others. Polygamy is absent. They must have tried it but then given it up because it leads to much trouble and expense. Divorce is rare, for then the man has to pay in money and goods and daughters are left with the mother."[2]

The woman is in fact the most important member of the traditional family, but her status both there and in society in general does not measure up to her role in production. This standing is nevertheless enhanced with age and increasing number of children. Naturally, I am not going to claim that women were free in traditional society. Any approach to this question from the standpoint of our present system of values would neither be appropriate nor necessary. And of course, we cannot really speak of the freedom of men in such a society either, because they, too did not take part in the process of production of their own free will. But the woman's dependence on the male members of the family extended beyond marriage, and she was in the position of a factor of production transferred from one family to another. The value paid in exchange for this transfer, variously called *başlık*, *kalın* or some other such name is, contrary to what is usually supposed, not peculiar to the Ottoman-Islamic society. For the *mehr* of Islamic law, paid in two parts *(mehr-i muaccel* and *mehr-i müeccel)*, is a payment appropriated by the women herself and as such constitutes some sort of economic security for her in the case of divorce or widowhood. Payments like *başlık*, *kalın*, etc., on the other hand, have nothing to do with principles laid down in legal *(fıkıh)* texts. In all traditional societies where women marry young into economic dependence, it is the custom for the groom to make such a payment for his bride. General characteristics of traditional agrarian societies clearly can be attributed to the specificities of neither Turkey

2 Salomon Schweigger, *Eine reyssbeschreibung auss Teutschland nach Constantinopel und Jerusalem*, R. Neck. Akad. Druck und Verlag. Gras, 1964, pp.201-210.

nor the other Islamic (Arab) societies only. Therefore the topic should be dealt with not from a narrowly legalistic viewpoint but also, more broadly, within a sociological perspective. Only in this way can the relationship between legal codes and actual social practices be clarified.

The customary explanation, then, is that the Turkish *başlık* payment or the *sada'k* – its Arabic counterpart – are extensions of the Islamic institution of the *mehr*. But *başlık* or *sada'k* have been present in the Orient from time immemorial. Undergoing very little change through the ages down to the modern era, such customs have also served again and again to establish legal precedent. Marriage involving the payment of brideprice has evolved naturally in the course of civilization as the transition from matriarchy to patriarchy deprived women of their equal status in matters of marriage, divorce and inheritance and eventually put them in the position of being given in marriage by their father or other kin in return for a payment by the groom. The new family formed under these circumstances is inevitably patriarchal and agnatic throughout the world.

Before Islam, marriage customs revolving around the payment of bride price as *mehr* or in some other from were already prevalent among the Arabs.[3] Such traditions reflect a patriarchal, polygamous

3 Among the Arabs of this period marriage had no further meaning than that of a simple sexual union. The married woman was not seen primarily as the wife of her husband. As long as she did not bear a son, even if she died, her husband would not be offered condolences: If she committed a crime, her indemnity would not be paid by the *huy* (clan) she belonged to by birth. The bride price *(sada'k or mehr)* of a young girl would be collected by her father, and in case he was not alive, by her nearest male relative. That the bride should go to the highest payer was the basic principle and it was commonly obeyed. There was also another type of marriage based on mutual exchange which was called *sığar nikâhı*. Since it was especially humiliating for women, it was outlawed by the Prophet of Islam. Still another type of marriage among the Arabs was the *mut'a nikâhı* which survived partially in later periods. Here the union was demanded by the women, and no *mehr* or other payment was accordingly

family structure. The pre-Islamic *mehr* was the purchase price for the woman. The Muslim religion, however, subjected this existing custom to new adjustments and constraints. Most importantly, it forbade the bride's father or other kin from appropriating the *mehr* and left it entirely in the hands of the woman to be given in marriage.[4] It is difficult to say that these Islamic injunctions have been universally or rigorously obeyed. It was always possible for ancient practices or deformations of new ones to spread for and wide under the force of socioeconomic circumstances.

As noted above, Islamic law demands that the *mehr* be paid in two parts: there is the *mehr-i muaccel* first, and then, the *mehr-i müeccel* to be paid out of the inheritance *(tereke)* in case of divorce or if the husband dies. In order for the act of marriage

---

involved. The marriage would take place on the demand of the women and without the consent of (her) legal protector(s). Any children to be born would belong to the mother. See: Şemsettin Günaltay. "İslâmdan Önce Araplarda Kadının Durumu"; *Belleten*, vol.XV, pp.702-705.

4 According to Islamic law, the payment of *mehr* was absolutely required. "A woman marrying a Muslim obtains a claim over some goods called *mehr* even if she is non-believer. Any interest capable of being exchanged with goods may also serve as *mehr*." (Ö. N. Bilmen, *Hukuk-u İslâmiyye ve Istılahat-ı Fıkhiyye Kamusu*, I.U.H.F., 1950, vol.II, pp.121-122). The last phrase in this definition has given rise to certain interesting applications which we are going to mention below. Apart from these two conditions, the payment of *mehr* had also to be specifically mentioned during the marriage ceremony. That is why researchers have time and again encountered recorded amounts of *mehr* and other payments in the *kadı* registers. See, for example, *Konya Şer'iye Sicili*, pages 74-76, for the amounts of *mehr-i müeccel*. Another entry in *Konya Şer'iye Sicili*, no.1, page 38, reads as follows: "Selime daughter of İbrahim and Mehmed son of Pir Ahmed were declared married with 2000 *akçes*' worth of *mehr-i muaccel* and 2000 *akçes*' worth of *mehr-i müeccel* paid." In case the husband died, the wife had first claim on the payment of the *mehr* out of the inheritance, and other heirs could not interfere. See *Çankırı Şer'iyye Sicili*. no.2, page 8, Verdict 20 – at the Museum of Ethnography of Ankara–: "I being Fahrüddin resident of the fort of Kengiri, my daughter Kerime being the wife of Ömer Agha, we had agreed upon a payment of 25.000 *akçes* and a shawl of value known to us after this death" (*Defter*, H.1069-1077).

to be formalized, the bride must have assented publicly that the *mehr* has been paid and this must have been duly recorded in the court register. There is disagreement among Islamic jurists as to what the minimum *mehr* should be, but 10 *dirhem*s of silver seems to have been most common. As the *mehr* belonged to the bride, neither her parents nor her husband could force her turn it into or add it to her dowry.[5] Nevertheless, comparison of such injunctions of Islamic canon law *(şeriat)* with actual practice in Ottoman society does reveal certain conflicts between custom and the letter of the law. Many entries concerning marriage recorded in the *kadı* registers of sixteenth century Ankara, Çankırı, Kayseri and Konya, for example, do not fit the requirements of any of the four Orthodox *(sünni)* denominations on the subject, indicating that marriage practices in Anatolia in that period did not always accord with Islamic regulations. In the light of such documents, it should be useful in this article basically devoted to family relations (marriage, divorce, extra-marital affairs) in Ottoman society to compare, from time to time, actual observed practices with the principles of Islamic law.

We know that in the Ottoman Empire, canon law *(şer-i hukuk)* was largely replaced by customary law *(örfi hukuk)* in the public field and especially in the area of land tenure. Conversely, it is often repeated that what we would today call the realm of private law was left to the *şeriat*. We are, however, unable to share this view since the abundance of observable practices in violation of the Orthodox *şeriat* shows that in familial matters like marriage and divorce "legality" extended way beyond the articles of canon law. Apart from the accepted domination of customary law in the fields of administrative and criminal law, it seems possible that further researches into family law might also uncover rich examples of non-canonical procedures, such divergences from religious principles usually being caused by the influence of local

5 Ö. N. Bilmen, *op.cit.* vol.II, pp.154-156.

custom and tradition. In the district or province to which he was appointed and where he would remain but for a short time, the typical Ottoman *kadı* refrained from strict implementation of standard legal rules and regulations. For him, it was better to conform to local traditions than to disrupt that local order and perhaps make way for chaos. Ottoman jurists never even tried to go beyond loyally copying the works of classical Islamic jurists when it came to writing a treatise concerning familial relationships (*feraiz or ahkâm-ı nikâh*). They were not nearly so orthodox, however, in actual practice. Thus, traditions such as *başlık* and *kalın* were legally validated by courts in Central Anatolia in the sixteenth-seventeenth centuries, and when it came to trying cases of adultery or divorce, Ottoman lawgivers once more proved more flexible than the harsh clauses of classical Islam. But one should not exaggerate: in the *kadı* registers we have cited, records conforming to the Islamic principles on *mehr* are as numerous as those that do not. Marriage, for example, was in all places recorded at the court register. It seems that this practice was indeed very widespread. Otherwise the man and woman concerned would be summoned to court for "cohabiting out of wedlock" and their illegitimate relationship also duly recorded at the same registry.[6] On the other hand, as Jennings has observed in the case of seventeenth century Kayseri,[7] in at least some localities the so-called Ottoman family was founded on the separation of property rights for husband and wife. But the best examples of customs

6 Thus according to any entry in the *kadı* registers of Konya for the year 1562-3 (II. 970), there arose a legal dispute as to whether a certain woman called Aynı binti Abdi presently in the household of one Süleyman Çelebi was properly married or not. There was no record of the marriage in the *kadı* register but the woman claimed that she had been properly married off by one Lutfi son of Berkuk. It seems that the verdict was one of "cohabiting out of wedlock," for the Subaşı's complaint to the *Kadı* was accepted and the woman's position recorded in the register as illegitimate. See: *Konya Şer'iye Sicili*, no.5, 79/5.

7 R. Jennings, "Woman in the Early 17th Century"; *JESHO*, vol.XVIII, part I, pp.101-102.

conflicting with the Islamic rules on marriage are to be found in Central Anatolia of the sixteenth century. Thus, on the basis of several entries in the Ankara court registers for that period, it would seem that a certain type of betrothal called *namzedlik* (literally: candidacy) was quite common.[8]

The father would promise his daughter in marriage to someone while she was still very young and would accept money or goods in exchange. This sum would then be consumed by the father and he would hand over his daughter to the man to whom she was betrothed when she finally came of age. *Zindegâne olmama* is the term employed in the *kadı* registers to denote real separation of a married couple or the fact that their joint existence has come to an end. Contrary to orthodox practice, in some places the wife who had left her husband's home would not be required to return.[9] Such a woman might instead forego her rights to the *mehr-i muaccel* and to alimony. A woman stated to be "henceforth divorced" by her husband was required by canon law to wait at least two months

8 According to an entry dated 1551 (H.958), a certain Edhem presented a complaint regarding a certain non-Muslim called İskender veled-i Devlet demanding that he pay a debt of 600 *akçe*s for which he had stood bond. It appears that this Edhem had a daughter by the name of Ayşe, for whose hand a janissary called Kara Yeniçeri presented himself. Edhem stated that his daughter was the "candidate" of one Simitçi Yusuf and that he had already accepted 600 *akçe*s himself, whereupon Edhem asked him to show bond. Kara Yeniçeri showed the non-Muslim called İskender as bond, took Ayşe from her father, and then disappeared without paying. That is why Edhem had to pay the 600 *akçe*s to Simitçi Yusuf himself and he was now bringing İskender to court since he had stood bond for the janissary. See: Halit Ongan, *Ankara* Şer'*iye Sicilleri* (TTK-1956), H.958 (A.D. 1551), no.2, Entry 1314. According to another verdict, a man called Cüneyd bin Mustafa brought another called Bâli bin Emir Ahmed to court, claiming that the daughter of the defendant's brother, called Katunbula, had been his "candidate" but then had been given by defendant to someone else in marriage. It appears that Bâli bin Emir Ahmed had been his niece's protector, he had violated the *namzedlik* bond by giving the girl to someone else and accepting *başlık*. This was in violation of the Islamic precepts concerning *mehr*.

9 Jennings, *op. cit.*, p.85; *Çankırı Şer'iye Sicili*, no.4.

before remarrying, and it seems that this particular injunction was commonly observed.[10] Payment of alimony would be decided by the court on the woman's application not just in case of formal divorce but when and if the husband simply left the house or failed to provide for his family.[11]

As in all traditional societies, extramarital relationships and bearing children of uncertain fatherhood were severely frowned upon by sixteenth century Ottomans. That *namus*, the Turkish word for honor – which, however, is just one of its meanings – derives from the Greek *nomos* should perhaps be sufficient indication of how universally prevalent attitudes were in this respect. Sixteenth century Ottoman society had nevertheless moved away from the much harsher punishments imposed by ancient oriental societies for such practices. According to Islamic law, for example, any adulteress upon proof or her "crime" was liable to be stoned *(recm)* in accordance with a provision adopted from old Hebrew law, but even in the earliest period of Islam, provisos were added which must have made inflicting this punishment all but impossible. That adultery had in fact been committed had to be proved through the testimony of at least four male witnesses. And the woman accused by her husband of adultery could evade punishment by denying the allegation and basing her denial on a solemn oath.[12] This particular ruling was commonly adhered to in Ottoman jurisdiction where *kadı*s generally refrained from deciding that "adultery had been formally

10 *Konya Şer'iye Sicili*, no.1, page 37.

11 *Çankırı Şer'iye Sicili*, no.2, page 32, Verdict 259.

12 The "Holy Light" verse of the Quran *(Kuran-ı Kerim*, "Nur Suresi") orders that 100 lashes be laid upon those who have committed adultery, the punishment to be carried out in the presence of believers. These who accused a chaste woman of adultery but were unable to provide four witnesses would be punished by 80 lashes and would not be accepted as lawful witnesses in the future. If the accused woman swears four times consecutively and in God's name that her husband is lying and in the fifth turn also adds the phrase: "May God's damnation descend upon my head if I am lying", she will not be punished.

proved". When residents of a quarter surprised a couple having an illegal affair and paraded and ridiculed them in the streets so as to bring them into court, the verdict would usually be one of "alleged adultery" and a prison term and/or condemnation to the galleys would be imposed.[13] Throughout Ottoman history, there was only one instance where *recm* was decided upon and carried out. This happened in a period of extreme religious fanaticism, and it encountered such opposition that it was not repeated. In 1680 a woman living in the Aksaray district of İstanbul whose husband was away at war was accused of having been caught in the act of adultery with a non-Muslim youth in the silk trade. The verdict of the Court was *recm* for the woman and the death penalty for the young man. The *kazasker* for Rumelia reluctantly assented, and the entire affair was much resented by the ulama.[14] The penalty was not repeated.

On the other hand, women who bore illegitimate children or cohabited out of wedlock were never regarded with tolerance, and urban security officers were enpowered to keep an eye on them. In the late sixteenth century, such women would be immediately placed in the custody of the *Subaşı* in the provinces.[15] And efforts were made in Ottoman cities to keep unmarried men out of the residential districts. Even in İstanbul, that megalopolis, the influx of single men looking for work would be channeled to special inns *(bekâr hanları)* in the central industrial district and quartered there under some sort of surveillance.

THE TRANSFORMATION OF FAMILY STRUCTURE

The last century of the Ottoman Empire was one of reforms, the main purpose of which might well have been, as is commonly asserted, the modernization of the army. However, it does seem

13 Başbakanlık Arşivi, *Kepeci Tasnifi*, no.252, page 22. Also see: Nejat Göyünç, "Osmanlı Ceza Hukukuna Ait Belgeler", *Belgelerle Türk Tarihi Dergisi*, 3.

14 *Silâhdar Tarihi*, I, p.750.

15 *Kayseri Şer'iye Sicili*, no.8 (H.1001), page 7, Verdict 52.

that the statesmen of the nineteenth century were aware of the necessity of a thoroughgoing modernization in the financial, judicial and administrative spheres as well. These nineteenth century reformers wanted a regime where the law was supreme. Social change, once it sets in, inevitably affects areas and aspects of society well beyond those for which it was initially intended. Hence, European civilization gradually but surely became the model not only for the army, administration and finances of Ottoman society but also for its culture, literature and daily life. The *Tanzimat* period was a time when a new type of Ottoman person began to emerge. Nineteenth century Ottoman society was obviously not yet in the throes of really radical, fundamental change. However, the onset of a certain modernization in practically every field remains hardly disputable.

And it was a time when significant changes also began to be felt in the life of Ottoman women whose existence took on a different hue. We should not suppose that this new coloration consisted solely of following the fashions, of differentation in consumption patterns, of learning a foreign language or playing the piano – in other words, that it was limited to the superficial tastes and behaviour of everyday life. In fact, the classical structure of the family in the rural countryside as well as in the larger cities came increasingly under the pressure of certain structural changes in agriculture and education in Ottoman territories throughout the nineteenth century and the eventual arrival there of the products of the global revolution in communications and technology. Finally, it should be noted that the problem of women's liberation occupies an important place in the Near Eastern modernizing ideologies of this period. From the Islamic modernists to the liberals, practically all thinkers of the region advocated changes in the classical family structure and in the social status of women.

As recent historical research into demographic movements

in the Balkans has demonstrated, the Rumelian provinces in the nineteenth century were the scene of developing commodity production for export to West European markets in both agriculture and semi-finished manufactures.[16] This led to considerable urbanization which in turn implied the initation of a modernization in family structure. In Anatolia too, an important turning point of Turkish social history was beginning to take shape. Forced sedentarization of tribes in the Çukurova, Antik and Maraş regions meant a new life for this previously nomadic population. Then, towards the middle of the century, the emergence of a class of agricultural wage labourers first in the Aegean region and then in Çukurova in connection with the spread of monoculture (cotton) lent further impetus to the transformation of the rural family's mode of existence and structure. Yet another factor was the Land Law *(Arazi Kanunnamesi)* of 1858 (H.1274) which was promulgated to put new legal shape on the classical system of land tenure that had long been undergoing dissolution and to promote the spirit of private enterprise in agriculture. While it is hard to say on the one hand that it effected a very rapid and efficient transition to private property or that it really helped to consolidate small and middle farming, the code also undeniably introduced some innovations in the tenure and inheritance of agricultural land. We are not going to analyse the Land Law here in detail except to point out that the issuing of title deeds for lands that had been held and exploited by custom by turning them into inheritable property, inevitably started the rural extended family down the path of eventual breakdown in conjunction with another important legal measure, the granting of equal inheritance rights to female children, acting as an additional accelerator. The new system of land tenure must have quickly made itself felt in regions with technically modern agriculture and developed commodities

16 Nikolai Todorov, *Ballanskii Gorod XV-XIX vekov*, Izd. Nauka, Moskva, 1976, pp.308-331.

markets. Quantitatively, these nineteenth century changes in the agrarian economy would certainly not stand comparison with the great transformation Turkey experienced in the 1920's and especially in the 1940's. Nevertheless, they clearly represented the beginning of something qualitatively new. Another qualitative change observable in the nineteenth century was in the migration from rural areas to the large cities like İstanbul, Beirut and Salonica. Whereas previously only unmarried men would move to the big towns and at least some would stay there only on a seasonal basis, migrations of entire families began around this time; and in İstanbul, in the vicinity of the Golden Horn close to the city walls, the first squatters' quarters *(gecekondu)* came into being. It would not be an exaggeration to call these the first signs of urbanization and a transition to the nuclear family.

The socio-cultural changes of the Tanzimat period constituted a golden age which introduced at least upper and middle class women to social life. While Islamic modernists came up with new interpretations of the sharia to justify abolishing or at least restricting polygamy, other thinkers and authors in both Ottoman territories and other Near Eastern countries as well as on the periphery of the Russian Empire were directly campaigning against the traditional type of marriage and family structure. Thus, İbrahim Şinasi Bey somewhat naively satirized these antiquated customs in his Şai*r Evlenmesi*, our first modern play. The founder of the dramaturgy of Azerbaycan, Mirza Fethali Ahundow and his followers also radically ciriticized in their works the sequestered existence of Muslim women, the patriarchal family set-up, and the ignorance to which female children were condemned. In the 1880's a group of women from among the Muslims of Russia started a women's journal called *Alem-i Nisvan* to spread the feminist movement. One of the most important undertakings of the Tanzimat in education was to provide schooling opportunities for girls by creating the intermediate level *İn'as rüşdiyeleri*. As the numbers of girls' schools increased and they came to include high schools or lycées by the end of the century, a new professional group arose: Female teachers That the initial entry of women into working life in Turkey took place in the field of education before their entry into industry partially accounts for the relatively strong position of women in the contemporary Turkish bureaucracy to this day.[17]

The new intelligentsia which emerged out of the intellectual ferment of the Tanzimat period included women of the upper class, Fatma Aliye Hanım, the daughter of Cevdet Pasha, being their prototype. In the larger cities women had broken out of the confines of the home and their visible presence in many types of social activity, ranging from moonlight excursions on the Bosphorus to shopping in Pera, made a Tanzimat statesman such as Cevdet Pasha anxious about the increase in womanizing and immorality.[18] In short, despite the slowness of industrialization and urbanization. Turkish women may be said to have entered a phase of moderate liberation in the nineteenth century. In newly industrializing Europe, women had paid a very high price for their liberation and encountered new difficuties in social life. A similar process is just beginning for the women of this society, but because of the difference in the general circumstances, the price paid by Turkish women for their liberation is probably not as high as that

17 When World War I broke out, women were already being employed as public servants at some ministries. Previously the Balkan War had set the stage for the entry of women into manual labour through the "battalions of women workers" that had been created. See: Zafer Toprak, *Türkiye'de "Milli İktisat"*, Yurt Yayınları, Ankara, 1982, pp.316, 341, 412. Truly exceptional was the fact that in the last years of the Ottoman Empire girls were allowed to register in various faculties of the University *(Darülfünun)* as well as in certain foreign institutions of higher education. At that time, many universities in Europe and North America still did not admit girls to either all or at least some of their departments; in some cases, girls were allowed to attend lectures and seminars but could not take the graduation exams, etc.

18 A. Cevdet Pasha, *Ma'ruzât*, edited by Y. Halaçoğlu; İstanbul, 1980, pp.9-10.

paid by their European counterparts. These different circumstances derive from the reforms in recent Turkish history which prepared a suitable ground for liberation *before* industrialization.

Statesmen of the Tanzimat period were aware that the existing family code and marriage customs were creating problems. Plans for legislation to cope with this date as far back as the attempt by Âli Pasha to adopt the French Civil Code. But since the level of social development had not permitted this, only certain decrees *(firman)* and edicts *(tenbih)* to bring traditional marriage under some control could be produced. As investigated by Ş. Turan, these decrees and edicts basically attempted to prohibit payment of *başlık* for marriage and to curtail great expenditures in general.[19] Thus, a *firman* of May 1844 (H. Cemaziyelevvel 1260) ordered that (1) daughters of age should be allowed to marry of their own free will without any interference from their parents, and that (2) payments such as *başlık* (in the text, *tekâlif*), being declared illegal, should not be rendered to brides' parents. Eighteen years later, on 23 Rebiülevvel 1279 (8, Sept. 1862), the governmental edicts in connection with the implementation of the said *firman* were issued: Ten articles in all, they prohibited extravagant weddings and the payment of *başlık* while setting the amounts of *mehr-i muaccel* and *mehr-i müeccel* at 100 kuruş, 500 kuruş and 1000 kuruş for the poor, the middle and the rich classes respectively. The very poor would pay nothing. All this was intended to make marriage easier. The edicts further abolished the custom of presentation of gifts by the groom to his bride's relatives after the wedding.[20] Weddings were also classified as first, second and third class types with the legal amount of expenditure for each category specified carefully. These edicts clearly resemble law number 55 dated 1336 (1921) "prohibiting extravagant expenditures at weddings" adopted by

---

19 Şerafettin Turan, "Tanzimat Devrinde Evlenme", *İş ve Düşünce Dergisi*, XXII, 182, İstanbul, October I, 1956, pp.14-15.

20 H. Berksun, "Düğün Geleneklerinde Yasak", *İdare Dergisi*, 1945, 174, p.14.

the Government of the Grand National Assembly during the Liberation War. That decree and the edicts obviously did not do away with customary practices overnight, but we must allow that they represented a certain progress. As is well known, the *Mecelle*, which was an important nineteenth century legal compilation, does not include articles on family law. Nevertheless, the decree and edicts mentioned above do indicate that the tendency to modernize marriage and the family was gathering momentum. At least among the urban population, ancient customs and polygamy declined during this period as a result of economic and social necessity.

In the Second Constitutional period, modernist ideological and political trends continued to focus on marriage and the family: There were polemics between administrators, lawyers and thinkers on this subject, and novelists of the time elaborated on the problems of Turkish womanhood in a rhetorical and didactic manner. Ziya Gökalp, the master theoretician of the Committee of Union and Progress *(İttihat ve Terakki)*, was drawn to this question in his youth and even wrote a short story titled *İbiş Dayi*, satirizing traditional marriage.[21] In this general climate, one would have expected the Young Turks in power also to undertake certain innovations in the realm of family law and, in fact, the Turkish Hearths *(Türk Ocakları)* were a hotbed of feminist activity. But the Union and Progress government was unable to make radical moves in this direction in its dictatorial phase after the Balkan War and then again during the great conflict of 1914-1918. In fact, those very government circles and Enver Pasha were busy trying to cope with the popular discontent of the squalid years of war and defeat by appeasing reaction. In this context, a special commission was even created

---

21 Ziya Gökalp, "İbiş Dayı" in: *Ziya Gökalp'in İlk Yazı Hayatı*, edited by Şevket Beysanoğlu, İstanbul, 1956, p.111.

to specify *çarşaf* lengths and standards for veils for women.[22] For all these reasons, the Decree on Family Law *(Hukuk-u Aile Kararnamesi)* of 1917 (H.1333), which had the status of law, did not introduce any deéppoing reforms. It was, however, considered binding for all Ottoman subjects regardless of religion, and in this respect it was the first standard legal text of its kind in any Islamic society. The decree lent women some protection against divorce and polygamy, and it imposed state supervision of marriage for Ottomans of all religions. While not going into the contents of this Decree on Family Law in any greater detail, we should point out that its claim of regulating marriage and family law for all Ottomans equally was somewhat damaged by the exceptions granted to non-Muslims through some of its individual articles.[23] Suffice it to say, then, that this never fully implemented *décret-loi* had a very short life, being abrogated in June 1919. It must have pleased neither fanatical Muslims nor those non-Muslim clericals who were afraid of losing jurisdiction over their respective congregations entirely.[24]

The daily life, socio-cultural behavior, earnings and consumption of typical families belonging to the various strata and regions of Ottoman society have yet to be researched intensively. Especially for the nineteenth century in which social change accelerated, such research should be based on combing a limited number

---

22 Falih Rıfkı Atay, *Çankaya*, İstanbul, 1968, p.407.

23 For the decree on Family Law and all other decrees issued up to the time of the promulgation of the Civil Code, see: Sabri Şakir Ansay, *Medeni Kanunun 25. Yıldönümü Münasebetiyle Eski Aile Hukukumuza Bir Nazar*, Ankara, 1952; A.Ü.H.F. This decree has also been summarised in some detail in the articles by Peter Benedict and Adnan Güriz cited below See: "Hukuk Reformu Açısından Başlık Parası ve Mehr" and "Evlilik Dışı Birleşmeler", both in *Türk Hukuku ve Toplumu Üzerine İncelemeler*, edited by A. Güriz and P. Benedict, Türk Kalkınma Vakfı, Ankara, 1974, pp.16-18, 106-109.

24 Gotthard Jaeschke, "Türkiye'de İmam Nikâhı", in *Ord Prof. Ş. Ş. Ansay'a Armağan*, Ankara, 1964, A.Ü.H.F., p.194, The translation is by Ahmet Mumcu.

of memories, birth und death registries which to be sure are not very orderly everywhere, and travelogues as well as literary works such as novels and short stories. Those of Hüseyin Rahmi Gürpınar and Ahmet Rasim, for example, as well as the scenarios for *meddah* (traditional mime) acts are of no small importance for an understanding of the way ordinary folk lived in that century. Of all Near Eastern countries in the past one hundred years, Turkey has undergone the most rapid economic change, to which not only purely agricultural and industrial growth but also legal and socio-cultural reforms have made an important contribution. Gaining an understanding of the transformation the family has gone through in the context of contemporary Turkish modernization may, therefore, be said to acquire some universal significance.

Today's Near Eastern Islamic societies survive on lands which witnessed the earliest agricultural revolution in history and, therefore, also the rise of the oldest urban communities. On the other hand, they still have not completed their industrial revolution and entered the stage of modern metropolitan life. By contrast, Europe and North America possess very brief pre-industrial histories. Hence, in investigating the family as well as many other institutions of these Near Eastern, Islamic societies, the dichotomy to keep in mind is not that between "Islamic society" on the one hand and "modern society" on the other, but that between underdeveloped metropolitan society on the one hand and developed metropolitan society on the other. It is our opinion that the seemingly different structural characteristics of the Near Eastern family should therefore be attributed to the heritage of an exceptionally long pre-industrial history of social development.

14

Ottoman Family Law and the State in the Nineteenth Century

Dedicated to Professor Ercüment Kuran for his pioneering scholarship in late Ottoman studies

The nineteenth century was an era of reform in the Ottoman Empire, not only in the administrative and military, but also in legal and cultural spheres. Compared to previous centuries, the nineteenth century Ottoman society witnessed changes in every aspect of life – and private life and family relationships were no exception. Put another way, the Ottoman citizen and the Ottoman family were much more affected by state initiated changes in legal codes and their application than ever before. The increased incidence of legal proceedings during that time is one measure of this. It is difficult to say whether or not traditional family structure and its legal status underwent the same density of change in every region of the empire, but the formulation of codes concerning the family and the mode of their implementation began in that century to lose many features they had acquired during the classical period, features which had persisted until the nineteenth century. Religious communities, which previously had followed their own socially and legally circumscribed lives and traditions, now come to be composed of family units which were required to adhere to laws promulgated by an increasingly penetrating state, were obliged to follow standard administrative procedures, and were themselves subject to a bureaucratic administrative recording system. These changes mark a transition to life in a modern state and a modern society, one based on a single universalistic legal code.

The reforms which took place during the reign of Sultan Mahmud II in the 1830s had begun the process of decreasing the jurisdiction of religious foundations *(vakıfs)* and religious *(kadı)* courts. However, despite the restriction in function, the actual volume of cases heard in such institutions had increased. During the reign of Sultan Mahmud II, changes were made in areas of concern to institutions such as the family and the inheritance system by reorganizing the pious foundations. The bureaucrats of the *Tanzimat* period attempted to implement a number of direct reforms of laws concerning inheritance, land, and the family. These developments finally bore fruit in the last years of the Ottoman Empire when the governmental Decree on Family Law, a statute considered the predecessor of the modern Republican Civil Code, was put on the books. While the *Hukuk-ı Aile Kararnamesi* of 1917, as it is known in Turkish, was a legal document which contained many contradictory provisions, it was, nevertheless, one which for the first time embraced all the subjects of the Ottoman Empire regardless of religious affiliation.

There are interesting parallels to be noted between certain changes in the family and in the law during the *Tanzimat* period. Changes in such institutions as marriage, divorce and inheritance oftentimes were surprisingly far reaching. The essential importance of these changes lies in the presence behind them of a modernist ideology and of a debate supporting that ideology. In Ottoman society, one not only encounters debates about the proper lives for modern men and women to lead, but also witnesses deviations from the moral values created by the closed environment of the traditional family. An examination of the travelogues of this period bear witness to these issues.[1]

---

1 See, for example, a German travelogue from the sixteenth century: Salomon Schweigger, *Eine Reyssbeschreibung aus Teuschland Nach Constantinopel*, Graz, 1964; İ. Ortayli, "16. Asır Alman Seyahatnamelerinde Türkiye", *Tarih ve Toplum*, 2, p.50.

In nineteenth century Turkey, the institution of marriage gradually became the focus of legal proceedings throughout the country, not just in the capital and the major cities. From that time on proceedings of that sort became subject to the knowledge and the registration of legal representatives. The fixing of marriage, divorce and guardianship and the recording of inheritance proceedings increased consistenly in the Shari'a court registers of the nineteenth century. Furthermore, these registers were not solely restricted to Muslims; beginning under the reign of Mahmud II, non-Muslims were also included in them. Even in the remote cities of Anatolia registration increased severalfold. By the end of the nineteenth century this increase had become especially striking. The impact of *Tanzimat* reforms was also very strong in a number of related areas: in the modernization of the legal system, in the transition to a fully monetary economy, in changes in land administration and in the development of a system of title deeds. In inheritance proceedings the increasing frequency with which registration of family-related proceedings took place was due in large part to the predominance of entries for assets such as vineyards, gardens and fields. We shall give examples of this below.

In the Shari'a Court registers for Ankara and Kayseri of both the early and late nineteenth century which I have studied, the number of Muslim marriage contracts shows in increase. These developments are very clearly connected with the beginnings of the practice of mandatory marriage registration. Previously, although marriages had not been registered as a matter of course, when necessary, witnesses to the marriage ceremony from the community, or the *imam* of the village or quarter were summoned, and the nuptial event was admitted to the court registers. Let us give an interesting instance of this practice. In this case a certain woman did not want to continue living with her husband. Because no record of her marriage had been made, she was able to declare to the judge that the man who claimed to be her husband had never been married to her. Her husband contested this and brought to court two people whom he claimed were witnesses to the marriage ceremony, and was therefore able to have their prior married state recorded in the registers.[2]

In almost every area of nineteenth century life the traditional social fabric of Ottoman society had to some extend begun to unravel. Such changes in social structure were to be reflected in the mechanisms of governance, and in an increasing penetration of civil authorities into the everyday and family life of its citizens. For example, the government came to accept prostitution as a reality in the big cities; it founded hospitals for victims of veneral diseases, and organized squads of moral police. Not infrequent were cases involving the abandonment of children born out of wedlock. When these children were found, they were usually delivered to the appropriate state institutions and had an allowance assigned to them. There exist many examples of this for various times and places. One or two will suffice here. In 1851, an allowance was awarded by the *Meclis-i Vala'* to a child who had been abandoned in the courtyard of a mosque in Mosul. In April 1854, in the Silivrikapı neighbourhood of İstanbul, a child who had been left in the street was handed over to the care of a woman named Hatice and had an allowance allotted to it. In a similar case occuring two years previously a child named Ferhad who had been abandoned in the street was given an allowance of 25 kuruş. There is no shortage of additional examples of this kind. In Rebiyulevvel 1268 (January 1854) a *ferman* was issued concerning the giving of allowances to children of this sort in Manastir (Vitola), İstanbul and in other cities.[3] Such allowances were even assigned for illegitimate children. In September 1854, an allowance was awarded to one Gülhiz Hatun because she

2 *Kayseri Şer'iyye Sicili*, no.194, p.9, 17 C, 1242 / January 1827 (the cases of Ali and Emine bint-i Hasan).

3 Başbakanlık Arşivi (hereafter BA), *İMV*, no.6682 and *İMV*, no.11567 (18 Safer 1270) and *İMV*, no.7822 (16 RA 1268) and *İMV*, no.8108 (2 C. 1270).

gave birth 26 months after her husband's death.[4] In addition to orphaned or abandoned children, allowances were granted to aid families with twins, triplets or handicapped infants. In 1851 in a place called Etropol near Sofia, a man named Hristos was given government money to help support his triplets. Such decrees are encountered frequently.[5]

The transformation of family law was a natural outgrowth of the other financial and administrative reforms and the social and legal changes initiated by the *Tanzimat* bureaucracy. In the centralized administrative system that Ottoman Turkey was becoming, the family was to be considered a financial unit in need of inspection and control by the state. In particular, this meant that the state needed to be informed of family events such as births, deaths, and marriages. As a consequence, in the nineteenth century, references to marriage, inheritance, and guardianship, found earlier only in the *kadı* registers also came to be inscribed in the population registers. The result of this bureaucratic imposition is the possibility of charting trends in this area to a degree not possible in earlier periods of the Ottoman Empire. It is unfortunate that the population registers for the nineteenth century have, by and large, not yet been classified, and are therefore not available for detailed investigation.

We shall see that at the end of the nineteenth and beginning of the twentieth centuries, regulations were promulgated which made mandatory the registration of such events as marriage and divorce with the Population Office *(Nüfus İdaresi)*. A number of government decrees were issued in this period in order to protect the rights of families and wives. In a document entitled *Sicill-i Nüfus Nizamnamesi* (Regulation of Registration) dated 2 September, 1881 (8 Şeval 1298), it is stated that weddings of both Muslims and non-Muslims must be performed with the

4 BA, *İMV*, no.13199 (23 Z. 1270/August-September 1854).

5 BA, *İMV*, no.7764 (28 Sefer 1268).

permission of the leaders of their spiritual communities and that these leaders as well as those registering their marriage must inform an official of the Population Office of that event. On December 18, 1884, a judgment was obtained mandating the punishment of an *imam* who had performed a marriage without receiving permission from the State Council Court. It seems clear that in circumstances where marriage did not follow legal prescriptions the state preferred that the legal authorities not intervene in such cases, but merely be cognizant of them. A decree dated 1881 impels local religious leaders, but more importantly male heads of household, to inform the Population Office in the case of a death or divorce. And finally, in the *Sicill-i Nufus Kanunu* of 27 August, 1914, some even more protective restrictions were imposed. According to this law, a husband was obliged to inform the Population Office in the event of his divorce. Likewise, the Population Office was to be informed of marriages.[6] By means of these procedures the state attempted to prevent the occurrence of marriages solely performed in the traditional fashion without the knowledge of a legal or governmental office. As a consequence, government offices took over from the religious establishment the control of the registration of the population. An important change was brought about in the penal code on 1 March, 1914, according to which the legal guardians of women under twenty years of age had to be present when a marriage permit was sought from the court. What is important is that for the first time, the rule gave women older than twenty years of age the right to apply for such a permit without approval.[7] Finally, two imperial decrees issued in 1916 increased the opportunities of women applying for divorce. As is well known, in previous eras these opportunities had been extremely limited.[8]

---

6 M. A. Aydın, *İslâm Aile Hukuku*, İstanbul, 1985, 136-148.

7 *Ibid.*, 140-141.

8 G. Jaeschke, *Yeni Türkiye'de Islamlık*, Ankara, 1972, 55; M. A. Aydın, *İslâm Aile Hukuku*, 145.

The social upheavals and reforms of the nineteenth century also had their impact on the status of women. As is already well known educational reforms led to the opening of girl's schools, and women began to enter society for the first time as teachers. Fatma Aliye, one of the first Turkish feminists and female writers was the daughter of the conservative Cevdet Pasha, whose roots extended back into the *ulema* class. Upper class women did not just follow European culture by learning to play the piano or speak foreign languages. Education had also begun to change their life style and world view. The issues of female emancipation concerned Ottoman intellectuals of all religious persuasions, indeed all Middle Eastern intellectuals. Intellectuals of all sorts, from the Azeri Mirza Fethali Ahundov to the Islamic modernist Namık Kemal, and from the Arab Muhammed Abduh to the Albano-Turk modernist Şemseddin Sami take up this issue, and it also found place in the first novels. We even know from his personal letters that the conservative Cevdet Pasha was violently opposed to polygamy.[9] Actually what we know of the pasha's behavior *en famille* refletcs a rather modern-minded approach. An interesting example exists, of the bureaucracy's attitude towards family life and women's rights in this period. In 1849, a session of the *Meclis-i Vala* (The Imperial Council of Judicial Affairs) punished a high-ranking bureaucrat, one Alaeddin Paşazade Celal Bey, for reprehensible acts against his wife.[10]

The state bureaucrats of the *Tanzimat* realized that the existing family law and marriage traditions were out of step with the world of the nineteenth century, and they attempted to work fundamental legal innovations on them. Mehmet Emin Âli Pasha even favoured adoption of the French Civil Code, but the Islamic party under the leadership of Cevdet Pasha blocked this

9 M. Kütükoğlu, "Cevdet Paşa ve Aile İçi Münasebetleri", *Ahmet Cevdet Paşa Semineri*, İstanbul University Faculty of Arts and Sciences, 186, 199-222.

10 BA, *İMV*, no.4234 (1265 H).

proposal. In spite of this, Cevdet Pasha was legislatively inactive in the field of family law, and one must point out that even in the Islamic civil code that he prepared, only the laws of goods and obligation were included; family law was entirely left out. Actually, his work was not a code at all in the modern sense of the word; it was a casuistically written legal document and did not attempt to codify and impose a standard system for all communities in the Empire. As we have indicated, it excluded the subject of family law. This work carries the name *Mecelle-i Ahkâm-i Adliye*. It has been characterized as an intellectual monument of the last century of the Ottoman Empire and the last great work of Islamic law by partisans of Cevdet Pasha and even by some contemporary legal scholars including the famous Italian scholar Giorgio del Vecchio.[11] Since it was promulgated in reaction to the French Civil Code, it must be seen as a document whose essential defect lies in its lack of courageousness in attempting to prepare a standard family code addressing all the peoples of the Ottoman Empire. It is this failing that drove progressive intellectuals in Turkey to attempt to find a modern solution to the problem of family law by continuously bringing onto the governmental agenda proposals for the adoption of a secular civil code. There was, of course the unsuccessful "Decree on Family Law" *("Hukuk-ı Aile Kararnamesi")* of 1917. These efforts to find a solution to this problem continued unabatedly until the Swiss Civil Code was adopted in 1926.

Despite the lack of success in preparing a general and secularized family code, the bureaucrats of the Tanzimat showed concern for the ordering of family affairs potentially via edicts *(ferman)* and admonitions *(tembih)* concerning family formation, that is, relating to marriage and the protection of family institutions. One of the goals of these edicts and admonitions was to do away with traditions viewed as having a negative effect

11 Giorgio del Vecchio, *Hukuk Felsefesi* (trans. S. Erman), İstanbul, 1952, 247.

on marriage. Şerafettin Turan has studied these *fermans*. He tells us that one dated May 1844 states that young girls may marry of their own free will, and that no brideprice should be paid (the word *tekalif* [tax fee] is used in the original).[12] Research that I have undertaken suggests that attention was indeed given to the implementation of this *ferman.* Decrees written for Bolu and Ankara in January 1865 state that spending moderately for a wedding strenghtens a marriage, that an Islamic dowry *(mehr)* should be fixed separately for the four classes of society and orders conformity to these structures.[13] Turan mentions another *ferman* dating from 1863 in which the Islamic dowry payment is differentiated into three classes, with one standard one for the poor, another for the middle class, and one for the rich, these being 100, 500, and 1000 kuruş respectively.[14] Were the structures of these *fermans* actually complied with? Except for a very restricted segment of society it is very difficult to say. But in the event of a dispute, the dictates of these *fermans* were binding in court. It is significant that for the first time, a topic directly concerning the Shari'a was reordered by subjecting it to the control of the civil authorities, that is to imperial decrees which were both binding and implemented in a standardized fashion. It is important to note that standardized norms were set forth without taking into consideration the differences between the norms and codes of the four schools of Islamic jurisprudence (Shafi'i, Maliki, Hanbali and Hanafi). Furthermore, in 1850 two imperial decrees were issued which stipulated severe punishments for a kind of "marriage by abduction" *(kız kaçırma)*, a practice still prevalent in parts of Anatolia.[15]

---

12 S. Turan, "Tanzimat Devrinde Evlenme", *İş ve Düşünce Dergisi* (22) 182 (1956), 14-15.

13 BA, *Cevdet-Dahiliye*, no.11586 (29 Z. 1261/January, 1845).

14 Turan, *op. cit.*, 15.

15 BA, *İMV*, no.5470 (16 Za 1266/September 1850), and *İMV*, no.4758 (22 Ra 1266/March 1850).

DEVELOPMENTS IN INHERITANCE LAW

During the *Tanzimat*, one is struck by the tendency toward creating a standardized legal structure in matters of family law concerning inheritance. It would not be an exaggeration to state that particularly in inheritance matters the law had begun to become both standardized and secularized. There were two essential stages to this process in relation to Ottoman law. The more important stage was the standardization of the codes themselves; the second began when both Muslims and non-Muslims showed an actual preference for utilizing the same legal institutions for matters of inheritance. A turning point in the Ottoman inheritance system came with the Land Law of 1858 (1274). Ö. L. Barkan, who undertook the first detailed study of this decree, emphasizes this aspect of its significance.[16] The purpose of the decree was the development of a liberal system of land ownership in the *Tanzimat* period, one which would replace the antiquated *tımar* system of landholding which dated from the classical Ottoman period. This law increased the distribution of titled land and in many places encouraged the development of medium and small-sized land holdings. The institutionalization of private landownership certainly reordered inheritance procedures in a way quite different that they had been in the past.

One important feature of the law was that in comparison with the past, it placed men and women on an equal legal footing with respect to the inheritance of land. Accordingly, daughters of the deceased were to receive the same share as sons, and even if there were no sons, they were to receive shares as if they were males, despite the existence of other more distant male heirs. In actuality, cases recorded in nineteenth-century *kadı* registers usually do not adhere to this law, and female offspring continued to receive only half shares, following earlier Islamic precepts. In

16 Ö. L. Barkan, "Türk Toprak Hukuku Tarihinde Tanzimat ve 1274 (1858) Tarihli Arazi Kanunnamesi" in Ö. L. Barkan, *Türkiye'de Toprak Meselesi*, İstanbul, 1980, 353-355.

practice a double standard for female heirs persisted into the twentieth century with respect to matters of inheritance.

Starting at the beginning of the nineteenth century, some non-Muslim groups seen to have adopted the standardized inheritance procedures as much as did Muslim groups. Here, it was not a case of everyone being forced by legal *ukaz* to conform to the same procedures. Particularly in cases involving land inheritance, non-Muslims also began to apply to *kadı* courts and thereby divide their inheritances according to the same system as that of the Muslims. In studies I have undertaken in the Ankara and Kayseri *kadı* registers from the beginning to the end of the nineteenth century, one witnesses Greeks, as well as Protestant, Catholic, and Gregorian, Armenians applying to the *kadı* courts for the settling of estates. This was not, however, the case for the small urban communities of Jews in those regions of the country. With the exception of Jews, all land-owning Ottoman subjects, regardless of religious affiliation, adopted the same system of inheritance. Let us list a few cases from the Ankara court registers from the reign of Mahmud II. There are many examples of the division of estates among Armenians. One of these even belongs to the famous *zengin* and *Amira* Düzoğlu Kirkor.[17] Also in this era one notes that female trustees received inheritance shares in preference to small children who were also heirs, and in the family women were appointed as guardians in preference to uncles and grandfathers of the deceased.[18]

By the end of the nineteenth century, we observe an increase in cases concerning the division of estates of non-Muslims. To give a few examples: there are records of the division of the estate of one Artin in Kayseri in January 1888 (CA 1305), in January 1891 (CA 1308) for the Greek Orthodox Karakuşoğlu Simon[19]

17 *Ankara Şer'iyye Sicili*, no.226, p.136.

18 *Kayseri Şer'iyye Sicili*, no.194, 7 Za 1242/June 1827, p.38; another case from (15 Za 1242/June 1827), p.41.

19 *Ibid.*, no.241, pp.7-8.

in the village of Kerim near Kayseri, and in the village of Nence for Serkis, son of the Gregorian Armenian Hacı Serkis in March 1888 (CA 1305). In the same register, the estate of Artin, son of the Armenian Cırcıroğlu Kirkor of Kayseri was assessed at 42,440 kuruş. In February 1888, this estate, valued at 41,080 kuruş after the deduction of legal expenses, was divided as follows:[20]

His Wife	5,135
His Son Artin	14,378
His Son Karabet	14,378
His Daughter Samnaz	7,189

As can be observed from these figures, the estate was divided in complete accordance with Islamic laws of inheritance *(feraiz)*, with the daughter receiving a half share.

The same *defter* records the case of one Kirkor, of the Tus quarter of Kayseri, whose estate was divided along similar principles. In this case, the division of the estate of the deceased also included an assessment of his land holdings.

Shares of Cash Assets Landholding		**Shares in Landholding**	
His wife	4722 kuruş		3644 kuruş
His son Kirkor	7439 kuruş	6378	2160 kuruş
His son Sevan	7439 kuruş	6378	2160 kuruş
His daughter	4219 kuruş	3189	1030 kuruş
His daughter	4219 kuruş	3189	1030 kuruş
His daughter	4219 kuruş	3189	1030 kuruş

In the Ankara *kadı* court records (number 306) one notes that the *kadı* received applications in inheritance cases from Armenian Protestants from Ankara itself, but especially from the district of Zir. As we have seen, the implementation of inheritance law in the nineteenth century runs parallel with the application

20 *Ibid.*, pp.10, 15.

of standardized procedures to law concerning land tenure and to the development of a monetary economy. These developments encompassed Ottoman subject of all religious persuasions.[21]

CONDITIONS PREVENTING MARRIAGE AND RELATED LEGAL PROCEDURES

In contrast to contemporary Turkish law, during the Ottoman period the state was not concerned with regulations requiring medical examinations prior to marriage or with other situations which might potentially prevent marriage from occuring. Indeed, Ottoman law had very few regulations which might prevent marriage. Only as late as March 23, 1916 did a decree allow courts to try divorce cases in which the wife had contracted certain specified illnesses from her husband.[22] According to classical Islamic law, only the marriage of a Muslim woman to a non-Muslim could be prevented. This rule also applied to the marriage of non-Muslims of different religions, so that a Christian and a Jew were not permitted to marry. Indubitably this was a situation that the non-Muslim communities would themselves have restricted. The essential principle of Ottoman law involved was that of preventing a female Ottoman subject of whatever religion from marrying a man of foreign nationality.

The origin of this principle lies in Ottoman law of the classical period, which forbids men who are not Ottoman subjects from marrying Ottoman females whatever their religion. This regulation was also adhered to in the nineteenth century, and even if they were Muslims, marriage to Iranians was forbidden. In other words, this was a requirement of Ottoman personal law which was applied without exception to all Ottoman women. For instance in accordance with the law, an imperial decree sent to the vilayet of Nish in eastern Serbia in January 1851 (25 RA

21 *Ibid.*, p.17, and *Ankara Şer'iyye Sicili*, no.306.

22 M. A. Aydın, *op. cit.*, 148.

1267) outlawed marriage of the women of this region to men of the Principality of Serbia.[23] Again, a decree issued in December 1853 forbade the marriage of the daughter of a Greek Orthodox sea captain named Anderliyo (?) to a doctor of Greek citizenship. Another decree dated August 1850 outlawed the marriage of Jewish women of Salonica to Tuscan Jews resident in that city. This same document orders the commissioner of nationality *(teba tefrik memuru)* Ahmed Rasim Bey to investigate and pursue any such cases.[24] As we have just indicated, this law also applied to Muslim women. For example, a woman who had married an Iranian man in Tire in the İzmir region had to have her marriage annulled.[25] The ban on Ottoman women marrying Iranian men remainted on the books up until the last days of the empire,[26] and was, as we have seen, part and parcel of the Ottoman state legal structure.

In the last years of the Ottoman Empire, a codified document on family law, the *Hukuk-u Aile Kararnamesi*, was issued. This document legally encompassed all subjects of the Ottoman Empire. As a document of family law it is far from perfect.[27] Indeed, like the nineteenth century adoption of French commercial, penal and administrative law codes, this law was the end product of a broader mentality which resulted in the Europeanization of many aspects of Ottoman law. Despite claims to comprehensive jurisdiction for Ottomans of all religions, it is a document full of contradictions and exceptions that violate the general principles it lays out. This law was short-lived, lasting only from its promulgation in 1917 until June of 1919. Its importance lies in the fact that it laid

23 BA, *İMV*, no.6185.

24 BA, *İ. Har.*, no.5109 and OMV, no.5129 (17 Şeval 1266/August 1850).

25 A. M. Armağan, *Batı Anadolu Tarihinde İlginç Olaylar*, İzmir, 1984, 15.

26 M. A. Aydın, *op. cit.*, 141.

27 For a study of the 1917 Family Law, see S. Şakir Ansay, *Medeni Kanunun 25. Yıldönümü Münasebetiyle Eski Aile Hukukumuza Bir Nazar*, Ankara, 1952; M. A. Aydın, *op. cit.*, 151-239.

much of the groundwork for the Republican Civil Code of 1926. The religious leaders of the non-Muslim communities, as well as fanatical Muslims, opposed the family law on the grounds that it deprived them of their jurisdictional authority over members of their religious communities.

CONCLUSION

The nineteenth century did not produce of secular and uniform family code law in the Ottoman Empire. However, the course of events during that century necessitated certain legal changes, palliative though they may have been. Though of an Islamic nature, such legal developments were open to the influences of European law. Numerous projects emerged during the century to provide all religious communities in the Empire with uniform marriage, divorce, and inheritance codes. Given the reception accorded to European procedure, criminal, and commercial law, there clearly was a leaning toward the acceptance of such a family code. There certainly was, at a minimum, a movement in the direction of a uniform code encompassing all the communities with respect to inheritance and the registration of marriages. The various regulations and family law projecs of the period never were actually implemented in full. And their eclectic structure, a dualism of traditional Islamic law and of European jurisprudence, was carried into the Republican period as part of the Ottoman legal heritage. The 1926 Republican Civil Code attempted to produce a radical solution to the various problems resulting from that dualist structure. Changing family structures in twentieth century Turkey provided impetus for the increasing influence of the new law and for its widespread implementation and acceptance.

15

Some Notes on Modern Turkish Historical Drama

In contemporary society, conciousness of history equates the consciousness of politics. The interpretation of history is the source which shapes political action and ideology. Eighteenth and nineteenth century nationalism perceives history as the proof of national rights and liberty. Consciousness of history is the principal instrument of society in constructing its own future. This situation does not apply only to the longing for independence of the dependent peoples of Eastern Europe. Guiding history teaching and the science of history in accordance with an official dogma and censorhip in Alexandre II's Russia and Abdülhamid II's Ottoman Empire is significant in this respect.

Liberal thoughts have found means to influence large segments of people through historical novels and historical plays. Historical subjects had offered enormous possibilities to the writers to outline the anatomy of the phenomenon of political power and to teach the role of the individual towards society, and history. As Lindberger puts it, "When history reaches its own consciousness it explains itself through the theatrical expressions."[1] In the novel and drama of the eighteenth and nineteenth centuries, works with historical themes contributed to the literary splendor of the languages in which they were written. Historical novel and drama reflect the intellectual level of the society which produces it.

1 Lindberger, H., *Historical Drama*, Chicago, 1975, p.29.

In 1788 Goethe, in his well-known drama "Egmont" introduces to us a hero displaying a new interpretation of history, a hero who dies for the freedom of Holland. Whereas, it is known that the real Egmont did not possess any of these virtues, Goethe's interpretation is based upon the nationalist and liberalist perceptions of the Enlightennment Age. "Jungfrau von Orleans" and "Wallestein" of Schiller were the new interpretations which were the product of this novel approach. The historical drama in the Western world underwent and is still undergoing an interesting evolution, from the nationalist and individual heroism – which changes history – of the Enlightenment Age up to the works reflecting the political trends of our era.

I.

Historical drama has been introduced rather recently in the history of Turkish theater.

It starts at the end of the nineteenth century and is still in its prime.[2] The contemporary Turkish drama writer although he gives some contradictory examples, is getting to be more and more experienced in the subject of using history as his material.

During the Hamidian era – also called the period of despotism – not many historical plays had been written, for it was the "censorship authorities" who were distrustful of the objectives supposedly hidden behind these plays. A play of Namık Kemal entitled "Vatan" which is an outsanding example and whose subject was the defense of the fortress of Silistra during the Crimean War, could have a certain effect on this.[3]

2 It is difficult to say that Turkish drama researchers and critics deal with historical drama seriously. Two descriptive works took into consideration these subjects: 1. Sevda Şener, *Çağdaş Türk Tiyatrosunda Ahlâk-Ekonomi Kültür Sorunları*, Ankara, 1971, 2. Metin And, *Türk Tiyatrosunun Evreleri*, Ankara, 1983. It is known that a thesis is prepared by Hülya Nutku in İzmir University covering this subject.

3 We can mention *Calaleddin Harzemshah* of Namık Kemal, *Fatih Sultan Mehmet* of Mehmet Rıfat, *Zuhur-i Osmanniyyan* of Ahmet Mithat (apparently)

Historical plays very rarely were written in the style of "heroic history" about the Ottoman dynasty. But it is known that some historical dramas have been written and printed secretly here and there (for example in Egypt). In 1908, with the proclamation of the Constitutional Monarchy *(Meşrutiyet)* for the second time, along with the publications of the Turkish authors on translated works, various dailies, novels and short stories dealing with near and far history, scores of plays began to be written in Turkish and even in some other languages practised in the Ottoman Empire.[4] Most of the themes of these plays dealing with Midhat Pasha, today in the 100th year of his demise, are hardly treated as enthusiastically as it had been then. Contrary to the 1908 writer who treats this subject in a rather naive style, today's progressist writer who discusses thoroughly the political personalities and the revolutionary movements of the nineteenth century acts quite timidly when it comes to deal with Midhat Pasha. Although Haldun Taner started to write a play on this subject he declared *(Milliyet* Doc. 18, 1983) that he would not continue this venture, and Orhan Asena who was writing about the trial in Yıldız, also could not terminate his play.

We observe that lots of plays have been written and staged during the period of Constitutional Monarchy. These plays written in an extremely naive way of thinking and style had a nationalistic and didactic nature as if they were written to teach history. The subject matter as well as the material source of these work were chronicles or history text books. As pointed out by Reşat Nuri Güntekin most of the historical plays of this period were childish and vulgar. Among these works we can mention *Feth-i Aydost Ghazi Abdurrahman, Kandiye Burcunda, Bizansın Sukutu, Sultan Selim'in Vefatı ve Alemdar Pasha, Sultan Mahmud-ı Sani, Deli*

among these. Metin And, "Türk Tiyatroşunda Tarihi Oyunlar", *VII. Türk Tarih Kongresi*, vol.II, Ankara, 1977, pp.769-70.

4 Metin And, "Türk Tiyatrosunda Tarihi Oyunlar ve Bunların Yazılış Gerekçeleri", *VIII. Türk Tarih Kongresi*, vol.II, Ankara, 1977, p.770.

Petro-Baltacı Mehmet Pasha. In a list established by Metin And one notes that several plays deal with Mehmed the Conqueror and the conquest of İstanbul.[5] The next popular theme is Selim III. It is strange that although plays on the subject of Mehmed the Conqueror and the conquest are still being written today (plays of Nazım Kurşunlu and Turan Oflazoğlu) these works have naive contents which cannot compete with the level of the modern Turkish drama literature. Somehow in the Turkish historical plays it appears that the subject of Mehmed the Conqueror can only be dealt with in the dullest and the most insipid manner.

A new conception of historianism from the standpoint of ideological fundamentals had emerged in the Republican era. One may safely argue that re-awakening of nationalist sentiments in Europe between two world wars might have, from time to time, had impacts on this ideology, but speaking in more basic or concrete terms the nineteenth century type of romantic nationalism made its appearance particularly on the stage with naive representations. Themes treated by these neo-nationalist playwrights were mostly those of pre-islamic Turkish history rather than of Ottoman history. Representative of the period in question: Faruk Nafiz Çamlıbel's *Akın*, Yaşar Nabi Nayır's *Özyurt ve Mete* and Behçet Kemal Çağlar's *Çoban ve Attila* can be cited as examples in this category.[6] The plays of this era give the impression of having been scribbled on the spur of the moment, as if swayed by the breezes of fashion of those days rather than being products which reflect a profound philosophy and "Weltanschauung". Let us add that most of those playwrights in their later works hardly ever returned to such works. At the time, needless to say, there existed quite a few writers who strongly opposed such preachings of romantic nationalism whose revelations came from the paganist era. One of such writers, Yahya Kemal, in one of his

5 Metin And, *Türk Tiyatrosunun Evreleri*, Ankara, 1983, p.339.

6 Sevda Şener, *Çağdaş Türk Tiyatrosunda Ahlâk-Ekonomi, Kültür Sorunları*, Ankara, 1971, pp.152-156, 158, 160.

essays criticized Hüseyin Cahit (Yalçın) in the following words: "Instead of writing of imaginary Turkish conquests of Japan, dwell upon the more recent and more real conquests, those of the Ottomans."[7] Speaking of fashionable movements, another one was set on its way out of respect for the tenth anniversary of the establishment of the Turkish Republic. Plays of this period do not occupy a significant place in the Turkish literature of drama, since they seem to be in tune with the conception of official historianism, resembling works designed for school and public centre representations subject matter of which are the War of Independence and Kemalist reforms.

Of the period, however, two historical playwrights appear to stand out: Musahipzade Celal Bey and Reşat Nuri Güntekin. The former has constructed his plays within the traditional technique of *orta oyunu* against a carefully designed setting of historic decor and costumes. In the spirit of republican propaganda he conveys to the audience not only decadence and bribery or other corrupt practices in the Ottoman bureaucracy, but also sufferings and suppression of ordinary people and artisans caused by the *ulema* and administrators. His plays are interwoven with pungent social criticism. The writer largely owes his enduring reputation and popularity to the skill with which he treats the old way of life and traditional drama as well as to the fact that he has so successfully utilized the traditional technique.[8] His social criticism, on the other hand, is depicted to have its limitations and is somewhat circumspected with a naive level of thought no matter how republicanist it may be.

The latter playwright, on the other hand, although not acknowledged by literary circles as an active one in the realm of historical drama, is worthy of noting especially for his play *Yaprak Dökümü* which Güntekin adapted from a novel of his

7 Y. Kemal (Beyatlı), *Tarih Musahabeleri*, 1975, p.83-85.

8 S. Şener, *ibid*, p.22; M. And, *ibid*, p.502.

under the same title. Performed at the Municipal Theater of İstanbul during the 1943-1944 season, the play brings to light how the process of modernization in the Republican era affected the life of a traditional middle class family living in İstanbul. The family under limelight due to a pointless passion for a modern mode of life, is gradually driven into a state of financial and moral decay thus compelled in the end to drift apart from each other. This play which is based on realistic descriptions as distinct from others, is not one of a naive structure. Therefore, it is of particular interest for students of anthropology. In fact, it was this play which, for the first time in the life of Turkish theatre, enjoyed such popularity as to have been successively performed over one hundred times, while the usual practice in show business in those days was to run only a limited number of performances. Thus, one may assume that the play which focused a criticism on the evolving Turkish society within a span of a decade or so, had led the audience to a rather serious contemplation of the issue.

II.

The fifties, perhaps mark off the beginning of a path whereby Turkish historical drama assumes more diversified forms, colour and flavour, especially when the peculiar development of social criticism following the sixties is taken into account. It goes without saying that the realm of historical drama is a cross-road where various ideas and residues of recent history find their expression. Consequently the playwright of our time also is in a day-to-day pursuit of updating himself with changing ideas just as Turkish society is. A prevalent view that radical reforms in Turkish society are consequently degenerated by residues of the ancient order has been transmitted into the stage through historical drama.

The tragedy of Alemdar Mustafa Pasha who with the Rumelian army had marched against İstanbul in 1809 was ironically re-lived a century later (1908) by revolutionaries who too marched from Rumeli to İstanbul. The first incident is depicted in Orhan Asena's *Tohum ve Toprak*, whereas the second one is to have found expression in Kemal Bekir's play *Düşüş* which is an adaptation from a novel called *Abdülhamit Düşerken* by N. Sırrı Örik.

Asena in *Tohum ve Toprak* construes the tragedy of Alemdar Pasha linking it to our time and drawing meaningful parallels between Alemdar and progressive, well-meaning army officers of the 1960 military coup who due to a similar unfavourable medium were also doomed to fail.[9] The Reformist is a good seed but the soil in which it is planted causes its decay. It is the rotten milieu and scheming bureaucracy which have obscured the well-meaning reformist's path to success as the Palace had done back in 1809. One can draw a certain parallel between Asena's *Tohum ve Toprak* and Kemal Bekir's *Düşüş*. Both of them have chosen their characters from among the officers who accomplished the military coup. In the adaptation of Kemal Bekir a young revolutionary officer who is a member of the Union and Progress Party joins hands in matrimony with the daughter of a Hamidian vizier, but provoked by his wife and overcome by his ambitions is driven to a point, in the end, where he betrays his ideals and friends. At the time when Örik was working on his novel, likewise, young bureaucrats and leading staff of the young Turkish Republic were making acquaintances and establishing ties both with business as well as other "in" circles in İstanbul. It has been argued that Kemal Bekir dramatized this same novel in order to show how reforms in Turkish history are being abruptly assimilated by the ancient order. In contrast to Örik's novel Kemal Bekir's adaptation displays a subtle sympathy for anti-Young Turk attitude and an inclination to the effect that the Hamidian regime possessed more *raison d'état*.

9 Orhan Asena, *Tohum ve Toprak*, Ankara, 1964, pp.10-12; Nahid Sırrı Örik, *Abdülhamit Düşerken*, 2nd ed. İstanbul, 1976.

The popular conception of history in the fifties, on the other hand, seemed to view the intrigues of the Harem in the Palace and the matrimonies of the Ottoman Sultan with concubines of foreign origin as one of the principal reasons for the decline of the Empire. As a matter of fact, such interpretations were even inserted into history textbooks taught in school curricula.[10] This same idea venturing to explain the decadence of the Ottoman dynasty is expressed in Orhan Asena's *Hürrem Sultan* which was written in the fifties. In this work grand vizier Rüstem Pasha and Hürrem Sultan[11] are depicted as accomplices masterminding the elimination of Prince Mustafa, the eldest son of Suleiman the Magnificent. Hürrem is portrayed as a sort of Lady Macbeth. It would not be unfair to say that the author failed to describe Hürrem as a *sui generis* character. She is merely depicted as a two-dimensional theatrical type and is presented as a character with general traits almost along parallel lines with Bafo of Venice (Safiye Sultan) or Kösem Sultan or like any other "Haseki Sultan" burning with desire for political power. In a more recent play written after 25 years by the same writer, however, Hürrem Sultan is portrayed with human characteristics which reflect the more refined conception of history of the society in which the writer lives.

Another misleading point, which found access to school textbook in the framework of the popular conception of history of the forties and fifties, was to attribute to a large extent the losses of the Pruth War by Baltacı Mehmed Pasha to the intrigues of Katharina and to his passion for earthly goods.[12] Haldun Taner, in a comedy *Lütfen Dokunmayın* challenged this conviction with a rather sceptical approach. In this comedy two characters are portrayed giving contradictory advice to a girl student doing

10 *Tarih III*, edit, by T. T. Tetkik Cemiyeti, İstanbul, 1933, p.118.

11 Orhan Asena, *Hürrem Sultan*, Ankara, 1959.

12 *Tarih III*, p.144.

research in a museum on the Peace Treaty of Pruth: Nesib Bey and Ekmel. In the eyes of Nesib Bey, a classical Ottoman scholar, Baltacı is a man of corruption and lust *(haza Kastamonu ayısı)*, whereas, according to Ekmel, a diplomat having studied the western historiographical sources on the subject, the real picture of Baltacı and the Pruth war is far from what had been painted until then, for the war was a risky adventure to start with and Baltacı, surely, was not to be blamed. In the views of a third character, Oktay, a guide interpreter in the museum, Baltacı Mehmed Pasha and Katharina are merely two people seized by fate in the course of history. They should be viewed in this perspective.

By the early sixties socialism and leftist thought have become an issue of extensive debate in the country. It was held that a kind of socialist progressist spirit no matter how naive it might have been, had run through the traditions of the Turkish people all along. It was this political climate which led Orhan Asena to draw up *Şeyh Bedreddin* in 1969. The same writer composed another drama *Atçalı Kel Mehmet* in those years in which *Atçalı*, an epic hero, is portrayed who resorted to robbery to serve the cause of justice during the reign of Mahmud II. Asena's interpretation of *Atçalı* is one of a historical personality with anti-feudal romanticist sentiments at times displaying progressist characteristics. A contrasting view holding that robbers who appear to be heroic can be nothing but a subject of mockery is elaborated in Kemal Tahir's novel *Rahmet Yolları Kesti*.

Similarly, such plays as İsmet Küntay's *Tozlu Çizmeler* and Ergin Orbey's *Birinci Kurtuluş* were drawn up during these years in attempts to bring into light the progressist spirit of the War of Independence. When political ideas and spirit of these days underwent change, such work fell out of grace.

As a matter of fact, the changing political atmosphere of the seventies led to the creation of a different type of historical drama.

During the 70-71 theater season Turan Oflazoğlu's *Murat IV* was staged as the main production of the State Theater.[13] This work portrays Murat IV as a despotic monarch symbolizing authority and power who has wiped anarchy out of the seventeenth century. The drama prossesses a chronological development and content. The first act is a description of the revolt and anarchy right outside the walls of the Palace, whereas the second act reaches a climax when an agreement among the people, the *ulema* class of the empire and the army is concluded to ensure complete allegiance order to Sultan Murat IV. Perhaps it is this scene which corresponds to the aspirations for authority and order to Turkey of the seventies. Throughout the third act, when everyone is annoyed with Sultan Murat's despotism, an inner conflict and a tragic dilemma prevail between despotic authority and liberty.

Orhan Asena's play *Ya devlet başa ya kuzgun leşe*,[14] which was performed by the State Theatre as a main production during the 82-83 season, was also drawn up in a similar atmosphere inciting the same aspirations for power. The sons of Suleiman the Magnificent are compelled to indulge in deadly struggles for the throne in order to avoid the alternative of being executed for the sake of public order. Of the rival princes Bayezid is an austere and rash person whose conduct and intrigues build up to an outright revolt. Upon this, Suleiman the Magnificent is faced with a tragic dilemma of choosing between protection of the authority of the throne and yielding to the love of his son. Not only the person of the Sultan, but others are going through the same dilemma; Hürrem Sultan as the mother of the princes, the viziers for the security of their future, Prince Selim and Bayezid. When judging Bayezid's rebellious attitude, Sultan Suleiman poses a question "What is crime, after all? Where does it start and where does it end?" and proceeds

13 Turan Oflazoğlu, *IV. Murat*, Ankara, 1982.

14 *Aut Caesar aut nihil.*

"Should thought be suppressed just because it might give rise to anarchy, what if there is a sparkle in it?" Nevertheless, this impasse is easily resolved by the writer in conformity with the political atmosphere of the day, for in a scene toward the end in which he is speaking to the ghost of Hürrem Sultan, we hear him saying "I am no more a kind father to my son, but a ruler against a rebel challenging the authority of the state."[15] With this practical but naive conclusion the work ceases to be tragedy. The resolution of the problem to this effect, in a way, exposes the prevailing spirit in recent Turkish history, in other words, there seems to be a trend in which periods of aspirations for more liberty and more tolerance paradoxically are followed by periods of intolerant authoritarian politics. Thus, in sharp contrast to tragic ends, Asena's drama concludes in a rather simplistic ejaculation.

Turgut Özakman is considered to be a humorist playwright in the Turkish historical drama. Although satirical or humorous elements are not depicted in his other works, Özakman particularly displays humour in his historical dramas. In fact, in their treatment of Ottoman history the generation of the 1920s appear to have adopted an ironic or satirical style of writing rather than reflecting a certain "Weltanschauung" or conscience. In the essayist Salah Birsel, for example, one can observe a similar attitude.

The same is true for Özakman's comedy *Sarıpınar 1914* which is an adaptation from a novel called *Değirmen* by Reşat Nuri Güntekin. Misinformed administrators in an Anatolian town, Sarıpınar, send an ill-founded message to İstanbul to the effect that the town is stricken by an earthquake. On receiving

15 This is an unusual instance of a soliloquy being written in capital letters, in the publications of the play by the State Theater: "benim sözüm bir baba sözüydü. Yüreği yufka insan sözü, şimdi bir çiğnenen DEVLET var. DEVLETİ ÇİĞNENEN HÜKÜMDAR. Bir de o DEVLETİ çiğneyen ASİ, p.103.

this message an international commission under the auspices of the crown-prince is set up and charity campaigns start. Finally members of the commission arrive at Sarıpınar finding the local administrators in a fit of fear. But their confusion and fears are in vain, because even the normal state of affairs in the town gives the impression of nothing else but a disaster-stricken area to newcoming observes from İstanbul and European centres.

Özakman, in his play *Resimli Osmanlı Tarihi* which was performed in the 82-83 season, employs a simple trick. A public functionary reading an illustrated Ottoman history in the year of 1960, goes back in time to 1875. From what he has read of the book in the

İstanbul of 1875 which happened to have been printed in Latin script, he is able to prophesy as a sort of *Nostradamus*. Since the truth he speaks annoys everyone, he finds himself in all sorts of troubles, but he is not in a position to change the course of events. The reactions of monarchs such as Abdülaziz, Murat V, Abdülhamid II and other statesmen, in the face of these developments, are described with colour and irony. Sultan Abdülhamid, for instance, a believer in the predictions of the book (an illustrated history) is aware of the fact that he cannot escape his fate. Keeping the book for himself he learns how to read Turkish in the Latin alphabet. Midhat Pasha, finding out that the predictor comes from Ankara inquires whether he happens to live around the Mosque of Hacıbayram. The answer he gets is shocking. The predictor lives right on the corner where Meşrutiyet Avenue crosses Midhat Pasha Avenue. Besides, jokes on the constitution of 1982 were very much appreciated by the audience at a time when the constitution of 1982 was in the making. With the exception of "Illustrated Ottoman History" which is in the style of a naive comedy, political cabaret theatre whereby powerful political criticisms are made has not fully flourished.

III.

Orhan Asena with *Gılgamış* and Güngör Dilmen with *Midasın Kulakları* have produced promising samples of drama-writing based on mythology. Later this trend, too, seems to have come to a halt.

The changing political trends of the day and some current topics occasionally serve to incite the writer to scribble historical plays, but these works are devoid of enduring values.

In the last analysis, in the domain of historical drama the Turkish dramatist is unable to create interesting characters, despite some recent endeavours.

RUSSIA AND TURKEY

Sultan Abdülmecid and Czar Nicolas I.

16

Reports and Considerations of Ismail Bey Gasprinskii in Tercüman on Central Asia

Russian expansion in Central Asia was a matter of greater concern for Ismail Bey Gasprinskii who closely followed local developments in the region, commenting about them in the columns of his paper *Tercüman*. His attention was mainly concentrated on the following points: (a) the issue of the integration of the central Asian provinces into the Russian Empire, (b) modernizing currents in the Islamic world and modern Islam, and (c) the westernization of the Oriental peoples in Russia. It should be clear that Gasprinskii was convinced of the benefits of the civilizing and westernizing role of Russia in its relations with Oriental peoples. This did not prevent him, however, from criticizing and attacking chauvinistic Russian Orthodox circles who opposed his conception of pan-Islam and reformist Islam.

Reports and articles on Central Asia, published in *Tercüman*, were all written by Gasprinskii himself and provide us with an insight on the views of a reformist Muslim thinker on such issues as cultural modernization, social evolution, Russian civilization and administration. It appears that the views on Western civilization of an Islamic reformist from Russia differ from those of his Ottoman-Turkish or Arab counterparts. Gasprinskii supports the Abdülhamid regime in the Ottoman Empire. This support is a genuine one, stemming not from a concern with censorship. In particular he is praiseful of reforms in the educational fields to which he devotes much space in his paper.

Gasprinskii was quite clear in his mind about the solidarity of the Islamic peoples. He never intended to open a discussion about rituals, faith, dogma and the legal structure of Islam, because he lacked a thorough knowledge of these questions. For him Islam was only a cultural and political entity, a cohesive defense against the West. Yet, he strongly advocated the adoption of Western institutions like secular education, women's emancipation, commercial and industrial enterprise and the development of capitalism. He naively notes that whereas all other native groups in colonial possessions had made great progress in education and trade, the Muslims were still lagging behind in a backward environment.[1]

His is a pan-Islam based on values adopted from the West. The great laboratory of westernization that was the Russian Empire encouraged Muslim intellectuals to adopt the institutions of Western civilization. Both Gasprinskii's predecessors and his contemporaries, men like Mirza Kazem Bey, Akhundov, and later Huseyin Zerdabi-Melikoff, A. M. Topçubaşev, or Akçuraoğlu, shared with him this *Weltanschauung*.

Gasprinskii's conception of Islam is a defensive one, rallying to the support of oppressed and backward Muslim peoples. The following quote is only one from the many appearing in numerous issues of *Tercüman* where he tackles this problem:[2]

> Whenever the Orient tries to organize itself and fight injustice and poverty, many reactionary European and Russian papers start a campaign against this Renaissance, talking of the resurgence of militant pan-Islam. If the Slavs are allowed to have their pan-Slavism and the Greeks their pan-Hellenism, why should we not have our pan-Islam.

Obviously Gasprinskii identified and interpreted the pan-Islamic ideology in secular and nationalist terms. In one issue of *Tercüman*, he even went as far as expressing a positive opinion

1 *Tercüman*, 26 November 1895.

2 *Ibid.*, 7 July 1909.

on Babism, albeit in a naive way. An Azerbaijani Babî with liberal views and a sound intellect had visited Gasprinskii in Baku and seems to have impressed him.[3] Gasprinskii pointed out that some Armenians and Jews had been attracted by the new faith which recognized equal rights to all religions and aimed at establishing a peaceful world order. Muslim modernists of that age seem to share a common interest and sympathy for Babism. Cemaleddin Al-Afghani's approach to Babism is now being widely criticized by Islamic fundamentalists.

Again like most of his Oriental contemporaries, Gasprinskii is full of praise for Japanese modernism. On the other hand, unlike the Young-Turk opposition, he is very respecful of the authority of Sultan Abdülhamid II. In almost every other issue of *Tercüman* there is a reference to the Sultanete and Caliphate. On March 19, 1895, there is a lengthy description of the state visit paid by the Sultan to the "Holy Relics" at Topkapı Palace, proudly emphasizing the imperial pomp and representative role of the Sultan-Caliph in the Muslim world.[4]

Making a clear distinction between British policy in the Afro-Asian colonies and Russian administration in Central Asia, Gasprinskii does not hesitate to state that the Muslim lands subjected to Russian role cannot be considered as colonies. These are provinces, he says, and he claims that Russians are not exploiting these lands since expenditures and investments by far exceed any revenue yielded: "In the Central Asian provinces, the Russian Treasury has spent during the past twenty-five years over 100 million rubles whereas the yearly revenues hardly reach 2 million rubles."[5]

Although he challenged and combated in *Tercüman* the views of the nationalist and reactionary Russian press, Gasprinskii was adamant in his advice to Muslim intellectuals, that they should cooperate with liberal Russian intellectuals and administrators to

3 *Ibid.*, 20 January 1895.

4 *Ibid.*, 19 March 1895.

5 *Ibid.*, 14 May 1895.

solve the educational problem in Central Asia.[6] In his paper he continuously stressed the civilizing role of Russia.

One of his leading articles provides a good example for his case: "The most powerful and gigantic state of our era, though looking at its 1,000-year history, Russia is still to be numbered among the young and promising countries, full of hopes to achieve the task of developing and enriching its resources."[7]

One of the aspects of Russian administration of Central Asia which Gasprinskii favored most was the sedentarization of the nomadic tribes. This dramatic operation, which he praises as a "civilizing process" – for which he was to some extent right – is covered in detail in several issues of *Tercüman*, which also applauds the opening of new Russian schools and the extension of cotton growing in Turkestan. Gasprinskii points out that Tashkent had greatly benefited from Russian rule and can be compared favorably with many Caucasian towns. "Locals have learned Russian and local craftsmen have improved their skills thanks to their exposure to Russia techniques and know-how." Yet he deplores that cultural and social structures have not evolved at the same pace, society retaining its backward patriarchal character.[8]

In June 1896, the paper contentedly announced that the Russian authorities had decided to change the local weights and measures system, replacing it with the metric system. As is well known, this attempt was largely unsuccessful even in the Caucasus, and, in Kars, the old Ottoman measures were used for decades.[9]

---

6 *Ibid.*, 1 August 1895; however for the activity of conservative Russian opponents of this education policy, see Nadir Devlet, *İsmail Bey Gaspirali*, Ankara, 1988, p.63.

7 *Tercüman*, 5 March 1895, "Rossia".

8 *Ibid.*, 25 February 1896, 14 January 1891, 17 March 1896, 19 November 1895, sedentarization of the Kirgizh in Semipalatinsk.

9 İ. Ortaylı, "Çarlık Rusyası Yönetiminde Kars" (Kars under Russian rule), *Tarih Enst. Dergisi*, İstanbul, Edebiyat Fak., IX, 1978, p.345; *Tercüman*, 30 June 1896, notes: "Although in Turkey the local measures are still in use, in Central Asia the Russian system is introduced since the beginning of this year (1896)."

In one of this articles, he acknowledges the efforts of the Russian governor of Samarkand, Count Rustovchik, to protect and preserve architectural monuments: "The imams and waqf administrators used to sell antiquities to Russian and foreign visitors. The governor has now prohibited this practice and put these monuments under state control."[10] Drawing a record of the Russian administration Gasprinskii wrote: "Fifteen years ago, we had no schools, no printinghouses, no newspapers. Today we have more than 100 schools, and the number of silk and cotton growers in the Caucasus and Central Asia has doubled."[11] On the other hand he conducts a bitter fight against chauvinistic pan-Slavist circles. In an article he refers to reports from these circles complaining about the resistance of the Ukrainians to russification and points out:

> In this Empire, we do not come across any russified non-Russian but many Russian communities in peripheral governments have changed their life style, adopting the language of their native neighbors or at least picking up some of it as it had been the case in the Crimea and the Caucasus...[12]

He was unable to convince local Russian authorities to apply his proposals, for cultural development. On the other hand he had good relations with the autonomous emir of Bukhara, Abdulahad who visited him in Bahçesaray and invited and honored him in Central Asia.[13]

To revert to the character and general nature of modernist Islam in the nineteenth century, the only genuinely internationalist pan-Islamist movement is to be found among Indian Muslims like Seyyid Ahmad Khan. The Arab pan-Islamists tended to favor the supremacy of their own kinfolk and so did the Turkish proponents

10 *Ibid.*, 11 August 1896.

11 *Ibid.*, 31 December 1895.

12 *Ibid.*, 25 February 1896.

13 *Ibid.*, 17 September 1895.

of pan-Islam, men like Said Pasha who stressed the pioneering role of his fellow countrymen.[14]Thus it is obvious that Turcophone intellectuals in Russia could hardly have a different vision of the movement and that the national idea would be actively pursued. Indeed Gasprinskii's historical mission has been his advocacy of Turkic culture and of a common Turkish language. But a more intriguing aspect of his personality is his westernizing laicist side. He discussed the problems of modernization without bothering about cultural influences or the structural and ideological aspects of the phenomenon unlike his Ottoman-Turkish contemporaries, he adopted a more pragmatic view giving priority to praxis and then discussing the implications of Westernism of anti-Westernism. This did not prevent him from viewing European civilization as based on injustice but yet promoting human progress. He is also critical of a European mentality which he outright rejects on the grounds that it could have harmful effects on the as yet politically immature Muslim intelligentsia, and of the illiterate people whose first need is an educational revolution and not a political one.

There is no distinct cleavage between Gasprinskii's Turkism on the one hand and his Islamism or his Westernism. He would judge every Turkist publication on its own merit, irrespective of whether it had Islamist, Turkist or Westernist leanings. *Tercüman-ı Hakikat, Sırat-i Müstakim, Çığır, Tanin*, etc., were all carefully scrutinized as helping to promote the case of Turkish an excerpts from these publications were extensively reproduced in his own newspaper. Gasprinskii's pragmatic approach is more evident in his educational activities. He can rightly be considered as the "Aprilof" of Russia's Muslims. He praised the importance given by Ottoman Jews, Armenians and Bulgarians to education and always encouraged the Turks to follow their example. He did not view Islam as an obstacle to progress though he did not

14 Ercüment Kuran, "Küçük Said Pasha as a Turkish modernist", *International Journal of Middle Eastern Studies*, 1, 2, Apr. 1970, pp.124-132.

expand at length on this matter. Convinced of the importance of education he devoted much space in his paper to every attempt to spread literacy. Czarist governors, Sultan Abdülhamid, local benefactors in small villages, westernizing wellmeaning Muslim circles, Crimean *mirza*s, progressive Kazan bourgeois, the emir of Bukhara were all irrespectively praised in *Tercüman* for their efforts in this field. He sums up he views on the matter in the following words: "The Eastern Question for me is neither Bismark's nor Gladstone's policy. The Eastern Question is basically the Educational Question." In 1884 the educational reform was started in twelve schools. Twenty years later, in 1905, it had been extended to 5,000 schools all over Russia.

17

Suleiman and Ivan: Two Autocrats of Eastern Europe

Sultan Suleiman was born in 1495 in Trabzon as the son of princegovernor Selîm (the Grim) and Princess Hafsa, the last noble bride to the Ottoman court, daughter of the Crimean Khan Mengli Giray.[1] On his accession he found himself in a position to head a well-established army and to lead a stable bureaucratic system. His brothers either had already died or had been executed. The fortunate man succeded to the throne during the golden age of the Ottoman empire to rule over a Middle Eastern-Balkan empire whose territories had been expanded by his conqueror predecessors. Since he was an able commander and statesman himself, expansion continued during his reign.

In those years Ivan IV succeeded to the Muscovite throne to become the head of an emerging power as the reigning monarch of the divinely respected dynasty of the Rurikids. He was born in 1530 as the grandson of Ivan III. An atmosphere of interregnum and intrigue dominated his childhood. At the age of 17 in 1547 he was crowned as the "Czar and Autocrator". But he was compelled to carry out drastic reforms in both the military and the administrative apparatuses. Ivan IV, the Czar, was the most successful conqueror of all of the rulers of sixteenth-century Russia. During his reign Kazan and Astrakhan

1 For a conflicting view of the identity of Suleiman's mother see, Alan Fisher, "The Life and Family of Süleyman II", in *Suleiman the Second and his Time*, (eds.) H. İnalcık and C. Kafadar, Isis, İstanbul, 1993, pp.1-20.

were conquered and boundaries on the northeast stretched by Cossak chief Yermak to Siberia. This expansion attracted little attention in Europe, and he was defeated in his struggle with Poland and Livonia and died in disappointment and grief, whereas Suleiman, with his conquests, altered Europe's map and is, therefore, known to history as one of the great conquerors. The epithets by which Suleiman and Ivan are known in Europe, in fact, give some indication of their reputation in the eyes of their contemporaries. The former ruled over a multireligious empire in magnificence, the latter headed an emerging power.

Some Western European historians, who are specialists of neither the Ottoman nor the Slavic worlds, tend to evaluate the two eastern European empires according to specific criteria. These evaluations all too often identify the term *autocracy*, in a derogatory sense, with the concepts of *tyranny* and *oriental despotism*. In an eighteenth century Austrian folk art print depicting the nations of Europe, the Turkish sovereign is shown as a tyrant whereas the Muscovite Czar appears as a "Freiwillige" (volunteer) a term which characterizes[2] someone who occupies a critical and dangerous position in a troubled and bloody time such as the late Rurikid period. It is difficult to claim that autocracy as a political institution has been properly understood ever since the Enlightenment. In fact, one cannot compare the Russian and the Ottoman empires of the XVIth century using the same criteria as one would in later centuries. Still, these two widely differing systems have certain things in common. The similarities are as striking as the differences. Therefore it is interesting to compare Suleiman with Ivan Groznij.

In the middle of the 15th century, many of the peoples who owed allegiance to the Eastern Orthodox Church lived under Ottoman rule; the second Orthodox state was Muscovite Russia.

2 İ. Ortaylı, "Avrupa'da Bulunan Milletin Kısa Tasviri", *Tarih ve Toplum*, nr.8, 1984 August, pp.36-39: description of a folk art print in Öst. Museum für Volkskunde in Vienna, lnv. 30905.

Mehmed II (the Conqueror) followed a deliberate policy of favoring unified rule in the Church. As Patriarch, he appointed Gennadios, virulent enemy of Rome, and displayed towards him a consideration greater than patriarchs had enjoyed during Byzantine times. The Patriarch of Constantinople now enjoyed a choice rank in the official protocol. In addition, the Bulgarian and Serbian Churches had been deprived of their autocephaly, with spiritual, administrative, financial and judicial authority over all Balkan Orthodoxy devolving on the Patriarch in Constantinople.

The main theme in Russian political literature of that period is the Byzantine inheritance. The Rurikids were matrimonially allied to Byzantine dynasties since the time of Vladimir Monomakh. Ivan III was the last Muscovite ruler to take a bride from the Palaiologan family. He based on this link his claim to the title of "Czar". This pretension was not acknowledged by the Ottomans and Western Europe before the seventeenth century. Popular tradition and official legends reported in the chronicles relate that the Byzantine cross and imperial sceptres which were thrown into the sea reappeared later in Russia. The attention of the Orthodox world focused on Russia ever since the sixteenth century and irredentist thoughts entertained by Balkan Slavs were focused on Russia. This is why Ivan Groznij's claim that Moscow was the Third Rome was not unfounded however early it may have been made. Still, it may be rash to talk of a Moscow-Constantinople rivalry as early as the sixteenth century. Likewise, the autocratic character ascribed to both rulers has to be evaluated differently in each case despite the obvious similarities.

If we look at the external paraphernelia of the ruler and the court life, the Kremlin appears to be as flamboyant in Ivan Groznij's time as Suleiman's palaces. This colorfulness which can be contrasted with the drabness of contemporary Western courts resulted from the importance of a pageantry created by, on the one hand, Russia's claim to be the center of the world, and on the other, Suleiman's *de facto* leadership of Islam. One can also find in the daily life and palace protocol of the two courts traces of a common past stemming from Asian traditions. These traditions are, if anything, more numerous in Moscow. The Russian crown stylistically comes from the Golden Horde; the Czars' clothes were auctioned off to the *Dvorians*; the Czars gave away caftans instead of medals and decorations.

In Ivan Zebalin's work, *Domashnii Bi't Russkih Zarei* one can find such traces.[3] Reforms introduced by Ivan IV lasted until the reign of Peter the Great just as Suleiman's court protocol has survived till the middle of the eighteenth century. However, whereas Ivan IV had himself set up the rules governing court protocol, Suleiman had largely inherited them from his predecessors. At the time of Suleiman the simplicity of the earlier times was gone and the ruler faced his subjects surrounded with a glittering display of magnificence. Both the Sultan and his subjects took this magnificence for granted. No doubt, Russia at the time of Ivan Groznij had no inkling of the splendor of XVIIIth century Romanovs nor of the respect their country would then command in Europe. Furthermore, titles of Russian Czars such as *Gosudar*, *Czar Vsiarusi*, *Samoderzhets*, *Velikii Kniaz* would only later be internationaly recognized. A point raised by Novaselski has been thoroughly studied by Halil İnalcık. In the 1640's the Crimean Khan did not recognize the title of the Czar equivalent to *âlempenâh* (refuge of the world). In spite of the insistence of the Muscovite ambassador, the Khan refused to use this special title reserved for the Ottoman Sultan, and instead used *Cümle Urusuñ Pâdişâhı or Uluğ ve Küçük ve Ak Rusuñ Penâhı*.[4]

Another similarity is in the system of inheritance. If the reigning monarch had two or more sons, the life of the Russian

3 Ivan Zabelin, Moscow, 1895, pp.142-160; vol 2, Moscow, 1915, p.15.

4 H. İnalcık, "Power Relationships between Russia, the Crimea and the Ottoman Empire as Reflected in Titulature" in *Passé Turco-Tatare et Présent Soviétique: Studies Presented to A. Bennigsen*, Paris, 1986, pp.175, 189, 201-202.

princes until their accession and the ensuing political instability was not very different from what prevailed in the Ottoman palace. Suleiman had the good fortune to be an only son. Ivan IV spent a harrowing childhood and youth before his accession to the throne. His life until then had been as bleak as that of an Ottoman *Şehzâde* in the *kafes* (cage). The real difference is structural. Ivan Groznij was forced to deal with landowning boyars of the *votchina.* Suleiman, however, was at the head of a different power structure. With the exception of a few provinces, the *kul* system was in force to rule the Empire.

Mustafâ Âlî in 1581 considers this as God's special favour to the Ottoman dynasty *(mevhibe)*:[5] In their rule, they are not hampered by relatives and surrounded only by devoted slaves *(kâr-ı sedefteki gevher-i yektâ gibi bir sarâyuñ içinde tek vü tenhâ dururlar ve akrabâ ve ta'allukât 'alâkalarını bi'l-külliye bertarâf kılurlar)*; they were also favored in that they always had enough men to govern outlying provinces and never had to resort to the local leaders. Their military power is unequaled, their finances are in good order. Taking the days of Suleiman as a perfect model, Mustafâ Âli reveals his disagreement with the political structure of his own days. He mentions, therefore, that "justice and prosperity should reign, but this can only be, if the Sultan does not leave the affairs of the State to the viziers;" furthermore, he does not fail to criticize the mistakes made by Sokollu Mehmed Pasha, the old Grand Vizier.

One can also find in the political literature of Ivan's times aspirations towards such a system.[6] Mustafâ Âlî is convinced of the need for an elite group in an autocracy of the Byzantine

5 A. Tietze, *Mustafâ 'Âlî's Counsel for Sultans of 1581* part II, Vienna, 1982, p.289 (38/122, 123).

6 A comparative study on the subject is done by Altan Aykut, "Ivan Peresvetov ve Sultan Mehmed Menkibesi" in *Belleten* 46 (1982), pp.861-882; see also the major work on the subject by A. A. Zimin, *I. S. Peresvetov i ego sovremenniki*, Izd. Akad, Nauk Mosva, 1958.

and oriental type. As a principle; "The Sultan has to find a worthy *muşâhib*, who is able to tell the thing, what others do not dare to tell him... The Sultan has to use trustworthy spies to be informed of the state of the country and of the actions of the administrators. The Sultan has to appoint highly educated men to the high offices..."[7] but, to be sure, neither wider public participation nor discussion by critics from the lower orders or the people at large was sought. As another principle he mentioned the suppression of demagogical preachers. "Vazında halt-ı kelâm ve mezemmet-i enâm iden vaîzler men oluna..."

The transformation of Czardom into a monolithic rule is a special circumstance related to Ivan Groznij's reign. Therefore, when one compares the reigns of Ivan and Suleiman in regard to administrative institutions, keeping in mind that the reign of Suleiman witnessed the institutionalization of Ottoman administration, to characterize these two systems as centralizing autocracies may be an overstatement. This could be all the more so in the case of Muscovite Russia; the title *Veliki Samoderzhets*, is the translation of the Byzantine "autocrat". This title should be viewed as the equivalent of the Latin "dictator" or Islam's *müstebidd*, but not as the contemporary *zulm* or tyranny with their negative connotations. To quote Bernard Lewis, "... traditional Islamic state may be autocratic, it does not mean despotic."[8] In this connection, one could mention the *fetvâ* of Şeyhü'l-islâm Mehmed Ziyâeddîn Efendi, issued at the time of the dethronement of Abdülhâmid II, which never used the terms *istibdâd* and *müstebidd*. Ivan Groznij started his reign as a lawgiver and was responsible for some of the most striking achievements of pre-Petrine Russia during the Rurikid period, though one should not exaggerate the impact of this legislation.

7 Tietze, *Mustafa Âli's Counsel*, p.290 (63/159).

8 B. Lewis, "On the Quietist and Activist Traditions in Islamic Political Writing", *BSOAS* 49 (1986); p.1 on *istibdâd*, see idem., *The Political Language of Islam*, Chicago, 1988, p.156.

One can still compare it with that of Suleiman. The latter's laws and codes have had long-lasting effects whereas those of the former underwent many changes before finally disappearing into historians' collective memory. Regarding Suleiman's legislation we can refer to İnalcık who cites an *'adâletnâme* proclaimed by Suleiman's great grandson Mehmed III in 1595, upon his accession to the throne, which reads: "In the time of my great ancestor Sultan Suleiman a lawcode *(kânûnnâme)* was composed and distributed to the provinces... then no one suffered any injustice or exaction... But now this law-code is discarded and forgotten..."[9] Certainly popular culture as well as chronicles and political literature referred forcefully to the times of Suleiman as an ideal model of bureaucracy, land tenure, protocol etc. The age of Suleiman was considered a perfect model during later Ottoman centuries. Yet as İnalcık has pointed out, Suleiman's legislation did not bring about any radical innovation; it was rather an evolution and expansion of existing codes.[10] Ivan Groznij, on the other hand, introduced what can be termed as important changes for Rurikid Russia, yet his code was destined to fall into disuse after having been heavily amended.

The *Czarski Sudebnik*, issued in 1550, is a code embodying with amendments and changes, the basic institutions of old Russia. This did not prove to be successful and durable legislation. It was not to be valid over a long period as its predecessors such as *Pravda Yaroslava* had been. Ivan IV himself was not acclaimed as a Czar of Pravda, the way his own grand-father Ivan III had been. The Russia of Ivan Groznij has been viewed both by historians and subsequent generations as an obsolescent system. However, it should be pointed out that the political interpretation of the *Pravda* concept by Rurikid Russia is akin to Ottoman thought.

9 H. İnalcık, "Adâletnâmeler", *T.T.K. Belgeler* 2 (1965), pp.104-105 (The *'Adâletnâme* of 1595).

10 H. İnalcık, "Suleiman the Lawgiver and Ottoman Law", *Archivum Ottomanicum* 1 (1969), p.117.

Pravda as such meant truth, justice and law. The "Russkaia Pravda" of Yaroslav and the fact that Ivan III was known as the "Czar of Pravda" reflect the adoption by Russia of a Byzantine theory. The Czar and his subjects must both abide by the *Pravda*. This is in conformity with Mustafâ Âlî's late sixteenth century description of what justice and imperial rule should be: gaining the affection of one's subjects.

Suleiman, known abroad as the Magnificent and at home as the Legislator, has been acclaimed by posterity as a sort of "Czar of Pravda". During the Ottoman centuries, Suleiman had the reputation of being a *Nûşirevân-i 'Âdil*, reflecting Sassanid Persia. Ivan Groznij remained plain Ivan Groznij. The translation of the epithet into European languages as "terrible" or "schrecklich" is inaccurate. Groznij is an epithet handed over to Ivan by his grandfather Ivan III. Groznij has no sadistical implications. Rumors that women fainted when faced with Ivan III's magnetic stare were widespread among the people. Ivan IV automatically took over this reputation and became Ivan Groznij. *Groznij* means not only "terrible" but at the same time "elevated, sublime, mighty, threatening"; the related noun *groza* can mean "Gewitter/thunderstorm" while the verb *ugrozit* can be translated as "to frighten." Peresvetov, the theoretician of the Russian polity of the 1550's, describes Ivan IV's autocratic character as follows:[11] "ugroşivse svojein grozoju czarskoi – he frightened them off, he awed them with his cesarian strength and might."

In fact Ivan, while trying to suppress in a blood bath the boiars of old Russia, was, despite the exaggerated statements of later day's

11 Peresvetov's main tract consists of two parts under the title of "chelobit'naia" in the form of a petition submitted to the Czar, where he points some cases and striking examples from the life and attitudes of rulers and even makes some comparisons to foreign rulers. Uwe Halbach: "Milost' and Groza-Fürstengnade und Ungnade in der Begriffswelt Altrussischen Quellen" in *Geschichte Altrusslands in der Begriffswelt ihrer Quellen*, Stuttgart, 1986, p.74. For Ivan Groznij's time, Herbert Spliet: *Russland von der Autokratie der Zaren zur imperialen Grossmacht*, Lüneburg, 1979, pp.46, 59 and 65.

historians, largely unsuccessful. Suleiman did not have to face, in the central lands of the Empire, either in Anatolia and Rumelia, a provincial landed aristocracy. This was not the case in the peripheral lands such as Lebanon, Arabia, Crimea, Transylvania, and Moldavia; but in Bulgaria, Serbia, Greece and Anatolia, the magnate families had been wiped out long before his time.

Ivan Groznij on the other hand, had to contend unsuccessfully with the boiar estates known as *votchina.* Even land-bound serfdom was not established before the time of his successor Boris Godunov.

The ordinances and decisions issued during Ivan's reign begin not with a clause "we order and want..." but with a formula such as: "by the direction of the sovereign (Gosudar) the boiars have decided..." It was pointed out earlier that Suleiman was not confronted with a group of magnates. It must be noted however, that *Bojarskoe Duma* which was opposed to Ivan Groznij was not comparable to the Seym of Poland. Kliuchevskij in his *Boiarskaia Duma drevnei Rusi*[12] mentions that this assembly in the mid-sixteenth century had 252 members in which the Suzdalian group was rather influential. We cannot say that each member of the Duma was an active participant in the debates. In fact some who were deaf, dotty, or idiotic are reported to have attented the meetings, dozing off most of the time and occasionally making their presence known with the help of their secretaries who used to sit beside them, unable to comprehend the decisions made. They were not accorded veto rights. As a matter of fact, not only the personal conviction of Ivan Groznij, but also the political

12 V. Kliuchevskij: *Bojarskaia Duma drevnei Rusi,* 4th ed. Moscow, 1910; and, A. A. Zimin: Sostav Bojarskoi Dumy v XV-XVI vekakh" in *Arheograficheskij ezhegodnik*, Moscow, 1958, pp.41-48. Thornton Anderson: *Russian Political Throught*, New York, 1965, p.86-87. Ruslan Grigorevich Skrynnikov: "Der Begriff Samoderzavie (Selbstherrschaft) und die Entwicklung Staendisch-Repräsentation vor Einrichtüngen im Russland des 16 Jahr" in *Geschichte Altrusslands*, pp.16-17.

thinking of the day was opposed to the domination of magnates. Maxim Grek, the so-called humanist author of the era, does not discuss the Duma's role in public affairs, but rather notes that the Czar has to be the sovereign of right and perfect legislation: - *Czar pravdaiu blagozakonyet*. Peresvetov, on the other hand, goes even further in criticizing the Boiars and argues that the "catastrophe of Byzantium had started with magnates." Speaking of the Czar, he used three epithets: threatening, strong and wise. The same idea prevails in Ivan's letter to Kurbskiis in which the czar writes:[13] "God has given a task to Kurbskiis and other boiars, to serve my grandfather Ivan III... *(v rabotu)*. Therefore, I cannot share my authority granted to us by God with the boiars," and adds, "we reward or punish our *kholop*s (he uses this very word) "the Czar has expressed his wrath and mercilessness for boiars *(opola)*..." In the 1930's it seemed exaggerated, when Soviet historians argued that centralization prevailed over the boiars with popular support, but in the *oprichnina* of the Czar there were hundred youngsters of boiar origin in 1565, and their numbers increased three fold within a decade.[14] Ivan attempted to strengthen *d'iachestvo* in order to reduce the role of *dvorianstvo*. He granted them land called *pomest'e* in return for their services. Certain *votchinas* were confiscated, on behalf of the *oprichnina*. Though this process was exaggerated by some historians for a while, recent research has shown that the scope of his operations were far from creating such a centralized absolutism. However Ivan's maneuver to create a new class was an accomplishment that survived. Owing to the creation of a *noblesse de robe*, fresh blood would be pumped into the aristocracy throughout Russian history.

In fact the consfiscation of some *votchinas* did not begin under the reign of Ivan Groznij. The process started with Ivan

13 *Ibid.*, p.21. S. V. Utechin: *Geschichte der politischen Ideen in Russland* (Kohlhammer-Mainz 1966), pp.30-31 and 37.

14 R. G. Skrynnikov: *Rossiia nakanune smutnogo vremeni* (Moscow, 1980), pp.40-46.

III after the conquest of Novgorod. In the 16th century it was a common practice to create a new courtly class. So Muscovite Russia was confronted with the emergence of this new class before Ivan Groznij. This process was also largely accepted by the political ideology of his age. Peresvetov pointed out that in order to limit the power of the hereditary boiars "the army and the government should not be left to the magnates, but rather to the warriors, freely entering the service of the Czar..." Peresvetov also clearly put a limit on the power of the aristocracy. This limit consisted of *starina* (tradition), divine laws, and the Czar's authority based on his own hereditary legitimacy.[15]

What were the limits on the potential of Suleiman's autocracy? The Ottomans were representatives of Islam and rulers of this world. But they were not alone. They had to compete with Iran and India. This was a fact which strengthened the claims to omnipotence of the Caliph and Sultan but also put a limit on such claims. Within the empire, there were autonomous governments, like the Crimea, Transylvania, Wallachia, and Moldavia. Furthermore, in such a multireligious empire, every community had its own privileges, rights, judicial organizations which put another limit, a legal one, on the powers of the Sultan, while Ivan Groznij, at the head of an Orthodox Christian czardom, did not tolerate any other belief.

Ivan Groznij is generally described negatively by modern historians whereas he was not always portrayed in the same light by his contemporaries; especially popular songs and *rasskazy* described him not as a mentally ill figure but rather as a despotic though strong czar. Suleiman, on the other hand, was exalted with the golden descriptions of Ottoman prose as in the *Tabakâtü'l Memâlik* of his own Head of the Chancery, Celâlzâde Mustafâ, and in many other works in later centuries.

---

15 Spliet, p.65 and Altan Aykut, p.864.

18

Reforms of Petrine Russia and the Ottoman Mind

Among the congratulatory messages read at the May 10th 1906 session of the first Russian Imperial *Duma* were a few telegrams sent by the Young Turk committees in Europe.[16] One, especially, was very meaningful; signed by A. Haydar Midhat, son of Midhat Pasha the father of the Ottoman constitution, read in part, "if the Russian people have been able to impose their administration and political rights and power on the Czar, this means that the same thing going to happen in Turkey also."

There was, of course, another section of the Turkish press which persisted in using the same language as the Russian conservatives and the reactionaries in Russia. In the March 1st 1907 issue of *Meşveret*, for example, the armed uprising in Russia was criticised as "an awful revolutionary crisis." An interesting background to this political atmosphere had taken place thirty year before. The inauguration of the first Ottoman parliament in March 1877 had touched off reactions in Russia, which infuriated St. Petersburg and caused Russian diplomat in İstanbul to declare: "For us Ottoman constitutionalism constitutes a challenge; we shall make the Turks pay dearly for the shame they have imposed on us of remaining the only country in Europe without .. parliament

16 *Stenograficheskii otchet Gosudarstvennoi Dumy*, tretii sozyv, sessiia II, zasedanie 331 (St. Petersburg, 1908); V.I. Shpil'kova, *Mladoturetskaia revoliutsiia*, Moscow, 1977, p.49.

and constitution."[17] Ottoman intellectuals and statesmen of the nineteenth century, in other words, whether they were conservatives or liberal felt themselves compelled to follow Russia's cultural and literary life and its state system closely, and Russians had a similar interest in Turkey. An officer of the Russian armies that liberated Bulgaria could not help wondering whose work the liberation of the Russian *mujiks* would be. In *Anna Karenina,* Tolstoy describe those who volunteered to fight for the liberation of Montenegro as follows: "Journalists without any newspaper and leaders of parties without any members were most vocal in supporting this cause." The Slavic question had come to provide entertainment for high society; those who volunteered were depicted by Tolstoy as adventurers who had been unsuccessful in their lives. Earlier in the same century Pushkin, too, had contemplated Turkey without hostility and with a critical sensibility devoid of exotism in his chronicle of Erzurum ("Puteshestvie v Erzurum"). This Pushkin, however, is neither a Lamartine nor a prejudiced Olivier. Gogol's famous comedy "Revizor" commences with ironical conversation in which the petty bureaucrats of the small provincial town are gossiping that "inspectors are being sent everywhere in connection with the war against the Turks that is about to start." The autocratic administrations of both empires cast their long shadows over the thoughts of their respective intelligentsias and pervaded both national literatures. For example, a dialogue in Midhat Cemal's novel *Üç İstanbul* between Adnan, a radical Young Turk, and Kerim Pasha, one of Sultan Abdülhamit's marshals, has the marshal reply to Adnan's criticism of the Hamidian despotism and censorship as follows: "Despotism and censorship exist in Russia too; why should you complain? Where are our Dostoyevski and Tolstoy? If you were to write as well, you would be read in Europe and in America even if we should ban you here. Have you written anything like

17 Y. Tiğin Kurat, *Henry Layard'ın İstanbul Elçiliği*, Ankara, AÜDTCF, 1968, p.167.

Anna Karenina?" To which Adnan retorts, "The Czarina wept as she read Tolstoy, and the Czar had him transferred to rear duty in order to safeguard his life during the battle for Sebastopol. Where in our society is there a comparable benevolence?" On the other hand, during the years of Young Turk opposition, Yahya Kemal, in comparing the Young Turk emigrants in Paris to Russian emigrants, accuses the first group of being ignorant and unconscious, equally impressed by the speeches of Jean Jaurès and the parades of "Action Française," at a time when Russians were leading politicians even among Western revolutionary circles.[18]

Western Europe in the first half of the nineteenth century saw both the Ottoman Empire and Russia as two Eurasian states, two states of eternal challenge. J. von Hammer dedicated his *History of the Ottoman State* to the Czar; Lamartine penned romantic histories of the two countries. These were still undiscovered, mysterious social entities in European eyes. The Brera Academy of Milan trained architects for Russia. The Fossati brothers from this circle impressed the Ottoman capital with the Russian embassy they built there; from then on they and their like would serve the officialdom of both empires.[19] So the striking resemblance between the residence of the Russian governor of Kars and the residence of the governor Midhat Pasha of Bulgaria in Rusçuk (Ruse) is not a simple accident. For even the official architecture of these autocratic empires was of the same origin.

One problem historians of Russia have never been able to resolve is the debate on whether this society belongs more to Asia or Europe. Of the Russians of the eighteenth century. V. O. Kluchevsky (1841-1911) has given us the following brilliant epigram: "they tried eternally to be at home among foreigners

---

18 Yahya Kemal (Beyatlı), *Çocukluğum, Gençliğim, Siyasi ve Edebi Hatıralarım*, İstanbul, s.a., pp.179-183. Another contemporary essay on Russia by Mehmed Ali Ayni was published in *Akşam*, 2 August 1338/1920, as "Rusya'yı tanıyalım."

19 Semavi Eyice, "Fossatiler" in *İstanbul Ansiklopedisi*, ed. R. E. Koçu, vol.11.

and succeeded only in becoming foreigners at home."[20] Taken in the West for Tartars dressed up to look like Europeans, they were considered by their countrymen to be Frenchmen born in Russia. This type of description would just as easily apply to the Ottoman elite of the nineteenth century.

The thoughts of the Turkish reformist of the nineteenth century also echoed the slogans of Russian populism and traditionalism, of which Tyutchev's lines are a good reflection:

> Not by the mind is Russia understood,
> Nor is she measured by a common rule:
> She has a special stature of her own;
> In Russia one can only put his faith.[21]

The motto of the Russian age of reformation –"we resemble only ourselves"– was raised again in nineteenth century Turco-Ottoman ideology. The famous eighteenth century Prince Cherkassky, who would allow only Russian to be spoken, and his wife, who declared that they wanted "neither foreigners nor their wares,"[22] appear in retrospect like somewhat ironic prototypes of Ahmed Vefik Pasha, who together with his family dressed up in products of native manufacture.

The Petrine reforms in Russia played an important role in introducing and accelerating military and administrative reforms in the Ottoman Empire. More important, however, was the mutual interconnection between the official ideologies and the ideological apparatuses of the two empires which began to manifest itself towards the end of the eighteenth century. It is as if the protectorate over Orthodox Christians of Ottoman

20 V. O. Kliuchevskii (Kluchevsky), *A History of Russia*, vol.5, London, 1931, repr. New York, 1960, p.147.

21 Translated by Jesse Zeldin, *Poems and Political Letters of F. S. Tyutchev*, Knonville, 1973, p.22.

22 H. Rogger, *National Consciousness in Eighteenth Century Russia*, Cambridge, Mass., 1960, p.48.

soil granted to the Russian sovereign by the treaties of Küçük Kaynarca, reminded the Ottoman sultans of their own title of "caliph." Thus political myths of both empires that had existed since the fifteenth century–namely, Russia as the official inheritor of the mantle of Byzantium, on the one hand, and the Ottoman sultan's caliphate over all Muslims, on the other–began to acquire a certain reality, giving rise to a new political ritual in the interior as well as exterior of the two empires revolving around the question of minorities.

A point quite often glossed over in Turkish historiography is that, just as the Russian czars acquired protectorship of the Orthodox Christians in Ottoman territories, so the Ottoman sultans, as caliphs, acquired similar rights over Russian Muslims and especially those in the Crimea. In 1784-85 Catherine II granted to the nobility of the Crimean Tartars status corresponding to the Russian *dvorianstvo*. This was the first rehabilitation of any Muslim nobility within the Russian empire. A *predvoditel' dvorianstva* (marshal of the nobility) was appointed to head this Crimean nobility. By the same act, the ancient ranks of the nobility dating from the period of the old khanate were made equal to each other. The Crimean squadron *(Krymskii Konnyi)* founded in 1784 was a special guard regiment directly patronized by the Empress, and the Czar was the ranking member of this regiment. This afforded opportunity for the Muslim Mirzas of the Crimea to enter the ranks of the officer corps.[23] The Ottoman Sultan, on the other hand, was considered the religious leader of the Crimea, and this right and ritual were jealously guarded. Thus the Russian imperial family, arriving at the Livadia Palace on an annual sojourn, would be welcomed there by a vizier (either the Foreign Minister or marshal of the palace) in the name of his Imperial Majesty, Sultan and Caliph, down to the Ottoman Empire's last years.[24]

---

23 *Krymskii konnyi eia velichestva 1784-1934. Iubileinaia spravka*, Paris, 1934.

24 İ. Ortaylı, *Türkiye İdare Tarihi*, Ankara, 1979, p.136.

Members of the Crimean Giray dynasty, refugees in Turkey, were paid salaries by the sultans until the last days of Ottoman rule.[25] İstanbul sent several *müderris* to Crimean *medresse*s to carry out religious education there and later even teachers for secular schools. Some Crimean youths, on the other hand, were educated in Turkey and even attended military schools there. From the eighteenth century onwards, the Ottoman sultans used the title of caliph pointedly and importantly vis-à-vis the Muslims of Russia, perhaps indicating that pan-Islamism was being resorted to as an ideology in a modern sense in opposition to pan-Slavism and pan-Orthodoxy. This phenomenon must be considered something of a turning point for the history of Ottoman ideas. The extraordinary interest exppressed by the Sublime Porte in the Polish National Committee in exile (up to the 1830s) and the granting of diplomatic status to the representatives of that same committee[26] may also be interpreted as probable responses to the policy pursued by the Russian Empire towards the Balkan-Slavs, and especially the Montenegrines and the Serbians.

The autocratic modernization drive of the Hamidian regime was woven of the same cloth as the Russian imperial system. In this context, technical and military training were given absolute primacy while the regime was decidedly allergic to philosophy and history as school subjects and did not break off from religious education as a manifestation of its *Weltanschauung*. One can say that the curriculum prepared by the Minister of Education, Prince Uvarov, was copied and imitated by the Ottoman educational establishment almost in its entirety.

Conservative official Ottoman ideology changed within one century of Petrine Russia and its reforms. The death of Peter the great was at that time recorded by Raşid, the offical chronicler

25 Başbakanlık Arşivi, İrad.-Duh. 1258, no.2593; 1260, no.1103, 4309; 1262, no.1540; İrad.- Mec.-Vala no.1436, are some examples.

26 Nigâr Anafarta, *Osmanlı İmparatorluğu ile Lehistan Arasındaki Münasebetlerle İlgili Tarihi Belgeler*, İstanbul, s.a., pp.117-119.

(vakanüvis) of the Ottoman State, in the following words: "The Muscovite Czar Peter being dead, his corpse was left lying in some quiet corner, he had tried to impose crazy new fashions on his people."[27] And Mehmed Ağa, an Ottoman ambassador who had visited Petrine Russia in those days, had gone so far as to heap scorn on a parade organized by the Emperor and the European protocol used there with the expression "The Czar's clownings *(Çarın maskaralıkları)*." Another Ottoman ambassador, Şehdi Efendi, left the following description of an opera he attended in 1757 at the invitation of Empress Elizabeth: "The singers and instrumentalists stroked their instruments in a strange fashion, shouting according to certain modes in their own language *(hanende ve sazendeler usul-i garîbe ile darb-ı evtar ve makâmat nevâz ve lisanlarınca velveleperdaz olmuşlardır)."* By 1794, however, Mustafa Rasih Pasha,[28] ambassador at the court of Catherine II, would leave us detailed information concerning the way of life and administrative and military organization of that period, expressed in an admiring way. It seems that this change in attitude took place around the time of the Treaty of Küçük Kaynarca. For nineteenth-century Ottoman thought and historiography, Peter was no longer "The Mad" *(Deli)* but "The Great." Thus, an official book of an unknown writer (probably a dragoman at the Sublime Porte) with the significant title "The History of Peter the Great–*Büyük Petro Tarihi*"[29] was printed at the very outbreak of the Crimean War. Cevdet Pasha, too, in his famous history spoke of Petrine Russia and Peter's reforms with unmistakable praise:[30] "The Russian never used to have a powerful state of great renown. Now he rules one-ninth of the world. The real founder of this state is Peter the Great." Also giving insistent credence to the myth of the "Testament of Peter the Great," the same author

27 A. Ubicini, *Lettres sur la Turquie*, pt.1, Paris, 1853, p.165.

28 F. Reşit Unat, *Osmanlı Sefirleri ve Sefaretnameleri*, Ankara, 1968, pp.62, 107, 162.

29 *Büyük Petro Tarihi* (by an unknown author), İstanbul, 1270/1853-54.

30 *Cevdet Tarihi*, vol.1, İstanbul, 1309/1890-91, p.241.

makes this interesting comparison between the reforms of Peter and of Mahmud II in his correspondence with Sadullah Pasha, the Ottoman ambassador in Vienna:[31] "The political organization of the two states is essentially similar and parallel." He believes that: "in England reforms were initiated by the gentry, that is, the upper class, and it was this that led to the creation of a constitutional monarchy, whereas in France, the upper class proving incapable of the same, the initiative came from below, and this resulted in a republic." To this he then adds that:

> Ottoman as well as Russian reforms were embarked upon by the Crown *(taraf-ı saltanat-ı seniyyeden)*. Even dissolution of the Janissaries resembles the dissolution of the Strelitsy, with the exception that, whereas the Janissaries had been a cancer in the very heart of our Sublime Porte, the Strelitsy had been a tumor on Russia's back *(lakin yeniçeri devlet-i aliyyenin kalbinde bir seretan idi. Strelitsler ise Rusya'nın sırtında bir ur idiler)*. Here, once the Janissaries were dispersed, continuous reforms in every administrative department became inevitable, but there (in Russia) a vacuum became apparent only in the military field and therefore Russian recovery was quickly completed.

Cevdet adds: "We do not possess cadres of the necessary courage and will," and concludes, "Peter was very determined and he acquired further learning in Europe. When he removed the Strelitsy, he knew what he was doing and how he was going to replace them. Sultan Mahmud was also a determined ruler, but he had not and would not see Europe. Our statesmen were not endowed with sufficient learning and determination." It should be pointed out that, instead of focusing on the personalities of Ottoman statesmen, Cevdet Pasha might have dwelt on the fact that the Ottoman reforms were retarded by a full century. Nevertheless, the comments reveal him to be a serious historian capable of approaching the Russian reforms analytically.

31 Cevdet Pasha, *Tezâkir*, ed. C. Baysun, pt.40, Ankara, 1967, pp.217-219.

INDEX

K

L

Ö

P

Discovering the Ottomans

İLBER ORTAYLI

What made the Ottoman Empire such an important chapter in world history? How did the Topkapı Palace manage to be both modest and sumptuous? What did the Ottoman sultans and pashas do on a daily basis? *Discovering the Ottomans* seeks answers to these and other questions, addressing key issues that continue to intrigue people in Turkey and beyond. It is the work of İlber Ortaylı, one of Turkey's foremost historians, and is memorable not just for its interpretations, which attest to the author's rich intellectual background, but also for its fluid and engaging style. The book invites history buffs of all ages to discover the Ottomans.